NANOSCALE SCIENCE

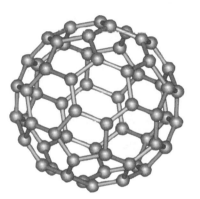

Activities for Grades 6–12

NSE Graduate Group
Univ. of California, Berkeley
210 McLaughlin Hall #1726
Berkeley, CA 94720-1726

NANOSCALE SCIENCE

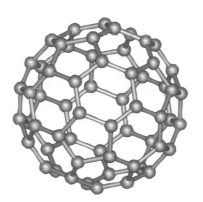

Activities for Grades 6–12

M. Gail Jones ● Michael R. Falvo ● Amy R. Taylor ● Bethany P. Broadwell

NATIONAL SCIENCE TEACHERS ASSOCIATION

Claire Reinburg, Director
Judy Cusick, Senior Editor
Andrew Cocke, Associate Editor
Betty Smith, Associate Editor
Robin Allan, Book Acquisitions Coordinator

ART AND DESIGN
Will Thomas, Director
Joanne Moran, Assistant Art Director, Cover and Inside Design

PRINTING AND PRODUCTION
Catherine Lorrain, Director
Nguyet Tran, Assistant Production Manager
Jack Parker, Electronic Prepress Technician

NATIONAL SCIENCE TEACHERS ASSOCIATION
Gerald F. Wheeler, Executive Director
David Beacom, Publisher

Library of Congress Cataloging-in-Publication Data

Nanoscale science : activities for grades 6-12 / M. Gail Jones ... [et al.].
    p. cm.
  Includes index.
  ISBN 978-1-933531-05-2
  1. Nanoscience. 2. Nanostructures. 3. Nanotechnology. 4. Science--Study and teaching (Secondary)--Activity
programs. 5. Technology--Study and teaching (Higher)--Activity programs. I. Jones, M. Gail, 1955-
  QC176.8.N35N35577 2007
  620'.5--dc22

                    2007006376

CONTENTS..........

PART I. SIZE AND SCALE

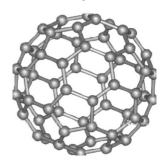

PART II. TOOLS AND TECHNIQUES

PART III. UNIQUE PROPERTIES AND BEHAVIORS

PART IV: NANOTECHNOLOGY APPLICATIONS

PART V: SOCIETAL IMPLICATIONS

THE AUTHORS

M. Gail Jones is a former middle and high school biology teacher and currently is a professor of science education at North Carolina State University. She leads the Nanoscale Science Education Research Group investigating effective ways to teach nanoscale science.

Michael R. Falvo is a research associate professor of physics and materials science at the University of North Carolina at Chapel Hill. Mike conducts research with nanoscale materials and teaches a special course on nanoscale science for undergraduates.

Amy R. Taylor is a former high school biology teacher and is currently a doctoral student in science education at North Carolina State University. Amy is conducting research on how students learn scale and scaling.

Bethany P. Broadwell is a former middle school science teacher and currently serves as a lecturer in science education at North Carolina State University. Bethany has conducted research on nanoscale science education and conducted workshops for teachers in nanotechnology.

ACKNOWLEDGEMENTS

The authors wish to thank the many people who inspired, reviewed, and helped craft this book. Our special gratitude goes to Adam Hall for his insightful cartoons and beautiful electron micrographs, Tom Oppewal for ideas for an early draft of the Shrinking Cups investigation, Jenn Forrester for reviewing the manuscript with a teacher's eye, and the many nanoscale researchers who shared their research and images. Thanks to Richard Superfine, Russell Taylor, Tim O'Brien, Sean Washburn and the rest of the nanoscience research group at University of North Carolina who have supported and collaborated with the authors in developing nanoscale science education. Thanks also to Robert A. Freitas Jr., senior research fellow at the Institute for Molecular Manufacturing, Thomas P. Pearl, department of physics, North Carolina State University, and Elizabeth Collie, Knotty Oak Middle School, Coventry, Rhode Island for their thoughtful reviews.

Our special appreciation goes to the National Science Foundation for supporting our nanoscale science research, our research into how students learn nanoscale science, and the development of new courses that focus on nanotechnology for undergraduates.

This material is based on work supported by the National Science Foundation under Grants Numbers 0354578, 0634222, 0507151, 0411656, and 0303979.

DEDICATION

This book is dedicated to Toby and Davis and all children who remind us that the smallest things can be the most important.

INTRODUCTION

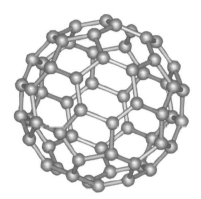

I magine you could build something from scratch atom by atom. What would you build? Would you build a robot that would move through your body gobbling up diseased cells or create a new molecule that when sprinkled on an oil spill would break down the oil, eliminating any risk to the environment? For the first time in human history we have the ability to manipulate and build materials from the atom up. New tools such as the atomic force microscope allow us to not only image atoms, but also move atoms into new arrangements that have never been attempted before. What makes all this particularly remarkable is that all this takes place at the nanoscale—one-billionth of the size of a meter. Futurists predict that nanotechnology will be the next major scientific revolution and will have greater impact on our lives than the industrial revolution or the great advances that have been made in genomics.

This book examines nanoscale science with an eye toward understanding nanotechnology. Geared toward middle and high school teachers, these investigations are designed to teach students about the unique properties and behaviors of materials at the nanoscale. The investigations were developed as a result of three National Science Foundation grants given to the authors for research examining effective ways to teach and learn nanoscale science. The investigations are designed as guided inquiry with open-ended exploration where possible. The goal of the book is to introduce the essential concepts that students need to understand nanoscale science while maintaining a broad inquiry approach. The activities of this introductory book may serve to whet the students' appetites to know more. The book is organized around five themes: scale, tools and techniques, unique properties and behaviors, nanotechnology applications, and societal implications (see key concepts listed in Table 1).

TABLE 1 ....
KEY NANOSCIENCE AND ENGINEERING CONCEPTS.

Size and Scale

Nanoscale	The unique placement of the nanoworld between atomic and micro/macro scales allows exploration of the regime where properties transition from atomic behavior to familiar macro behavior.
Relative Scale	How large objects are in relation to each other. (Which is bigger an atom, molecule, or a virus?)
Powers of Ten	What is a nanometer? How much smaller is a nanometer than a micrometer?

Tools and Techniques

Atomic Force Microscopy	Probing microscopes use a scanning tip to detect physical properties of materials.
Nanoimaging	The ability to detect the arrangement of matter at the nanoscale allows for the design of new materials.
Nanomanipulation	Manipulating matter at the nanoscale opens up whole new possibilities building new objects.

Unique Properties and Behavior

Stickiness	Intermolecular forces dominate familiar forces such as gravity (van der Waals bonding, hydrogen bonding…) at this scale.
Shakiness	Thermal energy produces strong effects (Brownian motion, thermally activated processes).
Bumpiness	Graininess of matter (atoms/molecules) and properties (quantization, quantum confinement) makes working at this scale bumpy.

Nanotechnology Applications

Nanomaterials	The ability to synthesize small materials means new functionality, improved materials properties, and revolutionary technology.
Textiles	Nano construction allows for the creation of new fabrics that resist staining or have antibacterial properties.
Building Materials	The ability to mimic nature at the nanoscale allows the lotus effect to be applied to objects such as windows.
Medicine	Medical applications include nanoshells that target cancers and tumors for detection and treatment.
Water Quality	Nanoparticles that can detect and combine with pollutants may provide more efficient ways to clean water.

Societal Implications

Environmental	What are the unknown dangers of generating new nanoparticles that may be released in the environment?
Ethical	What are the ethics of creating new materials and rearranging matter?
Social	How will society change as a result of using nanolabels to track the movement of people, animals, and materials throughout the globe?

Nanoscale science uniquely ties together all the science domains because it focuses on the raw materials—atoms and molecules—that are the building blocks of physics, chemistry, biology, and Earth and space sciences (Table 2). In unprecedented ways, scientists from different departments are collaborating in nanoscale research to explore science from multiple perspectives. For example, physicists are interested in the unusual properties of gold nanoshells. These tiny nanoparticles begin as glass beads that are then covered with gold. The nanoshell behaves differently depending on the size of the gold shell. Different-sized shells have different melting temperatures, different electrical conductivity behaviors, and are even different colors. These properties make it an ideal tool for use in medical testing and treatment.

Table 2
NANO INVESTIGATIONS AND THE SCIENCE DOMAINS.

Investigations	Biology	Physics	Chemistry	Mathematics	Environment
Introduction					
Fact or Fiction? Exploring the Myths and Realities of Nanotechnology	•	•	•	•	•
Size and Scale					
That's Huge!				•	
One in a Billion			•	•	
Nano Shapes: Tiny Geometry		•	•	•	
Biological Nanomachines: Viruses	•	•		•	
Tools and Techniques					
What's in Your Bag? Investigating the Unknown		•			
NanoMagnets: Fun With Ferrofluid		•	•		
Scanning Probe Microscopy		•			
Unique Properties of Nano Materials					
It's a Small World After All: Nanofabric		•	•		
Biomimicry: The Mystery of the Lotus Effect	•	•	•		
How Nature Builds Itself: Self-Assembly		•	•		
Physics Changes With Scale		•		•	
Shrinking Cups: Changes in the Behavior of Materials at the Nanoscale		•	•	•	
Limits to Size: Could King Kong Exist?	•			•	
Nanotechnology Applications					
NanoMaterials: Memory Wire		•	•		
Nanotech, Inc.	•	•	•		
NanoMedicine	•	•	•		
Building Small: Nano Inventions	•	•			•
Societal Implications					
Too Little Privacy: Ethics of Nanotechnology					•
Promise or Peril: Nanotechnology and the Environment	•	•	•		•

The gold that coats the nanoshell is an inert metal that easily absorbs light and the rate of absorption and reflection depends on the thickness of the gold layer. This differential rate of absorption means the nanoshell can be used for locating and treating cancer. When nanoshells are coated with antibodies and injected into the body, they are delivered by the body to a specific cancer where antibodies on the nanoshell attach to antigens on cancer cells. When a laser is shown on the cancerous area, the gold nanoshells heat up—essentially cooking the cancer while the surrounding healthy cells are unharmed. In addition to treating the cancer, a similar process is used to attach florescent dyes to nanoshells. When the florescent dyes are injected into the body the nanoshells glow in areas where there are cancer cells, which makes the nanoshells a remarkable tool that allows doctors to very specifically locate cancers and target specific areas for treatment. Not only is nanotechnology being innovatively used in medicine but also in environmental science. Scientists are exploring the use of nanoshells as a way to target and filter specific pollutants in water. The goal is to have a highly efficient way to provide clean water to countries around the Earth. As this example shows, a single application such as a nanoshell can be used in chemistry, physics, biology, and Earth and space sciences. By exploring science at the tiniest of scales, students can begin to understand the building blocks of materials and the properties of atoms and molecules that make up our world.

This book begins the study of nanotechnology for students by getting them to think about the very small size of a nanometer. Understanding size and scale at this very tiny level is difficult because we cannot easily experience things this small. Most students have trouble understanding the small sizes of things like cells or bacteria, and even more difficulty understanding the size of atoms, molecules, or viruses. The investigation of scale begins with a focus on relative size (understanding which is bigger, a virus or a cell) and moves to investigating the powers of ten, which are the foundation of the metric system. Students explore just how tiny one part in a billion really is through a series of investigations with dilutions (One in a Billion). Students explore the size and geometry of nanomaterials such as buckyballs, carbon nanotubes, and even viruses (Nano Shapes: Tiny Geometry). Next students take a look at viruses as self-assembling nanomachines (Biological Nanomachines: Viruses). These activities lay the foundation for later concepts that focus on molecular self-assembly and the introduction of unique properties of nanotubes.

TOOLS AND TECHNIQUES

Just as the microscope and the telescope opened up new worlds that had never been seen before, the atomic force microscope and other new nanoscale tools have enabled significant advancements in nanoscale science. But unlike the telescope and microscope, the nanoscale world is too small to be seen and can only be detected through other more indirect means. Students explore what it is like to try to detect unknown materials bound inside a black bag (What's in Your Bag: Investigating the Unknown). They must think like scientists to detect the properties and shape of their unknown materials. Next, students explore how an atomic force microscope (AFM) works to probe these tiny materials. Using a pen flashlight they model how an AFM scans back and forth to detect shape (Scanning Probe Microscopy). Next, students use magnets to shape ferrofluid into new forms and explore how magnetism can be a tool for detection and manipulation (NanoMagnets: Fun With Ferrofluid).

TABLE 3 ....
INTERDISCIPLINARY NANOSCIENCE:

Links to the Science and Mathematics Education Standards.

Physical Sciences
Motions and forces
Interactions of energy and matter
Entropy and conservation of energy
Life Science
The cell
Molecular basis of heredity
Matter, energy, organization in living systems
Earth Science
Properties of Earth materials
Geochemical cycles
Science and Technology
Abilities of technological design
Understandings about science and technology
Mathematics
Measurement
Proportionality
Mathematical modeling and representations
Problem solving
Unifying Concepts and Processes
Constancy, change, and measurement
Systems, order, and organization
Science in Personal and Social Perspectives
Health
Risks and benefits

UNIQUE PROPERTIES AND BEHAVIORS

The section on unique properties and behaviors of nanoscale materials introduces students to the structure of these materials. They begin their investigations exploring how nanofabrics are able to repel a range of stains and liquids (It's a Small World After All: Nanofabric). This effect is explored further with living materials as students explore biomimicry of the lotus effect using plant leaves. This remarkable activity shows how the structure of some leaves makes them highly resistant to dirt, giving them a self-cleaning mechanism. Using magnifying glasses, students can see water bead up on leaves like cabbage and then watch as water droplets pick up other solid materials and as it rolls off the leaf (Biomimicry: The Mystery of the Lotus Effect). This macroscale investigation models the behavior of new self-cleaning glass that is used in skyscraper windows.

Materials behave very differently at the nanoscale than they do at the macroscale that we usually experience. The investigations Physics Changes With Scale, How Nature Builds Itself, and Shrinking Cups are designed to explore the shaky, bumpy, and sticky nanoworld. At this tiny scale materials are very bumpy and are highly influenced by changes in thermal energy. Students model this behavior through a self-assembly activity using Legos and magnets. After placing pieces of magnets and Legos into a box and shaking the box repeatedly, uniform structures form. This investigation models self-assembly that occurs with structures such as virus capsids at the nanoscale. The magnets in this activity model the intermolecular forces that dominate other forces such as gravity. Students explore how different scales influence each other by looking at the relationships of surface area to volume (Limits to Size: Could King Kong Exist?). By measuring different sized cubes and examining how the volume differs when surface area decreases, students are encouraged to think about why friction and heat play major roles in nanoscale manipulation.

NANOTECHNOLOGY APPLICATIONS

An examination of new applications in nanotechnology challenges students to think about the tremendous potential nanoscale engineering may offer to our society. Students conduct investigations with memory wire (NanoMaterials: Memory Wire) and nanofabricated socks that are antibacterial (Nanotech, Inc.). Using gelatin and gel, students explore how gold nanocapsids are able to kill tumors without damaging the surrounding healthy tissue (Nano Medicine). This section ends by challenging students to think of their own inventions that could be created with nanotechnology. Students imagine a world where nanobots can reshape their eyes so they don't need glasses or a world where nano-machines move around their mouths mopping up bacteria. This futuristic writing activity places them in the shoes of modern engineers who apply nanoscale science to human problems (Building Small: Nano Inventions).

SOCIETAL IMPLICATIONS

One of the greatest changes that nanotechnology may bring is the use of tiny labels and tracking devices that will allow us to monitor the movement of most materials around the globe. The changes in our privacy may be dramatic, from diamond rings that can have nanosized names and addresses tagged in them, to explosive materials that are embedded with distinctive markers (Too Little Privacy). What are the ethical implications of engineering new and totally different materials that are released into the environment? Should we build self-assembling robots just because the technology is available? Furthermore, what are the potential problems that can occur from this type of invisible engineering (Promise or Peril)? The last section of this book examines the ethical and societal implications of nanotechnology. Students consider how this remarkable technology could alter the way we live and imagine a new world where we can build nearly anything from the bottom up.

FACT OR FICTION: EXPLORING THE MYTHS AND REALITIES OF NANOTECHNOLOGY

OVERVIEW

Will clouds of self-replicating nanobots take over the world, or is this just a scene from a science fiction novel? Nanotechnology is a rapidly growing field that has huge potential for transforming our world. But the reality of advances in nanoscale science falls short of the hype that has emerged from the imaginations of many futurists. Students consider a series of nanotechnology claims and decide if each one represents fact or fiction or somewhere in between. This activity is designed to capture students' imagination and to spur their interest in learning more about nanoscale science and technology.

OBJECTIVES

- Raise awareness of the current state of nanotechnology.
- Promote healthy critical thinking about the benefits and harmful effects of nanotechnology.

Process Skills
- Predicting
- Inferring

Activity Duration
20 minutes

Extension Activity
90 minutes

BACKGROUND

In Michael Crichton's best-selling book *Prey*, a swarm of nanobots is released into the desert where they evolve quickly and develop new behaviors that go beyond their computer programming. The swarm replicates and becomes more intelligent as time goes on. The book captures our imagination as Crichton skillfully weaves science into an amazing fictional story. Recent advances in nanoscale science have produced amazing new products and materials that make us wonder if they are fact or fiction. There are also a number of fantastic claims about nanoscale science that fall purely on the side of science fiction.

Nanotechnology is the design and production of structures, devices, and systems at the size of the nanoscale, or a billionth of a meter. For the first time, scientists are able to manipulate and control matter at this very tiny scale. But being able to synthesize, image, move, and detect nanoparticles is far removed from creating something as incredibly complex as self-assembling nanobots that are capable of existing outside of the laboratory. Building such complex machines remains a distant future goal of nanotechnology.

THE FACTS

Recent advances in the development of new forms of microscopy now allow scientists to see and manipulate matter atom by atom. These new microscopes, the atomic force microscope and the scanning tunneling microscope, have provided the ability to investigate properties and behavior of materials at the atomic scale. Scientists can now image and probe molecules and atoms. Furthermore, scientists can move individual atoms and build new molecular arrangements. This new capability opens up the possibilities for new technologies that are cleaner (less wasteful by products of manufacturing) as well as more efficient (gears that fit exactly together). The small scale of this type of engineering means that machines can be made at scales that have never been possible before.

One amazing phenomenon that has been documented at the nanoscale is the process of self-assembly. Under certain conditions, materials will self-assemble into organized structures without external intervention. Although this seems like science fiction, this type of behavior occurs frequently in the natural world with DNA and RNA replication or virus capsid construction. The idea of self-replication is a potentially powerful tool for technologists to use to manufacture tiny devices and materials at the nanoscale in large numbers with little energy input. Already scientists can take a series of atoms and build two tiny rotating gears or an axis with two wheels. These tasks are not trivial and take considerable time. Scientists are

(used with permission. www.rice.edu/media/nanocar.html)

Nanocar Model

exploring new ways to not only create the parts of machines with nanotechnology but to harness the potential power of self-replication to create tiny machines in large numbers (see chapter 11, *How Nature Builds Itself: Self-Assembly*, for further information).

The field of nanotechnology is moving so rapidly that what we deem as science fiction today may become part of tomorrow's reality. The challenge is for us to think about where we want technology to go in the future while keeping a critical eye out for potential harmful effects. Furthermore, this challenge must be balanced with understandings about what is realistic and what is impractical. Nanotechnology provides this generation with the opportunity to harness these new technologies to make a real difference in our environment and our lives.

MATERIALS

For each student:
- Copies of *Fact or Fiction: Exploring Myths and Realities of Nanotechnology*

For the teacher:
- Transparency of *Fact or Fiction: Exploring Myths and Realities of Nanotechnology* answer sheet

PROCEDURES

ENGAGE Ask, *What have you heard about nanotechnology? What is nanotechnology?* Encourage students to share their ideas and experiences with nanoscale technologies.

The first response that students typically mention is the iPod nano that plays music. The name iPod nano builds on the idea of making things smaller and smaller. You might follow up and ask if anyone has read the science fiction novels *Prey* by Michael Crichton, *The Diamond Age* by Neil Stephenson, or *The Snow Queen* by Joan Vinge. Students may have seen the *Star Trek: The Next Generation* episode entitled "Evolution" where nanites take over the ship (season 3, episode 1).

Share with students that the goal of this activity is to think about what we know about nanotechnology and to think critically about which aspects of nanotechnology are fact and which are fiction.

EXPLORE Ask students to stand up and gather in the center of the room. Put the "Fact or Fiction" statements (page 3) on the overhead projector or computer display and read the directions to the students. Ask students to think about each statement after you read it aloud and to align themselves across the room according to whether or not the statement is fact (one side of the room), fiction (the other side of the room), or somewhere in between. Label the sides of the room as "Fact" and "Fiction" so students know where to go. Read each statement and ask students to move and then select a couple of students from each location to explain why they placed themselves there for that statement.

EXPLAIN For each item discuss students' ideas and then share the explanations provided on the teacher key for "Fact or Fiction." Encourage students to investigate these issues and learn more through library research.

EXTEND Provide students with time to do web searches to investigate many of the ideas introduced in this activity (space elevators, nanobots, toxic nanoparticles, and nano-treated pants). Have them share any false ideas that they come across during their research. Encourage them to think creatively about new possible uses for nanotechnology. Highlight careers that utilize nanoscale science, such as biomedical research, chemical engineering, materials science, physics, or environmental engineering.

EVALUATE Although this lesson is designed to engage your students and motivate them to learn more as part of their study of nanotechnology and nanoscale science, you may want to assess their learning by asking them to discuss in groups or write responses to these questions:

a) What do these emerging new technologies have in common?
b) Why have new advances in nanoscale science happened only in the last few years?
c) What are the potential benefits and harmful effects of significant uses of nanotechnology?

FACT OR FICTION STATEMENTS

Fact ....**Fiction**

Directions: Position yourself on the side of the room that best represents whether you think the statement is a fact or fiction. If you believe that the correct response lies between the two sides you can place yourself in the middle. Be prepared to share the reasoning you used to make this judgment.

1. There are currently biological nanomachines that naturally exist in your body.

2. Tiny nanotweezers can be used to pick up nanometer-sized molecules and move them around to build different structures.

3. Gold nano-sized bullets can be injected into the body to kill cancer cells.

4. Scientists have created a nano-sized car that has four doors, tires, and tiny seats and can move around freely.

5. There are clothes that don't stain due to nanotechnology. You can throw coffee on khaki nanopants and the coffee just rolls off.

6. Through nanotechnology ice cream is being made that is lower in fat and better for you.

7. NASA plans to build a space elevator that would use carbon nanotubes to move materials from Earth to outer space.

8. Nanoparticles have been shown to cause liver damage and can move into the brain.

9. Self-cleaning toilets are now available. These toilets are made with nanotechnology that keeps the porcelain clean.

10. Through nanotechnology, steaks can be made atom-by-atom such that cows are no longer needed to produce the meat.

FACT OR FICTION STATEMENTS

1. There are currently biological nanomachines that naturally exist in your body.

Answer: True

Explanation: Viruses are nano-sized biological machines that currently exist inside the body. Viruses are capable of self-replication within a cell. This means that the virus parts spontaneously come together to create new viruses. There are many proteins in your body that also act as machines. Myosin, for example, is a very large protein that uses ATP as its energy source to produce small movements that are the source of muscle contraction.

2. Tiny nanotweezers can be used to pick up nanometer-sized molecules and move them around to build different structures.

Answer: True

Explanation: True, but a major challenge is the stickiness of materials at the nanoscale. Many materials simply adhere to the tweezers and refuse to be released making the tweezer a difficult nanoscale tool. Picking up is easy, putting down is hard.

Source: Collins, P. G., and P. Avouris. 2000. Nanotubes for electronics, *Scientific American* 283: 62.

3. Gold nano-sized balls can be injected into the body to destroy cancer cells.

Answer: True

Explanation: Tiny gold capsules (a few nanometers in diameter) are coated with antibodies. When injected into the body the antibodies adhere to tumors and when irradiated with a laser, the gold capsids heat up destroying only the tumor while leaving the surrounding healthy tissue unharmed.

Source: Hirsch, L. R., R. J. Stafford, R. E. Price, J. D. Hazle, N. J. Halas, and J. L. West. 2003. *Targeted hyperthermic cancer therapy using immunoconjugated nanoshells.* Paper presented at the Summer Bioengineering Conference, Key Biscayne, Florida.

4. Scientists have created a nano-sized car that has four doors, tires, and tiny seats and can move around freely.

Answer: False

Explanation: Amazingly scientists have created a chassis and axles made of organic molecules with pivoting suspension and freely rotating axles. The wheels are made of buckyballs, spheres of pure carbon containing 60 atoms apiece. The entire car is about 4 nanometers across. However, the car does not have doors, tires, or seats. The car can move but not freely.

5. There are clothes that don't stain due to nanotechnology. You can throw coffee on khaki nanopants and the coffee just rolls off.

Answer: True

Explanation: Textile chemists can now treat fabric with a special process to alter the fabric's properties at the nanoscale. The fabric resists stains and repels spills.

Source: www.nano-tex.com

6. Through nanotechnology ice cream is being made that is lower in fat and better for you.

Answer: True

Explanation: The use of nanotechnology in food processing is resulting in the production of products such as ice cream that have lowered fat content. The technology works by creating a tighter matrix in the ice cream that results in a reduced size of ice crystals. This makes an ice cream that is smoother and creamier.

Source: Heller, L. 2006. Flavor firm uses nanotechnology for new ingredient solutions. *FoodNavigator-USA* (July 10). Available online at *www. foodnavigator-usa.com/news/ng.asp?id=69008-blue-pacific-flavors-taste-nanology-stabilease.*

7. NASA plans to build a space elevator that would use carbon nanotubes to move materials from Earth to outer space.
Answer: False
Explanation: Reportedly Liftport, a space-infrastucture company supports the construction of a space elevator. The idea is to use a long thin cable made of carbon nanotubes anchored to a platform that would extend out into space. The cable would be held in place by the Earth's rotation. The space elevator could then be used to move materials into outer space. But all of this is just an idea and thus far there are no serious plans to build a space elevator.

Source: Kanellos, M. 2005. Nano skyscrapers may precede space elevator. CNET News. Available online at *http://news.com.com/Nano+skyscrapers+ may+precede+space+elevator/2100-11397_3-5914208.html*.

8. Nanoparticles have been shown to cause liver damage and can move into the brain.
Answer: True for Fish
Explanation: A recent study showed that nanoparticles called fullerines induce an immune response in the large-mouth bass and molecules may have traveled to the brain and central nervous system. This landmark study has spawned a series of studies that examine the safety of manufactured nanoparticles in the environment.

Source: Thompkins, J. 2004. Nano-pollution: No tiny issue? *Popular Science* (July). Available online at *www.popsci.com/popsci/science/ 1bfc0b4511b84010vgnvcm1000004eecbccdrcrd.html*.

9. Self-cleaning toilets are now available. These toilets are made with nanotechnology that keeps the porcelain clean.
Answer: True
Explanation: Toilets are now available that are covered with a ceramic glaze that covers the toilet bowl with a non-porous, super smooth, nanometer-sized coating. By eliminating tiny nooks and crannies there are no places for dirt to adhere to the toilet bowl. This coating is called CeFiONtect (Ceramic Fine Ion Technology) or SaniGloss and is now available for purchase.

Source: *http://www.toto.co.jp/en/products/technology/cefion.htm*.

10. Through nanotechnology, steaks can be made atom-by-atom such that cows are no longer needed to pro-
   duce the meat.
Answer: False
Explanation: Although food chemists are looking at new ways to make new food additives and to keep food from spoiling though nanotechnology, currently there is not a way to make complex proteins, like those found in steaks, artificially. Our current abilities to manipulate atoms are very, very primitive as compared to nature's bottom-up manufacturing capabilities.

PART I

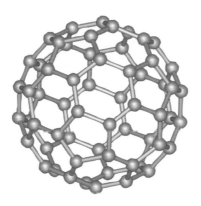

SIZE AND SCALE

THAT'S HUGE!

OVERVIEW

Just how big is a billion? How tiny is a nanometer? Five hands-on inquiry activities are presented that use measurement and calculations to help students visualize one billion. Students develop mental anchors or references to use when conceptualizing quantities of a billion.

OBJECTIVES

- Build an understanding and a mental visualization of one billion.

Process Skills
- Observing
- Predicting
- Measuring
- Collecting Data

Activity Duration
60 minutes

BACKGROUND

Students learn about place value and how to read the number 1,000,000,000 in elementary school. They see and hear the number "one billion" everyday whether it is on the national news discussing the cost of war or when their science teacher discusses the world population. Imagining a billion of anything can be mind boggling, whether it is the number of stars in the Milky Way (~100 billion) or the number of H_2O molecules in a drop of water (billions of billions). Students are fascinated with huge numbers, but do they really understand the magnitude of things like a trillion-dollar deficit? If they have difficulty understanding very large numbers, it is likely they will have the same difficulty understanding very small numbers as well. It is believed that connecting science and math concepts to real-world examples helps students conceptualize the sizes of things found at the nanoscale. By applying very large and very small numbers to real-world examples also helps students develop a mental visualization of the actual sizes of these numbers.

WHAT IS A BILLION?

A billion is a thousand million, or in numerical form, 1,000,000,000. In exponential form it is written 10^9. A nanometer is one billionth of a meter, 0.000000001 or 10^{-9}. A few examples of quantities in the billion-size range include:

- On October 12, 2006, the U.S. Census Bureau announced that the population of the United States would reach 300 million (or just under one third of a billion) on October 17, 2006. (*www.census.gov*)
- On September 7, 2003, President Bush announced on national television that he was asking congress to grant him an additional $87 billion for the fiscal year, beginning October 1, 2004, to continue the fight on terror in Iraq and Afghanistan. (*www.crunchweb.net/87billion*)
- There are approximately 250 million molecules of hemoglobin in a red blood cell, and each of these molecules is capable of picking up four molecules of oxygen. As a result, one red blood cell can deliver up to one billion molecules of oxygen. (*www.meds.com*)
- There are one billion nanometers in a meter.

Getting students to conceptualize one-billionth at the nanoscale is probably a more difficult task than learning a billion at the macroscale. The purpose of this activity is to help students understand one billion and ultimately one-billionth. By taking a top-down approach to developing a number sense of a billion, students can then move to conceptualizing a billionth of a meter, a nanometer.

Each group will need:

- Triple beam balance
- 1 small cup with about 3 tablespoons of raw sugar
- Ruler
- Meterstick
- Golf ball
- 25 sheets of plain white paper
- Stop watch
- Tweezers
- Calculator
- Student Sheets 1–5
- Article – "Nanotech: A Billion Computers in a Drop of Water" for background reading: (*www.newsfactor.com/perl/story/15100.html*)

For engagement activity:

- One gallon jug filled with salt

PROCEDURES

ENGAGE

Show students a one-gallon jug or jar filled with salt. Ask the students, *How many grains of salt are in the jug?* Have them record their answers on paper and set it aside.

Students' responses may vary from 10,000 to one trillion. Record some of the responses on the board and tell the students to remember their guesses. You will reveal the answer at the end of the class. (Optional: Award the student with the closest estimate.)

As a transition into discussing one billion, ask the students to describe a billion in their own words. You may hear responses such as "a very large number, the number of stars in the sky, it's larger than a million but smaller than a trillion," and so on.

Write the number 1,000 on the board. Ask the students, *How many times larger than 1,000 is a billion?* The correct answer is that one billion is one million times larger than one thousand.

Write on the board $1,000 \times 1,000,000 =$ and ask the students how many zeros one billion should have. Write the answer 1,000,000,000 on the board. Next, ask the students how would one billion be written in exponential form. The correct answer is 1×10^9.

EXPLORE

Explain to the students that they will be working in groups of four to solve some mysteries about the concept of a billion. There are five activities they will need to complete, and some of the activities will require them to move around the classroom. Students need about 25–30 minutes to complete the activities. At this point, pass out the packet of activities.

Circulate the room throughout the activities to check on their progress. Some groups may need additional assistance, depending on their mathematics and problem-solving skills.

EXPLAIN

Review the activities after the students have finished. Start with Student Sheet 1. Ask the students, *How big would a container need to be in order to hold one billion golf balls?* The correct answer is a box 50 m (160 ft) on a side (see calculation on the teacher key). This is equivalent to the volume of approximately 400 classrooms that measure 10 m × 10 m × 3 m. Ask each student to place a golf ball in the palm of his or her hand, and tell the students it is one-billionth the size of the container.

Continue reviewing the remaining activities. Encourage students to try visualizing the size or amount of one billion and to compare that size to one-billionth. For example, ask the students to imagine a stack of paper that is 66,667 stories high. Next, have them hold one piece of paper in their hand. Ask the students what fraction of 66,667 stories high is this single piece of paper. The correct answer is one-billionth.

EXTEND

Ask the students to get out their paper from the beginning of class. Give them a chance to change their initial estimate of the number of grains of salt in the jar.

Write on the board:

1 Pinch =

1 Cup =

Ask the students, *How many grains of salt are in a pinch?* The correct answer is about 1,000 grains. Write 1,000 grains on the board beside 1 pinch. Next, ask the students to estimate how many grains are in a cup. The correct answer is about 1,000,000 grains. Write 1,000,000 grains on the board beside 1 cup.

Write on the board 16 cups = 1 gallon and ask the students to calculate how many grains of salt are in the one gallon jug. The correct answer is $16 \times 1,000,000 = 16,000,000$ grains of salt. Ask the students if this is an exact answer. Discuss with the students that the answer is an approximation and how it would be almost impossible to count every grain of salt.

EVALUATE Lastly, ask the students, *How big would a container need to be in order to hold one billion grains of salt?* It is estimated that one billion grains of salt would fill a bathtub! Ask them to imagine a bathtub full of salt and to also imagine one tiny grain of salt. Ask the students, *What fraction is a single grain of salt of the full bathtub?* This will give them a mental reference point that may help them later when conceptualizing the size of a nanometer.

THAT'S HUGE!

TEACHER KEY

Student Sheet 1
Process

1. Approximately 5 centimeters.
2. Answers will vary.
3. Answers will vary.
4. Answers will vary.
5. Answers will vary.

Challenge: The container could be 1,000 golf balls × 1,000 golf balls × 1,000 golf balls. Knowing that each golf ball is about 5 cm in diameter, this would mean the container must be 5000 cm (50 m) on a side. This is a volume of 50 m × 50 m × 50 m = 125,000 m^3. A box 50 m on a side is the size of a medium size office building (approximately 160 ft high) or the volume of approximately 400 classrooms (10 m × 10 m × 3 m).

Student Sheet 2
Process

1. Approximately 5 mm. (The remaining answers will be based on 25 sheets being 5 mm in height, however actual measurements may vary by several millimeters.)
2. 2 cm.
3. 20,000,000 cm or 200,000 m.

Challenge: approximately 66,667 stories (or 125 miles).

Student Sheet 3
Process

1. 7 seconds. (The remaining answers will be based on 7 seconds, however actual measurements may vary by one or two seconds.)
2. 70 seconds.
3. 700 seconds.
4. 700,000,000 seconds.
5. 11,700,000 minutes.
6. 22.3 years.

Student Sheet 4
Process

1. Answers may vary.
2. Answers may vary.

Challenge: One granule of raw sugar is approximately 1 cubic mm. Therefore, the volume of 1 billion granules of raw sugar would be 1 billion mm^3. To determine the size of the container in cubic meters, divide by $(1,000)^3$ to get 1 m^3.

Student Sheet 5
Process

1. 0.25 nm.
2. 1 cm is 10^{-2} m. 0.25 nm is 0.25×10^{-9}. The number of atoms placed side to side is therefore $10^{-2}/(0.25 \times 10^{-9}) = 4 \times 10^7$. An alternative way of solving the problem is to recognize there are 10^7 nm in a cm and 4 atoms per nm.
3. $(4 \times 10^7) \times (4 \times 10^7) \times (4 \times 10^7) = 6.4 \times 10^{22}$. This is an incredibly big number. Perhaps ask the students to calculate how long it would take to count to a number this big (10^{15}, or a million billion years, or much longer than the known lifetime of the universe). Also emphasize that this gives them a sense of how many atoms there are in objects that they interact with.

    The number of atoms in their body could be another calculation they could attempt. An easy way to do this is to assume your body is only water. You should get a number of approximately 10^{27} or so. Or a billion billion billion. The molecular weight of water is approximately 18 g. The weight of a typical middle school student is approximately 50 kg. So there are the equivalent of 50 kg/0.018 kg = 2800 moles of water in the body. $2800 \times 6.02 \times 10^{23} = 1.7 \times 10^{27}$ water molecules.
4. Avogadro's number is 6.02×10^{23}. This number of atoms or molecules is known as a *mole*. There are this number of atoms in a chunk of material whose mass in grams is equal to the molecular weight in an atomic mass unit (amu). So a 1 cm^3 chunk of aluminum (Al) is about one tenth of Avogadro's number which means this is one tenth of a mole of Al.

    As a check, we can determine the number of atoms an alternative way using Avogadro's number. The density of Al is 2.7 g/cm^3, so a 1 cm^3 chunk of Al is 2.7 g. Al's molecular weight is 27 amu. This means that one mole of Al weighs 27 g. So a 2.7 g chunk of Al is one tenth of a mole.

THAT'S HUGE!

Name _____

Problem

How many golf balls would it take to fill this classroom?

How big would a container need to be in order to hold one billion golf balls?

Prediction

• I predict this room will hold _____ golf balls.

• I predict the container would have to be _____ in size to hold one billion golf balls.

Materials

• Golf ball
• Meter stick

Process

1. The diameter of the golf ball is _____.

2. The length of the room is _____, the height is _____, and the width is _____.

3. It would take _____ golf balls to make a line the length of the classroom, _____ golf balls to make a line the width of the classroom, and _____ golf balls to make a line the height of the classroom.

4. The dimensions of this room in golf balls is ___ golf balls × ___ golf balls × ___ golf balls.

5. The volume of the room in units of golf balls is _____ golf balls.

Challenge

How could you determine the size of a container that would hold one billion golf balls?

What size would the container need to be?

THAT'S HUGE!

Name _____

Problem
How tall would a stack of a billion sheets of card stock be?

Prediction
I predict that a stack of a billion sheets of card stock would be _____ tall.

Materials
- 25 sheets of card stock
- Metric ruler

Process
1. The height of 25 sheets of card stock is _____ mm or _____ cm.

2. Therefore, the height of 100 sheets of card stock would be _____ cm.

3. Based on the information in #2, the height of one billion sheets of card stock would be _____ cm or _____ m high.

Challenge
One story of a building is approximately 3 m high.
How many stories would a billion sheets of card stock be?

THAT'S HUGE!

Name _____

Problem

If you counted from one to one billion, how long would it take?

Prediction

I predict that it would take _____ to count from one to one billion.

Materials

• Stopwatch

Process

1. Have someone time you while you count from one to ten at a normal speaking rate. It took _____ seconds.

2. Based on the information in #1, it would take _____ seconds to count from one to one hundred.

3. Based on the information in #2, it would take _____ seconds to count from one to one thousand.

4. How many seconds would it take to count from one to one billion? _____

5. How many minutes would it take to count from one to one billion? _____

6. How many years would it take to count from one to one billion? _____

THAT'S HUGE!

Name _____

Problem
How many bags of raw sugar would you need to have one billion granules of sugar?

Prediction
I predict that you would need _____ bags of raw sugar to have one billion granules of raw sugar.

Materials
- Small cup of raw sugar
- Small empty cup
- Balance or scale
- Calculator
- Tweezers

Process
1. Using the equipment and supplies devise a plan with your group to determine how many bags of sugar you would need to have one billion granules of raw sugar.

Results
1. One billion granules of raw sugar weighs _____ kg or _____ lbs. It would take _____ bags of sugar to have one billion granules.
2. Describe how your group made this calculation.

Challenge:
How could you determine the volume of one billion granules of raw sugar?

FIGURE 2.1 ....
SCANNING ELECTRON
MICROGRAPH OF SUGAR
CUBES AT 1MM, 50 μM,
AND 30 μM

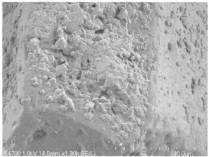

Hint:
1 bag sugar = 5 lbs
1 lb = 453.6 g
1 kg = 2.2 lbs

Name _____

Problem

Atoms are a little less than 1 nm in diameter. An aluminum atom is roughly 0.25 nm in diameter. If you have a cube of aluminum 1 cm^3 on a side, how many atoms are there in the chunk?

Prediction

I predict that there are _____ atoms in a 1cm^3 chunk of aluminum.

Materials

Look up Al at *www.webelements.com* to find the density, molecular weight and atomic diameter of aluminum.

1. The diameter of an aluminum atom is _____ nm.

2. Based on the information in #1, it takes _____ atoms to lie side to side across one edge of the aluminum chunk.

3. Based on the information in #2, the total number of atoms in the whole chunk of aluminum is _____ .

4. How does this number compare to Avogadro's number?

CHAPTER 3

ONE IN A BILLION

OVERVIEW

How do you get students to understand a number as small as one-billionth? Through a hands-on dilution activity using food coloring, students will learn about parts per billion. A matching card game helps students further understand one-billionth by giving real examples, including nanoscale examples.

OBJECTIVE

- To build an understanding and a mental visualization of one-billionth.

Process Skills

- Observing
- Predicting
- Measuring
- Collecting Data

BACKGROUND

"Seeing is believing," as the saying goes. Students are more readily able to put concepts in their working memory when they are able to see and experience the concept. But how do you see or show extremely small numbers such as one-billionth? The same problem is encountered when attempting to show one billion. It is recommended that the students complete "That's Huge!" before doing this activity, because they should more readily understand one-billionth if they have an understanding of one billion. One billion is significant because a nanometer is one-billionth of a meter and nanotechnology involves the building of materials at this tiny scale.

Activity Duration

60 minutes

····MATERIALS·········

Each group will need:

- White paper
- 1 ml dropper
- Food coloring
- 200 ml of water
- Rinse cup of water
- 9 small cups (clear or white) or beakers
- 1 ml mouthwash (Not to be distributed until the Extend section)
- 2 graduated cylinders (10 ml)
- Student Sheets 1 and 2

PROCEDURES

ENGAGE Begin the activity by asking students, *Which number is larger: one billion or one million?* Then ask, *Which quantity is bigger: one part per million or one part per billion?*

Students may respond that one part per billion is larger because they know that one billion is larger. Some students may understand that one part per billion is smaller than one part per million, however, they may not have an accurate conception of the actual size of one part per billion.

Ask students, *Would you prefer to have a concentration of toxic substance in your drinking water at one part per billion or one part per million? Please explain why.* Listen to their responses to get an understanding of their prior knowledge.

Ask the students to give you some examples of "things" that could represent one billion. They may give examples they learned from the *That's Huge!* activity, such as, "It would take one billion grains of sugar to fill a bathtub." Write their responses on the board.

Once you have written down five to six examples of one billion, draw a line beside it to make a two-column chart and write *One-Billionth* at the top of the new column.

Tell the students: Many people have a difficult time understanding very large numbers and very small numbers. In the last

One Billion	One-Billionth

activity you all learned about very large numbers, numbers in the billions. Today we are going to travel to the opposite end of the spectrum and learn about very, very small numbers. After the activity we will complete our chart by filling in examples of one billionth.

EXPLAINING "PARTS PER" AND PERCENT

Students will need to have an understanding of solutions and how their concentrations are calculated in order to complete the activity.

Ask students, *What does it mean to say that you have one in ten chances of winning a game?* Ask them, *Is there another way of stating that you have one in ten chances of winning a game?*

Students may say that out of ten people playing the game, only one person is going to win. Others may explain that one person has a 10% chance to win the game. This will lead you into a discussion on the term *percent*. Ask the students, *How many cents are in a dollar?* They will say one hundred. Ask the students, *How many years are in a century?* (You may want to write the underlined words on the board so that students can see the words.) Ask the students, *How often does the federal mint make centennial quarters?* Then ask the students, *From the terms we've discussed that are written on the board, what do you think the word "cent" means?* After discussing that cent means one hundred, write the root word *percent* on the board and explain that percent means "part per hundred."

Hold up a beaker with 95 grams of water (95 milliliters). Ask the class, *If I wanted to make this a 5% sugar solution, how much sugar do I need to add to it?* Write "95 grams of water" on the board. Once you have received the answer (5 grams), write "5 grams of sugar + 95 grams of water = 100 grams of solution." Write the fraction "5 grams of sugar/100 grams of solution." If the students seem to have difficulty understanding percent then you may want to be prepared to add other examples.

Check for understanding: Hold up a beaker of water and red food coloring (a 10% solution). Tell the students that this is a 10% solution. Ask them, *How did I make this 10% solution out of water and food coloring?*

Further explain that 10 parts of food coloring were added to 90 parts of water. You could demonstrate this by putting 9 drops of water in a clear cup or test tube and then adding one drop of food coloring.

EXPLORE It is suggested that students work in pairs. Each pair should have nine small cups or beakers placed on a blank white piece of paper to help them see the color change. Explain that they will perform a series of dilutions, each larger by a power of ten. This is referred to as a serial dilution. Distribute Student Sheet 1.

You may need to get them started by doing cups 1 and 2 as a class. You may also need to help them calculate the concentrations for these cups. Explain and write on the board that cup 1 has a 10% solution or 1/10 solution. If they add 1 ml of a 1/10 solution to 9 ml of water the solution will now be 1/10 of 1/10 which equals 1/100 (a 1% solution), or 1 part per hundred. Have them calculate the concentration of cup 2.

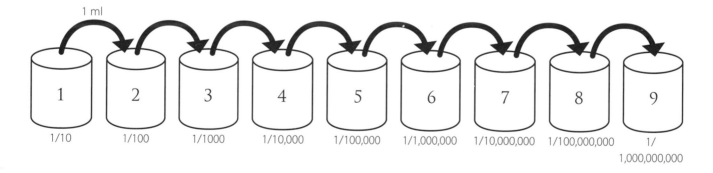

1 ml

| 1 | 2 | 3 | 4 | 5 | 6 | 7 | 8 | 9 |

1/10 1/100 1/1000 1/10,000 1/100,000 1/1,000,000 1/10,000,000 1/100,000,000 1/1,000,000,000

EXPLAIN Ask students to discuss the results of their investigation.
Discuss with the students that "parts per billion" typically is used when working with extremely small amounts. Nanotechnology is a field that works at this tiny unit. Discuss that a nanometer is one-billionth the size of a meter. The students could no longer see the food coloring at a certain solution level, however the pigment was still present. We cannot see objects that are at the nanoscale, but they do exist. It is important for students to understand that even though things are too small to be seen, it does not mean that they don't exist, or that they are too small to have an effect.

The next investigation will further develop their understanding of the size of one-billionth by repeating the dilution activity using their sense of smell.

STUDENT SHEET 1 ANSWER KEY.....................................

Students' results in the data table may vary.

Cup	Color	Concentration
1	Black-green	0.1
2	Dark green	0.01
3	Medium green	0.001
4	Very light green	0.0001
5	Slightly green	0.00001
6	Clear	0.000001
7	Clear	0.0000001
8	Clear	0.00000001
9	Clear	0.000000001

1. In which cup did the solution first appear colorless?
Answer: This may vary but should become colorless at cup 5 or 6.

2. What is the concentration of food coloring in this cup?
Answer: Cup 5 = 1/100,000 or 10 ppm
Cup 6 = 1/1,000,000 or 1 ppm

3. Do you think there is any food coloring present in this cup of diluted solution even though you cannot see it? Explain.
Answer: Yes, the solution is still present with each dilution because a tiny amount was transferred from one cup to another.

4. What is the concentration of cup 9? Explain your answer in your own words.
Answer: 1/1,000 ppm or 1 part per billion. There is one part of the dye for every billion parts of water.

EXTEND Distribute 1 ml of mouthwash to each group, nine clean cups (or beakers), and Student Sheet 2. Students will use smell in this investigation as well as color as they make serial dilutions. Students are able to detect the presence of mouthwash by smell even after they can no longer see it. This provides an opportunity to discuss how things at the nanoscale are present even though they can't be seen.

EVALUATE

Cup	Color	Smell	Concentration
1	Slightly green	Strong	0.1
2	Clear	Medium	0.01
3	Clear	Medium	0.001
4	Clear	Slightly	0.0001
5	Clear	Slightly	0.00001
6	Clear	Barely	0.000001
7	Clear	Barely	0.0000001
8	Clear	None	0.00000001
9	Clear	None	0.000000001

Prediction: At what point do you think you will no longer be able to smell the solution?
Answer: This will vary.

As an entire class, talk about the answers to the Discussion questions on Student Sheet 2.

STUDENT SHEET 2 ANSWER KEY...

1. In which cup did the solution first appear colorless?
Answer: This will vary depending on initial darkness of solution.

2. In which cup did the solution first appear odorless?
Answer: Around cups 6 or 7.

3. Which cup holds the "nano" concentration solution?
Answer: This can vary as well. If they followed the same procedure used in the previous dilution activity, then the answer is cup 9.

4. What is the actual percent solution of this "nano" mixture written in numerical format?
Answer: 1 ppb or 1/1,000,000,000

5. Explain how you made a "nano" concentration solution?
Answer: This may vary; however, you should take a close look at their procedures to assess their understanding of 1 ppb.

STUDENT SHEET 1

Name _____

Problem
At what concentration (which cup) will the solution appear colorless?

Prediction (Write your hypothesis in the space below.)

Materials
Each group will need:

- White paper
- 1 ml dropper
- Food coloring
- 200 ml of water
- Rinse cup of water
- 9 small cups (clear or white) or beakers
- 2 graduated cylinders (10 ml)

Process
1. Number the cups or beakers 1–9.

2. Place white paper under the nine cups or beakers.

3. Using a graduated cylinder, put 1 ml of food coloring and 9 ml of water in cup 1. Be sure to rinse the graduated cylinder with water each time. Swirl cup or beaker gently to mix solution.

4. In the results chart, describe the color of the solution in cup 1 and write 0.1 under concentration to represent a 10% solution.

5. In cup 2 add 1 ml of solution from cup 1 and 9 ml of water. Again, describe the color and calculate the concentration of the solution. Record results in the results chart.

6. In cup 3 add 1 ml of solution from cup 2 and 9 ml of water. Record results in chart.

7. Continue the dilution process as done above for cups 4–9. Record all results in chart.

Results

Cup	Color	Concentration
1		
2		
3		
4		
5		
6		
7		
8		
9		

Conclusion

1. In which cup did the solution first appear colorless?

2. What is the concentration of food coloring in this cup?

3. Do you think there is any food coloring present in this cup of diluted solution even though you cannot see it? Explain.

4. What is the concentration of cup 9? Explain your answer in your own words.

ONE IN A BILLION

Name _____

Going Further

Your challenge is to dilute mouthwash to the point that it is a "nano" percent solution. You will use the same process as you did for the first dilution investigation. In cup 1 add 1 ml of mouthwash and 9 ml of water. As you continue the dilution process for cups 2–9, record your observations of color and smell. Calculate and record the concentrations.

Prediction: At what point do you think you will no longer be able to smell the solution?
(Write a hypothesis in the space below.)

Cup	Color	Smell	Concentration
1			
2			
3			
4			
5			
6			
7			
8			
9			

Discussion

1. In which cup did the solution first appear colorless?

2. In which cup did the solution first appear odorless?

3. Which cup holds the "nano" percent solution?

4. What is the actual percent solution of this mixture written in numerical format?

5. Explain how you made a "nano" percent solution.

NANO SHAPES: TINY GEOMETRY

OVERVIEW

Advances in nanotechnology are due in part to the unique structure and properties of carbon nanotubes and buckyballs. These unusual structures are being studied for their potential use as vehicles for drug delivery, to strengthen materials, and as miniature circuits. Through an examination of the geometry of nanoscale materials, students explore the possibilities of nanoscale technologies.

OBJECTIVES

- To describe the geometry of a carbon nanotube and a buckyball.
- To understand the relationship between geometry of nanoscale objects and the behavior of the materials.

Process Skills
- Predicting
- Inferring

Activity Duration
20–30 minutes

BACKGROUND

Carbon atoms have long been recognized as the stars of the molecular world because of their unique properties. Carbon is special for a couple of reasons. First of all, the carbon-carbon bond is the strongest chemical bond in nature. This is what makes diamond the hardest material in nature. Secondly, carbon has a unique ability to use its four chemical bonds in very flexible ways. It can make what are called "hybrid bonds" that allow it to form chains, rings, or networks. This flexibility is what gives rise to the myriad complex structures of organic materials in nature. In diamond, carbon bonds to four neighboring carbon atoms forming a three-dimensional network. The geometry of the diamond bonds is *tetrahedral*. In graphite, the carbon atoms bond to three neighboring atoms and form two-dimensional sheets that look like honeycombs or chicken wire (scientists call it a *hexagonal network*). In biological polymers (DNA, proteins) and industrial polymers (polyethylene, polystyrene, etc.) carbon bonds to two neighboring atoms to form chains. Two newly discovered carbon structures, the buckyball and the carbon nanotube, have received a lot of attention over the last 15–20 years for their potential scientific and technological promise.

THE BUCKYBALL: SOCCER BALLS OF THE NANO WORLD

Buckyballs look like soccer balls but are incredibly tiny. These molecules, discovered by three scientists, Richard Smalley, Harry Kroto, and Bob Curl, are composed of 60 carbon atoms bonded together to form a sphere. These scientists found that when graphitic carbon was vaporized with a laser, tiny buckyballs formed. They were awarded the Nobel Prize in Chemistry in 1996 for this discovery. Further research has shown that these tiny balls have unusual physical properties. The molecule is particularly stable because the 60 carbon atoms are arranged into 20 hexagons and 12 pentagons linked to form a sphere.

Scientists formally named buckyballs buckminsterfullerenes, in honor of the architect Buckminster Fuller, because buckyballs have a shape similar to the geodesic dome buildings that Fuller designed. The geodesic dome design results in a particularly strong structure. Fuller liked the design for buildings because not only is it stable but it also encloses the greatest volume while taking up the least surface area. Fuller hoped that the design would produce large numbers of inexpensive homes for soldiers returning from World War II. The geodesic dome can been seen in a number of buildings that exist today including the Biosphere, the Climatron at the Missouri Botanical Garden, and Spaceship Earth at Epcot Center in Disneyland. The shape of the building makes it ideal for withstanding high winds such as those found in hurricanes. To see geodesic domes under construction visit *www.bfi.org/domes*.

Just like the buildings, the buckyball molecules have remarkable characteristics such as a high surface area-to-volume ratio. Buckyballs are being explored for a wide range of applications, including as vehicles for drug delivery, as tiny environmental sensors, and as light detectors.

NANOTUBES

In 1991 in Tsukuba Japan, Sumio Iijima was looking at electron microscope images and noticed unusual threads lying in carbon. These regularly shaped threads—nanotubes—were made of carbon and have emerged as valuable tools for nanotechnology applications. Nanotubes have unique properties including unusual strength, electrical conductivity, and thermal stability. Nanotubes have now been used in a wide variety of products including plastics and displays. Nanotubes have shown great promise to push computer miniaturization even smaller than ever.

Geodesic Dome

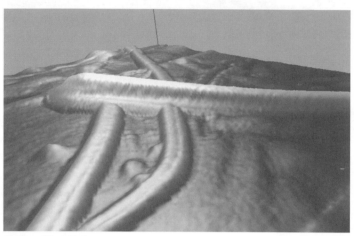

Carbon Nanotubes

The strength of nanotubes comes from the way the carbon atoms link together. The hardness of diamonds is a result of the tetrahedral arrangement of the carbon atoms and the strength of the carbon-carbon bond. We now know that nanotubes exist naturally in soot, and scientists are now creating nanotubes artificially for potential uses in a number of products. In nanotubes, the carbon atoms are arranged in hexagonal rings that look like a roll of chicken wire. There are both single-walled nanotubes (like a cylinder) and multiwalled nanotubes (like a cylinder within a cylinder; similar to Russian nesting dolls). Some nanotubes are open at both ends and others taper off to a rounded point and are closed at the end.

There are three different shapes of nanotubes: zigzag, armchair, and chiral (Figure 4.1). To visualize these different arrangements, imagine that you bend chicken wire in different directions to form a cylinder. Although all three arrangements are made of the same chicken wire and have the same hexagonal arrangement of atoms, the different wrapping directions give the nanotubes slightly different configurations.

Nanotubes have remarkable properties, including unique electrical properties, great tensile strength, resilience, and thermal stability. These are the properties that engineers and materials scientists are harnessing as they design new products and applications. For example, paint manufacturers are using the electrical properties of nanotubes to create new forms of paint that will better stick to plastic. Engineers are experimenting with nanotubes as tiny wires that could replace wires in electronic circuits.

NANOCONSTRUCTION

In this activity students explore the unique geometry of the carbon nanotube and the buckyball. Students examine the patterns of carbon bonding that lead to these unusual structures.

FIGURE 4.1 ....
THREE TYPES OF CARBON NANOTUBES: ARMCHAIR (TOP), ZIGZAG (MIDDLE), AND CHIRAL (BOTTOM)

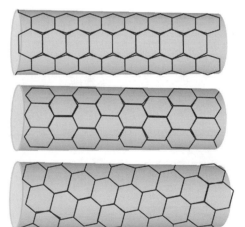

MATERIALS

For each student:
- Copies of the *Build a Buckyball* pattern (page 30)

PROCEDURES

ENGAGE Ask the students, *What are some things that are made of carbon? Have you ever heard of carbon?* You may have carbon graphite in your pencil or a ring or earrings with a diamond, a very hard form of carbon. It is the arrangement of carbon atoms that results in the different forms from soft (graphite) to hard (diamond). Brainstorm all the different types of carbon that you may have encountered (carbon in a grill, activated carbon in a fish tank filter, carbon in smog, or carbon in carbon dioxide that we exhale).

Buckyballs and carbon nanotubes are two types of carbon molecules that have been shown to behave differently from most carbon-containing substances and the differences in behavior that buckyballs and nanotubes exhibit are due to the differences in arrangements of the carbon atoms.

EXPLORE Directions: You can make a buckyball (looks just like a soccer ball) by connecting the carbon atoms in a distinctive pattern. Each buckyball is composed of 60 carbon atoms and is called C_{60} for short. The official geometric pattern is a truncated icosahedron. The ball has 32 faces including 20 regular hexagons and 12 pentagons.

The hexagon has six equal sides and angles are equal (the points where the sides meet). The pentagon has five equal sides and angles. When all the sides are the same length it is called a "regular" hexagon or pentagon.

Build a buckyball by cutting out the C_{60} pattern and taping the sides together. The sides are labeled with a letter so that you know to match side A on one face to side A on the corresponding face. Experiment with enlarging the buckball pattern to make larger models. Copying the pattern on card stock paper will make it easier to fold and tape. Your finished buckyball should look just like a mini soccer ball.

EXPLAIN Encourage students to examine the pattern and identify where the carbon atoms would be located and where the covalent bonds are found. Ask them, *Are all the faces composed of a hexagon? Count the vertices to see if there are really sixty carbon atoms in the model.*

EXTEND Investigate geodesic domes in your community. Encourage students to bring in photographs of geodesic domes that they have seen. Explore how domes are being used in playgrounds, camping equipment, homes, and businesses. How are these homes more or less efficient and more or less comfortable than traditional buildings?

Do a web search and investigate new applications for carbon nanotubes and buckyballs. How are these molecular structures being used in new products? Scientists are now investigating the use of nanotubes to make tear-resistant fabrics, concrete that won't crack, lighter tennis rackets, stronger bicycles, lightbulb filaments that will last longer, and water filters that can be used to desalinate water.

Encourage your students to make larger models of buckyballs and carbon nanotubes out of different materials. Use a molecular modeling kit to make a buckyball. Challenge your students to make models of the three types of nanotubes (zigzag, armchair, and chiral.) Make inexpensive nanotubes from coffee stirrers (the plastic hollow type) and pipe cleaners. Cut the coffee stirrers in half and cut the pipe cleaners into 4 cm sections. The pipe cleaners can then be inserted into the ends of the stirrers and can join one stirrer to another.

EVALUATE Assess students' understandings of nanogeometry by asking them to respond in groups or individually in writing to these questions:

1. What unique properties do nanotubes have?
2. How are buckyballs and nanotubes being used in new products and manufacturing?
3. What aspects of the geometry of the nanotube contributes to the unique properties of this molecule?
4. Are nanotubes found only in laboratories or are they found in nature?
5. Show your students several types of three-dimensional iscohedral shapes and ask them to identify which are not accurate representations of buckyballs.

Make your own Buckeyball!

Just print out the figure below, cut out the hexagons, and start folding along the lines common to two hexagons. You will find that the flat sheet neatly curls up into a sphere-like object as rings of hexagons are connected by pentagons (really this is easy! The figure practically makes itself once you start folding). This clearly illustrates how a graphite sheet rolls up into a buckyball. A few pieces of tape, and you'll have your own truncated icosahedron. Enjoy!

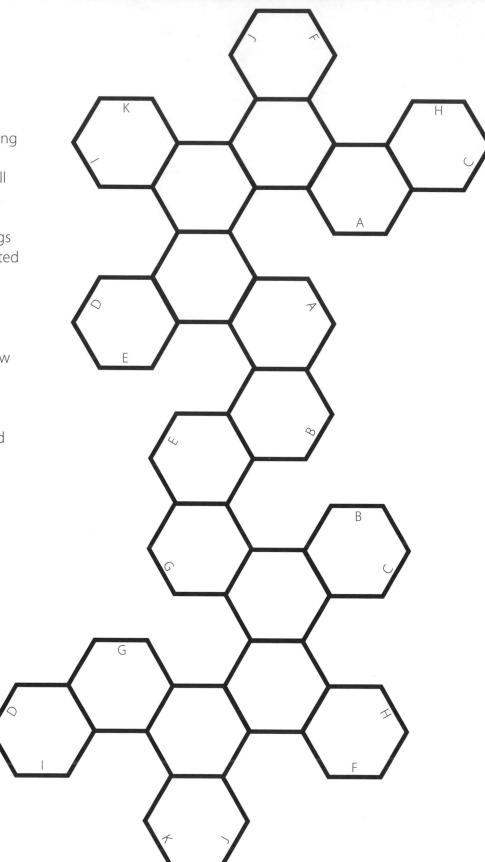

CHAPTER 5

BIOLOGICAL NANOMACHINES: VIRUSES

OVERVIEW

Although nanotechnology is a new and emerging field, nanoscale structures are not new. Small molecules such as water, large molecules such as proteins, and larger, more complex objects such as viruses and nanotubes are naturally occurring and exist all around us. Viruses are particularly interesting nanoscale objects because of their precise geometrical shape, their self-assembling capability, and their fascinating ability to invade cells and alter their function. Nanoscale science researchers are studying virus properties with the aim of developing new treatments for human disease. The virus is also being studied as a model for how to make materials and engineer products at the nanoscale through a process called "self-assembly." In this investigation, students create an icosahedral virus model and consider how virus structure and behavior could be mimicked in nanotechnology applications.

OBJECTIVES

- To be able to describe the morphology of a virus.
- To be able to describe how viruses function as nanomachines.
- To be able to describe how viruses self-replicate.

Process Skills
- Observing
- Predicting

Activity Duration
30 minutes

BACKGROUND

Viruses are natural nanomachines. They are exquisitely well designed to enter the body, travel through the bloodstream, and then attach, invade, and infect cells. They accomplish this complex task through the use of a host of protein machines that act at each stage of the infection process. Scientists are very interested in viruses both for their efficient biological function, as well as their beautiful architecture and assembling behavior.

The typical virus is 20 to 250 nanometers in length. This is incredibly tiny. A single nanometer is 0.00000004 inches. If a cell were the size of a classroom, then an average virus would be the size of a softball. Research has shown that most students think a virus is much larger than a bacterium since they hear about serious viral diseases. But in reality, most bacteria are a few micrometers (a millionth of a meter) long whereas viruses are nanometer-sized (a billionth of a meter).

As biological machines, viruses are interesting because they are able to perform complex targeted tasks at the molecular scale where the environment is so very different. At this scale thermal energy makes the world very shaky, gravity has almost no effect, there are huge frictional effects, and tiny attractive forces (van der Waals forces) make things stick together. But even with these adverse environmental conditions, viruses exist and find ways to locate their specific target receptors on cells, invade them, and multiply. Given that viruses lack a brain, sensory receptors, a reproductive system, or independent movement, it is clear that the virus is able to perform these tasks purely through its architectural and biochemical design. Unraveling the mysteries of virus design and function provides scientists clues as to how we might design artificial machines that could function at this tiny scale.

ARE VIRUSES LIVING OR NONLIVING?

This is a difficult question to answer because we have yet to define what it means to be living. Does having genetic material mean that it is living? Does having the ability to reproduce mean that it is living? Does needing food and metabolizing mean that it is living?

Clearly, viruses are more complicated than simple molecules or even complex proteins. Yet, they are much simpler than the most basic single-celled organism. Similar to organisms, viruses are made up of proteins and nucleic acids, which are organic compounds. Some viruses have a lipid membrane. They evolve and mutate. A virus has the potential to reproduce with the aid of their host cell, but it does not require food to exist. So it has the ability to reproduce but has no metabolism, which many biologists hold as one of the requirements for being defined as living.

So, depending on how you define living, a virus can be either living or nonliving.

Viruses are essentially nucleic acids packed in a "box" made of proteins. The nucleic acid can be either ribonucleic acid (RNA) or single-stranded deoxyribonucleic acid (DNA) or double-stranded DNA. The protein coat (or capsid) is typically an assembly of one to several protein subunits.

Icosahedral Virus

WHY ARE SOME VIRUSES HARMFUL?

Phage

Viruses can infect many living organisms, from bacteria to plants to animals. However, a single type of virus cannot infect all cell types. Your dog cannot catch a cold from you, for example. Viruses invade cells and force the host cells to produce multiple copies of the virus. In some cases, so many viruses are made in the cell that the cell eventually explodes and dies. Other viruses incorporate their genetic material into the host's chromosomes and stay dormant and then multiply with the cell. Often the host cells are eventually destroyed. When you are infected with a virus, your body's immune system kicks in to start destroying the virus. Many of the symptoms that those who are infected with mild viral infections suffer are actually caused by the body's immune response. For example, fever is one of the body's quick responses to help slow down virus multiplication. The higher the temperature in the body, the more difficult it is for viruses. Eventually, enough antibodies are produced to overwhelm the viruses and the infection and illness subside.

ARE VIRUSES DANGEROUS OR NOT?

Viral infections vary in severity from those that cause warts to those that are very serious (such as Ebola). Surprisingly, viruses can be used to help cure diseases rather than causing them. Scientists have found ways to modify the virus so that it acts as a *gene vector* rather than a parasite. They remove the viral genome so that the virus can no longer replicate and replace it with human genes that direct proper cell functioning. A vector is an object that can be injected into the bloodstream and get into target cells. A gene vector is then a carrier for a gene that arrives at a target cell, invades it, and alters the cell's nucleus by inserting the gene into the cell's genetic material. This is what is known as "gene therapy" and is still very much in the developmental stage as a therapy for human disease. One example of proposed gene therapy uses the viral vector to insert a gene into a diabetic patient's cells that produces insulin.

DEFINING PROPERTIES OF VIRUSES

What makes something a virus? There are common characteristics that viruses share. Viruses are parasites that invade cells. Without the cell the virus cannot survive. Viruses have either DNA or RNA that are gene codes for reproduction of the virus and other reprogramming of the host cell viral characteristics and behavior. As parasites, viruses direct the synthesis of new viruses within the host cell. Newly made viruses infect other cells. This infection process is highly specific and critical for the virus to keep the replication process going.

VIRUS STRUCTURE

Viruses are covered by a protein coat known as a capsid. Viruses are usually shaped somewhat like rods or spheres. A closer look at viruses reveals that there is a remarkable geometry to each virus shape. Furthermore, viruses utilize a highly efficient shape to ensure replication within a cell.

In 1956, Francis Crick and James Watson noticed that the genetic material in small viruses was probably insufficient to code for more than a few protein molecules of limited size. They speculated that the only way a virus could build a protein coat was to use the same type of molecule over and over again. They called this theory the theory of identical subunits. Crick and Watson noticed that the only way to provide each component of a virus with an identical environment was by packing them to fit some form of cubic symmetry. We now know that Crick and Watson were right and that viruses are composed of repeated, identical subunits. Furthermore, scientists have found there are only a very few shapes of viruses, that differ externally only slightly. There are two primary shapes that make up most viruses: helical capsids (rod shaped) and icosahedral (spherical shaped).

COMMON VIRAL DISEASES

Disease	Virus	Image
AIDS	HIV	
Wart	Herpes Simplex Virus	
Flu	Influenza	
Measles	Morbillivirus	
Cancer	Hepatitis B	

Helical Capsids

Helical capsids are filament-shaped structures with the RNA in the center of an outer helix. The helix is made by stacking repeating protein subunits in a spiral of RNA. Tobacco Mosaic Virus (TMV) is an example of a virus with a helical capsid.

TMV Virus

Icosahedral Capsids

The icosahedron is the most common virus structure, with 20 triangular faces and 2-fold, 3-fold and 5-fold symmetry axes. These are the axes about which the virus may be rotated to give a number of identical appear-

Adenovirus

ances. The icosahedral geometry is found in a number of unrelated viruses, suggesting that the shape is highly functional for virus replication. DNA or RNA is found in the center or the core of the capsid. Examples of icosa-hedral viruses include the adenoviruses that cause diseases like pinkeye or the common cold. The bacteriophage (phage) is a virus that infects bacteria and has an icosahedral head and a rigid tail. This "space ship" looking virus injects DNA or RNA into the bacterium and hijacks its internal operation. The stages of the process include

1. Viruses attach to the bacterium.
2. Tail penetrates inside the bacterium.
3. The virus protein coat is lost.
4. The virus tricks the bacterium into making more DNA.
5. The bacterium makes proteins for new phage capsids.
6. New phages are released outside of the bacterium.

Enveloped viruses

Enveloped viruses are viruses that have a lipid bilayer membrane coat surrounding the protein coat. These viruses are common in animal viruses, but are uncommon in plant viruses. The membrane comes from the host cell, either from the plasma membrane, golgi membrane, or nuclear membrane. Herpes and HIV are examples of envelope viruses.

An example of an enveloped virus is the Herpes Simplex Virus that causes cold sores.

LIFE REVISED

Are viruses living or not? The answer depends on how life is defined. Viruses do not breathe, me-tabolize, or grow. However, they do reproduce. Not only do they reproduce but they self-assemble (see *How Nature Builds Itself: Self Assembly* in Chapter 11). Researchers have found that virus capsids spontaneously form when given a solution that includes proteins, the right temperature, pH, and salinity. Using traditional criteria for life, such as breathing, metabolism, or growth, viruses are not living. But if one defines life from the bottom up—that is, from the simplest forms capable of displaying the most essential attributes of a living thing—the criteria for life rest on the ability to reproduce. As engineers learn to create machines that can self-assemble and replicate themselves, we might ask again, are these living or not?

VIRUSES AS NANO TRUCKS

Like the buckyball, scientists are exploring ways to use viruses as tiny trucks to deliver drugs, repair DNA, or act as tiny sensors. Each virus has specific bonding site requirements, which means that viruses are highly specific in the type of host they will invade. Already viruses are being used in gene therapy as vehicles that can carry and deliver DNA to a host cell. The host takes in the virus and assimilates the viral DNA into its own genetic code. The goal is to use this form of gene therapy to repair mutated DNA or replace a faulty code with a functioning gene sequence. The hope is that through gene therapy, diseases like diabetes, cystic fibrosis, or Parkinson's disease could be eradicated.

BUILD A VIRUS

···MATERIALS···

Each individual will need:
- Virus capsid template
- 10 meters of yarn
- Tape

Optional materials
- 3 pipe cleaners
- 1 pencil

Note: Copy virus capsid pattern on card stock for best results

ENGAGE

Ask students to work with a partner to brainstorm as many names of different types of viruses as possible. Ask them, *What viral diseases have you heard of?*

Show the class a series of photographs of different types of viruses. Ask them to describe the shapes of the different viruses. A great source for images of viruses is the *The Big Picture Book of Viruses* available online at *www.virology.net/Big_Virology/BVHomePage.html*. Viruses are not only beautiful to look at but they have amazing details and configurations.

EXPLORE

Explain to the students that they will create a model of an icosahedral virus—a biological nanomachine. The icosahedral shape is very common and includes viruses such as the polio virus, adenovirus (common cold) and the virus that causes hepatitis A. Review the characteristics of viruses and the morphology of viruses. Point out the 20 triangular faces and 2-fold, 3-fold and 5-fold symmetry axes found on the icosahedral virus. Note that DNA or RNA is found in the center or the core of the virus capsid.

INSTRUCTIONS FOR BUILDING AN ICOSAHEDRAL VIRUS

1. Make a copy of the virus pattern (page 37).
2. Cut along the outer edge of the pattern.
3. Fold and crease the bold lines.
4. Tape the edges together, leaving one side open.
5. Cut 10 meters of yarn to represent the DNA and place it inside your virus.
6. Tape the virus model closed.

Example of a Virus Model

EXPLAIN

Review the components of the virus. Describe the different shapes of viruses and the process viruses use to infect a host cell, replicate, and infect new viruses. Discuss theories about why viruses are symmetrical and have repeated faces composed of regular subunits.

EXTEND

Invite your students to find the most unusual virus they can locate on the internet. What is the shape of the virus? What is the host cell for this new virus?

Encourage your students to add to their virus model to more accurately represent specific viruses. What would it take to make the model look like HIV or herpes simplex?

Ask students to decide if a virus is living or nonliving. What defines life in this context? If a human engineered nanomachine could self-assemble and self-replicate, would it be considered living or not?

Research how viruses recognize and attach to specific types of host cells. How does a virus know when to penetrate a cell?

EVALUATE

Show students a series of different virus images and ask them to identify whether or not it is an icosahedral or helical capsid virus type.

Check for understanding:
1. What is the shape of the virus model that you made?
   Answer: icosahedral
2. How many faces are there on the virus model?
   Answer: 20
3. What is the protein shell called?
   Answer: capsid
4. Why do most viruses take the form of one or two basic shapes? Why would two very unrelated viruses have the same shape?
   Answer: Given the small size of the virus and the limited amounts of DNA or RNA, scientists speculate that using repeated faces and a regular symmetry allows the virus to replicate with the fewest number of unique parts.
5. How is a virus like a machine? If you could alter a virus to benefit humans, what would you engineer the virus to do?
   Answer: This question allows students to think creatively about how viruses might deliver drugs, clean out plaque from arteries, gobble up fat cells, or provide extra calcium for bone repair or growth.

BUILD A VIRUS

Make a Virus Model
Using the pattern on the next page, you can make an icosahedral virus like the adenovirus.

Instructions for Building an Icosahedral Virus

1. Print the virus pattern.

2. Cut along the outer edge of the pattern. Students may want to color the capsid.

3. Fold and crease the bold lines.

4. Tape the edges together, leaving one side open.

5. Cut 10 meters of yarn to represent the DNA and place it inside your virus.

6. Tape the virus model closed.

Optional
To add the tail to the capsid, insert a pencil into the bottom of the capsid and tape the paper "capsid" to the paper "tail." Use pipe cleaners or paper clips for tail fibers.

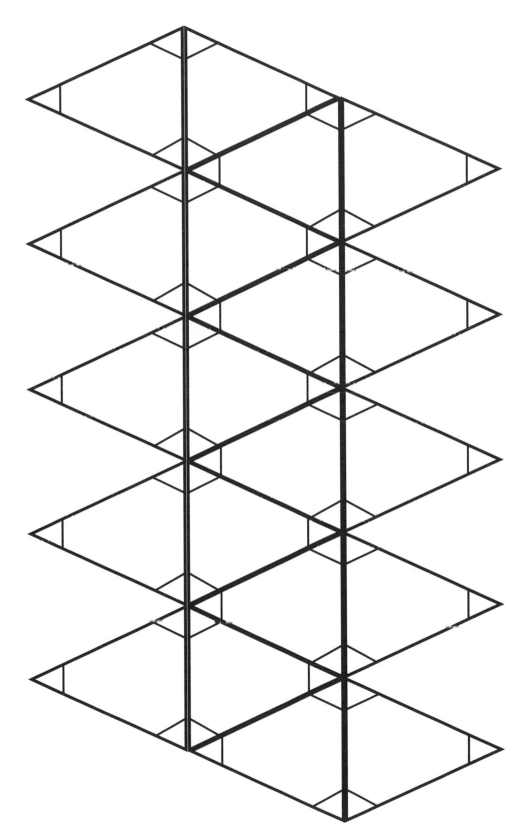

PART II

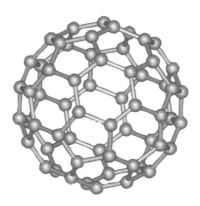

TOOLS AND TECHNIQUES

WHAT'S IN YOUR BAG?
INVESTIGATING THE UNKNOWN

OVERVIEW

In nanoscience, like all scientific endeavors, asking the right questions is a vital part of progress. Our ability to observe how things work at the nanoscale is very limited. We need the use of very advanced microscope technologies as well as other analysis tools to get even a hint of what is going on at this scale. As is the case in all science, the analytical and creative mind of the investigator remains the most important tool involved in the scientific process. Asking the right questions about a particular system helps us develop models of that system. In the end, our scientific understanding of the universe is a collection of models that help us make predictions. These models are constantly debated, refined, amended, and in some cases discarded as evidence and consensus dictate.

OBJECTIVES

- To be able to describe the characteristics of nanoscience work:
  A. Our ability to access scales beyond our senses is limited.
  B. Model building is a central activity in science.
  C. Science is a creative process and includes debate, opinion, and consensus making.

Process Skills
- Observing
- Predicting
- Measuring
- Model Building

Activity Duration
60–90 minutes

BACKGROUND

How do we evaluate things that are smaller or larger than we can see, hear, or touch with our own senses? We use telescopes, microscopes, and a variety of other advanced techniques that give us particular *limited* information about the system. In this exercise, students are given the task of determining what is inside a black bag by feeling it with their hands. They will build models depicting the unknown structure inside. They will come up with tests and controls to validate or discard aspects of these models. Scientific conferences will be held in which each group will display their models and debate the strengths and weaknesses of each. In the end, the class as a whole will attempt to (though may not) come to a consensus on models for each unknown object.

This activity is aimed at helping students understand that scientists are usually working with an incomplete picture when developing an understanding of the universe. Science is essentially a process that includes model construction based on this limited information as well as a debate among peer scientists about the strengths and weaknesses of each model. In the end, a consensus is formed and a model is agreed upon that best describes the system of interest. This exercise is designed to help students appreciate science as a process of model building that requires human creativity, analytical thinking, debate, and cooperation. It is particularly relevant to nanoscale science in that almost everything we know about the structure and function of nanoscale objects is through the indirect means of advanced microscopy and other analytical tools.

PROCEDURES

Advanced Preparation

Several models must be constructed by the instructor and placed within the plastic bags prior to the investigation. The effectiveness of the investigation depends on the students having no prior knowledge of the unknowns within the bags. There are several ways the investigation can be prepared. Several duplicates of the same model can be made and placed within their own plastic bags. Each team is given the same duplicate unknown in a bag. Or if time and resources permit, several unknowns are made that are circulated to each group. In this case there is the possibility that the model will be altered by

Each group will need:

- A sealed black plastic bag with an unknown (Lego model) inside. Note: It is critical that the black plastic be opaque and completely obscure any visual identification of the unknown. Heavy black trash bags can be cut up into smaller pieces of plastic and sealed using duct tape.
- Paper and colored pencils for sketching out model ideas.
- A set of Legos or other building materials available to build trial structures modeling the unknown.
- Student Sheets 1 and 2

the students probing it as it travels between groups. Though destructive interrogation of the unknowns should be discouraged, it can be an interesting point of discussion (in real scientific investigations, samples are altered or destroyed in the process of probing their properties). The most elaborate setup is to make two or three models for each group (again each group should have the same individual or set of models). It is important to the discussion and consensus building part of the exercise that the groups have access to the same model: either duplicates of an unknown or through circulation of a particular unknown.

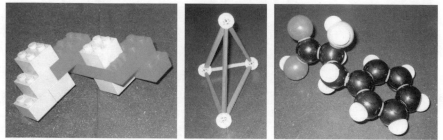

Black Bag Models

HELPFUL HINT: In preparing the models, it is best to err on the side of making them more complicated rather than less. The more challenging the modeling of the unknown, the more effective the exercise. In fact, making the unknowns complex enough such that it is unlikely that the students will be able to reproduce them exactly is preferable. It makes for a richer, more interesting exercise, as well as being a better analogy for real scientific work.

ENGAGE Role-Play: Divide the class into groups of 3–5 students. Explain that each group is a world-renowned research laboratory racing to determine the structure of a set of unknown samples. Hand the unknowns (sealed within the black bags) to each group and explain that the exact structure of the unknown within the bag is of profound scientific and biomedical interest. They are not allowed to cut or compromise the bag in anyway but can use any other means to determine the structure of the unknown inside.

EXPLORE Students investigate the structure of the unknown by feeling the model through the barrier of the plastic bag. They may come up with other tests such as applying magnets for example to glean materials information. The students should be encouraged to discuss/debate what they are determining, and to sketch out ideas about their guesses of the unknown structure on Student Sheet 1.

Once the students have gained some understanding of the unknown's structure, they will then begin building their approximation of the model. The same building materials of which the unknowns are built should be made available to the students (Lego, Tinker Toys, ZOME tool, or molecular models as shown in the figure above). To make the exercise more interesting, the students should be given a choice among several sets of building materials so that they have to choose which will best model the unknown. Encourage the students to test their theories about the unknown object's structure (hypothesis and subsequent test of hypothesis). Are there experiments they can perform to verify or discount a particular aspect of their model? The clever tests that students come up with at this stage can be some of the most rewarding and revealing parts of this whole exercise. Clever tests and controlled experiments are what push scientists beyond the limitations of their instrumentation.

The instructor can decide on how to manage communication between groups at this stage. One option is to simply let the students decide whether to collaborate, be secretive, or to negotiate information trading. If it is done this way, the instructor should observe and note the nature and content of the communication between groups. If more control is desired, simply encouraging students to focus on their own group's work and to ignore other groups at this stage will work fine as well. Give the students 15–20 minutes to work on their models.

CONFERENCES

The second stage of this investigation is to bring the groups together to discuss their models. If several different unknowns have been explored by each group, each group will send a representative to a "conference" for each unknown type. At these conferences, the students present the models that they've built and discuss and debate the strengths and weaknesses of each based on the evidence they collected. Some time should be allotted for the groups to refine their models based on the outcomes of these conferences. One possible outcome is that there may be consensus or agreement between groups on the correct model for a particular unknown. But this may not be the case and is perhaps more interesting if it does not occur (the more complex the unknown structure the more likely this becomes). Each group will submit a final model that they believe best represents the unknown. If there remains a discrepancy between groups, each group should defend their model and describe the evidence and tests that support their view.

THE LAST LESSON: THE BAG REMAINS CLOSED!

If the instructor thinks she or he can pull off this last step without mutiny, it can be a wonderful point of discussion. Scientists don't get to "open the bag." We never have complete knowledge of a system under investigation. Scientists' models and theories are based on the information collected from their instruments, their ingenuity and intelligence, and the outcomes of discussion and debate among their peers. The nanoscale of molecules, viruses, and DNA is a realm of which we have an increasingly refined view using the latest technology but there are large gaps in our knowledge. Much remains within the bag. Much remains to discover!

EXPLAIN Hand out Student Sheet 2 and use it as an outline for a class discussion. Or have students write down answers as an in-class assignment or as homework. There are several general themes that motivate the entire exercise that should be addressed. How is science really done? How do we really "know" what things look like at the nanoscale? How are models used in the scientific process? Is creativity a human quality that plays a part in science?

EXTEND The third section of Student Sheet 2 asks students to do a web search for images of DNA and to answer some questions as homework. The exercise is intended to point out to students that scientists (and teachers) use a variety of different models to describe the same thing. Each model has strengths and weaknesses and may emphasize one aspect or another of a particular system. Models are a way of conveying information about the object in question in the most clear and accurate way. The pictures of water molecules in chemistry textbooks may have red balls depicting oxygen and white balls depicting hydrogen. Of course these colors are made up for the purpose of conveying meaning. The model is very useful in helping the student (or scientist) understand the structure and make predictions about the behavior of the system. But these models are not and cannot be perfectly accurate pictures of the systems they represent.

OTHER HELPFUL HINTS

Ideas for unknown objects:
- Use rubber bands (How many are wrapped on the structure? One, two, three?)
- Thread attaching two pieces (Are the loose pieces attached? How many threads are in there?)
- Include magnets in the unknown structures. Have magnets available to the students but don't make it obvious. Make them figure it out.

Things to encourage and emphasize during discussion:
- What clever tests were used to determine the validity of particular ideas? Example: "We used a magnet to see if there were magnets in our unknown object." "We felt on our model with our eyes closed to see if it felt like the unknown object." Celebrate these clever tests if they happen. This is one of the ways in which creativity is crucial to scientific work. One must design experiments with disciplined creativity.

WHAT'S IN YOUR BAG?

Name _____

Problem: What's Inside the Bag?

The unknown object inside the black plastic bag is of profound scientific importance. You and your colleagues are members of a famous scientific laboratory. You have been given this sample because of your reputation for solving difficult scientific problems. Your job is to figure out the structure of the unknown object. The only rule is that the black bag must not be looked in, or damaged in any way.

Prediction:

Use the materials supplied by your teacher to construct a model that best depicts your vision of the unknown object's structure. As you discuss your ideas with your colleagues, draw diagrams of your trial models.

Drawing:

What tests can you perform to determine your model's accuracy? Be careful not to damage your unknown object while you investigate its structure (if you come up with a test that requires altering the model, check with your instructor).

Tests:

Process: Scientific Conferences

1. Once you have come up with a trial model that you are happy with, you will go to a conference attended by the other prestigious research laboratories that are investigating the same thing.

2. Discuss and debate with your colleagues from other labs the advantages and disadvantages of each model. Though the goal (as in real scientific work) should be consensus, be loyal to those aspects of your model of which you are most confident.

Name _____

Questions: Modeling and Science

1. Are any of the models you built perfect representations of the objects in the bag? To what degree?

2. Can a model be perfect?

3. If a model is not perfect, can it still be useful? Why or why not?

4. Is this exercise a good analogy to scientific work? Discuss ways in which you think it is and ways in which it is not.

5. What is the point of this exercise within the context of nanoscience? How do we "see" things of nanometer scale?

6. If you had to rebuild one of your models from memory a week from now, do you think you would be as successful if you had just seen a picture of your model (not built it)? Why or why not?

Questions: Communication and Science

1. How did you communicate with your partners about the structure of the object?

2. Were the models redone after discussion with other groups?

3. Did you use what you would call "creativity" in solving your model problem?

4. How do you think this process compares to actual scientific work?

Homework: Models of DNA

What does DNA "look like"? On your home or classroom computer, do an internet image search for "DNA." You will see a whole host of different representations of DNA. All of them are models of one type or another.

1. Which model/picture is "best" and why do you think so?

2. Describe what "best" means in this case or use some other word that you think is more appropriate.

3. Which model/picture do you think is different than the rest? Describe in what way you think it is different.

CHAPTER 7

NANOMAGNETS: FUN WITH FERROFLUID

OVERVIEW

Ferrofluid provides an easy opportunity to introduce students to the fascinating properties of the nanoscale. It is essentially a liquid magnet made of nanosized magnetic particles suspended in water or oil. Not only does it demonstrate the strange and beautiful properties of the nanoscale, but is also illustrates a case where nanoparticles and their associated properties provide interesting opportunities for technological applications.

OBJECTIVES

- To investigate the properties of ferrofluid.

Process Skills
- Observing
- Predicting
- Modeling

Activity Duration
30 minutes

BACKGROUND

Did you know that the dollar bill in your pocket is magnetic? The United States Treasury uses magnetic ink in the one-dollar bill! Magnetic fluids have a variety of interesting technological uses. One particularly fascinating type of magnetic liquid is called *ferrofluid*. Ferrofluid can be purchased relatively cheaply and with the aid of a strong permanent magnet and close supervision, students can experience a truly amazing example of the beautiful phenomena that can occur using magnetic fields and nanomaterials.

WHAT IS FERROFLUID?

Ferrofluid is a colloidal suspension of small magnetic particles, usually made of iron oxide (magnetite). These particles are extremely small: about 10 nanometers in diameter. A coating, called a "surfactant" surrounds each particle and keeps them from sticking together and falling out of solution. Though the name suggests ferrofluids are made up of ferromagnetic particles (permanently magnetized like a refrigerator magnet), the particles are in fact "superparamagnetic." Superparamagnetism is a special property of the nanoscale. When a normally ferromagnetic material like magnetite is shrunk down to the size of a nanoparticle (<20nm or so), it loses its permanent magnetic capability. Ferromagnetism depends on many (thousands) of neighboring ferromagnetic atoms reinforcing each other to sustain a collective magnetic moment. When the particle gets too small, the reinforcing effect becomes too weak to achieve this phenomena. The particle instead is "paramagnetic," which means it becomes magnetic when in the presence of a magnetic field. The particles in the ferrofluid are just normal metal particles when there is no magnetic field near them, and the fluid as a whole acts like a normal fluid. However, when a strong magnet is brought close to the fluid, something very unusual and amazing happens. The fluid becomes more solidlike as the magnetic particles are magnetized by the applied field. The particles attract each other and

Ferrofluid in a small petri dish. Top: Ferrofluid with no applied magnetic field. Bottom, Ferrofluid "spiking" in the presence of a strong permanent magnet on the underside of the dish.

form structures within the fluid. At the human scale, we see "spikes" and other strange shapes forming. The petri dish figure (p. 49) shows a case of some subtle "spiking" behavior. A small, strong magnet usually produces the best results.

USES OF FERROFLUIDS

Ferrofluids were originally developed at NASA for use as a liquid seal between moving parts. Because the fluid is magnetic, it can be held in place without leaking out of designated areas such as bearing surfaces. Ferrofluids are also regularly used in high performance speakers. All speakers use magnetic fields to produce the movement that ultimately produces the sound. Ferrofluids are incorporated into the speakers to damp out vibrations that create unwanted overtones. Ferrofluids are also being studied for use as inks in encryption or tagging technologies. In this case, very small patterns of magnetic material could be printed on important documents or objects that could be read later by magnetic sensors. In this way, these items could be identified uniquely using invisible and microscopic "bar codes."

···MATERIALS········

Each group will need:
- Ferrofluid kits or vials
- Magnets (different shapes and sizes)
- Paper and pencil to draw resulting shapes

Note: Ferrofluid can be obtained from a variety of scientific supply companies. Ferrotec Corporation makes a demonstration kit that may be useful (see *www.ferrotec. com* for further information).

PROCEDURES

ENGAGE Ask students to share different uses for magnets in and out of school. Challenge them to see if any of their coins or folding money is magnetic. Provide strong magnets and invite them to explore their money. Warn students to keep strong magnets away from their watches and electronic equipment.

Amazingly, American paper money has magnetic ink on it. See if your students can attract the bill with the magnet. Explain that ferrofluid is a colloidal suspension made up of many nano-sized particles. These particles (usually made of iron oxide) show interesting behaviors when brought into close contact with a strong magnet.

EXPLORE Distribute a small glass vial of ferrofluid and a magnet to each group and ask students to make predictions and observations about what will happen when the magnet is brought near the vial.
Note: Ferrofluid is a very messy substance that needs to be handled with care. To keep the mess to a minimum, you may want to use it in small vials rather than allowing students to explore it in an open container. Gloves and goggles are needed if the ferrofluid is investigated outside of a vial.

Have students draw what they observe when the magnet is placed in different locations near the vial. Encourage them not to shake the vial of ferrofluid. Shaking it causes the ferrofluid to separate into droplets and reduces the spiking.

Ask the students to think about their observations and propose an explanation to describe the strange behavior of the fluid.

Challenge them to make as many different shapes with the magnet as possible.

EXPLAIN Demonstrate the spiking that occurs when the magnet is brought close to the ferrofluid. The spiking is a result of the ferrofluid aligning to the invisible magnetic lines of force. The spikes occur when the lines of force are perpendicular to the ferrofluid.

Turn the magnet and show students using an overhead projector what happens when the magnets are not perpendicular but are parallel to the ferrofluid.

Discuss the colloidal properties of ferrofluid and explain that the particles are about 10nm in diameter. Note that ferrofluids are made up of ferromagnetic particles that are superparamagnetic, a property that is found at the nanoscale. When a normally ferromagnetic material like magnetite is shrunk down to the size of a nanoparticle (<20nm or so), it loses its permanent magnetic capability. Ferromagnetism depends on many (thousands) of neighboring ferromagnetic atoms reinforcing each other to sustain a collective magnetic moment. When the particle gets too small, the reinforcing effect becomes too weak to achieve this. The particle instead is paramagnetic, which means it becomes magnetic when in the presence of a magnetic field. So the particles in the ferrofluid are just normal metal particles when there is no magnetic field near them. So the fluid as a whole acts like a normal fluid would act. However, when a strong magnet is brought close to the fluid, the fluid becomes more solid as particles are magnetized by the applied field. The particles attract each other and form structures within the fluid.

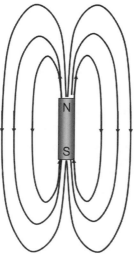

Magnetic Lines of Force

EXTEND Ferrofluid can be used to create wonderful designs. Take several small magnets and glue them into an interesting shape (a star, flower, or symbol). Place the magnet in the bottom of an aluminum pie pan and slowly add ferrofluid to the pan using a syringe. Watch as the ferrofluid takes on the shape of the magnet creating a three-dimensional design.

Ask students to think of new products that could be made or enhanced with ferrofluid. Explain that ferrofluids are often used in high performance speakers to dampen unwanted vibrations. What new applications could be made that use the unusual properties of ferrofluid? How would the ferrofluid enhance the product?

Homemade ferrofluid can be simulated with corn syrup, iron filings, and magnets. Stir the iron filings into the corn syrup and pour the mixture into a shallow dish. Use the magnet to manipulate the fluid into odd forms.

EVALUATE Check for understanding:

1. What makes ferrofluid behave the way it does?
2. Why is the behavior of ferrofluid considered to be a nanoscale phenomena?
3. Where might you encounter ferrofluid in your home?
4. Imagine you had a spill of ferrofluid in a creek or waterway. How could you clean it up efficiently?

CHAPTER 8

SCANNING PROBE MICROSCOPY

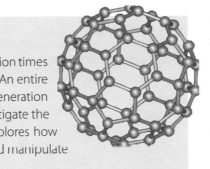

OVERVIEW

Imagine you could build an object that is a billion times smaller than a meter. What would you build? An entire new field has emerged as a result of a new generation of microscopes that allows scientists to investigate the world at the tiniest of scales. This activity explores how Atomic Force Microscopes work to image and manipulate materials at the nanoscale.

OBJECTIVES

- To be able to describe how an atomic force microscope and a scanning tunneling microscope work to create images at the nanoscale.
- To be able to describe the benefits and limitations of using probing microscopes.

Process Skills
- Modeling
- Collecting Data
- Inferring

Activity Duration
45 minutes

HISTORY OF MICROSCOPES

The first microscopes used glass lenses to magnify tiny objects. The highly advanced modern versions of these *light microscopes* are still used regularly in laboratories and remain invaluable tools in the physical and biological sciences. But these light microscopes cannot resolve objects that are much smaller than the wavelengths of visible light. Most protozoans and cells that we examine with optical microscopes are microns (a millionth of a meter) in size. The wavelength of white light is approximately 0.5 micrometers. What if we want to look at viruses, proteins, or molecules that are smaller than microns—smaller than the wavelength of light?

Following Anton van Leeuwenhoek's simple optical microscope built in 1674, scientists realized that in order to create images of objects smaller than the wavelength of light it was necessary to find ways to image without visible light. This led to the development of the electron microscope in the 1930s. Electron microscopes accelerate electrons in a vacuum and focus a beam of these electrons on a sample. The electrons are either absorbed or scattered and an electron-sensitive photographic plate or detector captures the electron scattering to form an image of the sample.

There are two predominant types of electron microscopy: Transmission Electron Microscopy (TEM) and Scanning Electron Microscopy (SEM). TEM was invented in the 1930s by German physicists Ernst Ruska and Max Knoll. Ruska was awarded a Nobel Prize for this invention in 1986. A TEM passes a focused beam of high energy electrons through a very thin sample and records an image on a surface below the sample (on film or an electronic sensor). A TEM works very much like a light microscope except that electrons are used instead of light and magnetic fields are used (called magnetic lenses) instead of glass lenses. High-energy electrons have very small wavelengths (smaller than the size of atoms or less than one angstrom) and this allows for very high-resolution imaging.

The SEM was developed in the 1950s and had the advantage of not requiring electrons to pass through the sample. This allows for much more general applications of surface imaging. This form of microscope uses electromagnets to steer an electron beam and scan it over the sample. The electrons bounce off the sample (or produce other electrons that are emitted from the sample) that are collected in a detector and processed to make an image. The SEM typically requires considerable sample preparation and in many cases objects to be imaged must be frozen or coated with a metallic coating.

Electron microscopes (EMs) provide the ability to study materials at the nanoscale, allowing scientists to see down to the molecular and in some very special cases the atomic level. Within both materials science and biological contexts, EMs have become a central tool in evaluating materials. One constraint of electron microscopes is that objects that are imaged must be placed in a vacuum and covered with a conducting layer (usually a thin gold film). Living materials cannot survive these conditions. Electron microscopy is regularly used to look at biological samples to investigate structure, but these samples are "dead" and are not in their natural biological environments. Much extremely valuable biological structural information has been and continues to be gained through use of electron microscopes despite these limitations, but there are other techniques now available that address their shortcomings.

SCANNING PROBE MICROSCOPES

Over the past 20 years, a new class of microscopes has been developed, which are collectively known as Scanning Probe Microscopes (SPMs). These microscopes all share the common feature of employing a very sharp tip that is scanned over a sample surface to measure some property. These probing microscopes bypass the problem of using glass lenses by directly probing materials. The process is similar to rubbing a sharp pencil across a quarter to detect the shape of the face and locate the words and numbers by feeling the small changes in the metal.

SCANNING TUNNELING MICROSCOPE

The first SPM invented in the early 1980s was the Scanning Tunneling Microscope (STM) which was the first microscope to image individual atoms. Gerd Binnig and Heinrich Rohrer of the IBM Zurich Research Laboratory won the 1986 Nobel Prize for Physics for their invention (a prize which they shared that year with Ernst Ruska, the inventor of the TEM!). The STM uses a very sharp metallic wire that is brought within a few angstroms of a surface and scanned over that surface. A tunneling current is collected that is used to create an image of the surface. Tunneling current happens when electrons move through a barrier that they classically shouldn't be able to move though. When the tip is brought very, very close to the sample, the wavelike nature of the electrons in the tip allow it to "tunnel" or jump over to the sample surface. This only happens when the tip is within atomic distances of the sample. A current of these tunneling electrons is then measured. This current is very strongly (exponentially) dependent on the tip-sample distance and therefore modulations in the tunneling current provide information about the topography of the surface.

In some very cutting-edge experiments, scientists have been able to manipulate atoms one at a time using the STM. In one famous experiment, researchers at IBM spelled out the name IBM with atoms. What if one day you could have atomic labels in your clothes that had your name spelled out in a single layer of atoms?

ATOMIC FORCE MICROSCOPE

Following the STM, Gerd Binnig, Christoph Gerber, and C. F. Quate invented the Atomic Force Microscope (AFM) in 1985. This first AFM used a tiny diamond tip glued onto a piece of very thin gold foil that acted as a spring. Over the past 20 years, AFM technology has advanced significantly and it has become the most prevalent form of scanning probe microscope. AFMs are now a common and essential part of research in many areas of science including physics, chemistry, biology, geology, materials science, forensic science, as well as myriad biomedical contexts.

HOW AN AFM WORKS

The sharp tip of the AFM probe is very small and looks a bit like the tip of a needle. The tip is attached to the end of a flexible cantilever which bends up and down as the tip moves over the hills and valleys of the sample. The up-and-down movement of the tip is measured by the movement of light from a laser reflected off the back of the flexible cantilever and picked up by a laser detector connected to a computer (see Figure 8.1). As the reflected laser beam is deflected up and down on the laser detector, a measure of the motion of the tip can be estimated. The computer essentially graphs the light position and as the tip moves back and forth in a series of parallel lines, the tip movement is translated into a three-dimensional image.

The resolution of AFM, as well as all other scanning

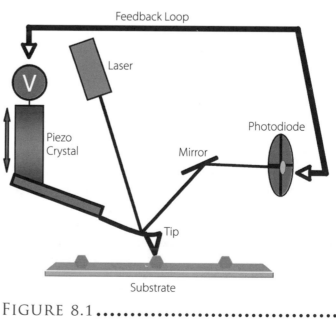

FIGURE 8.1 ....
ATOMIC FORCE MICROSCOPE FEEDBACK LOOP

probe microscopes, is limited in part by the sharpness of the tip. The sharper the tip, the better the image. Also, the tip can only scan over the tops of things and is unable to reach under them. One major advantage of AFM over STM or electron microscopy is that live biological samples can be imaged in their native biological solutions. This is extremely difficult and usually impossible with STM or electron microscopies.

The AFM is able to not only image a sample but can also manipulate a sample since the tip that does the imaging is actually touching the sample. The side-by-side figures below show an adenovirus before and after being pressed by the AFM tip.

In work done by our research team, the tip has been used in virus research to squash the virus capsid (releasing the DNA), roll the virus (allowing us to investi-

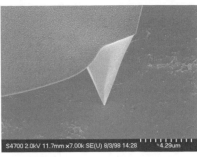

AFM Tip

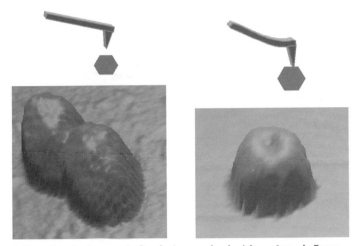

Adenovirus before and after being probed with an Atomic Force Microscope.

gate the morphology of the capsid), and probe the elasticity of the virus capsid. When imaging, the tip is pressed against the sample very lightly so it does not alter the sample and a clear image can be constructed. When manipulating, the force of the tip on the sample is increased to move or deform the sample. Researchers are now using the AFM to image individual DNA strands and pull and stretch individual protein molecules.

What makes an AFM such an amazing tool is that it allows scientists to manipulate matter directly for the first time at the tiniest of scales. Imagine the challenges of trying to build and experiment with individual molecules when you couldn't pick one up or image it. Not only can researchers explore how things are constructed (probing and imaging) but they can also try to build materials in novel ways.

AFM Sequence image generated as the tip moves back and forth across the sample.

IMAGES FROM PROBES: MODELING AN ATOMIC FORCE MICROSCOPE

··MATERIALS········

Each group will need:
- 2 wooden barbeque skewers (Snip off tip of skewers)
- Metal twist tie
- White paper (11 × 14 inches is ideal but any size as large as a shoebox top will work)
- Pen
- Shoebox with unknown object taped to the floor of the box (tape sides of shoebox)
- Graph paper
- Tape
- Quarter
- Pencil
- Paper
- Student Sheet 1

PROCEDURES

ENGAGE
If possible have students complete the *What's Inside the Bag* investigation before beginning this modeling activity. Ask, *How can you figure out what is inside an object that you can't see or cut open?* Encourage them to think about a range of ways to investigate an object. Typical responses include: Using x-rays, weigh the object, use magnets, and shake or squeeze the object.

Explain how an Atomic Force Microscope works (see introductory information). Model the general approach by having students place paper over a quarter and rub with a sharp pencil. The image that appears will provide clues about the topography of the coin.

EXPLORE
Launch the investigation by explaining that the task is to use the wooden skewers to determine the shape of an unknown object inside the shoebox. Note that this activity models the way an Atomic Force Microscope scans back and forth across a sample to create an image. Review the directions on the student investigation sheet for making the box, probe, and data recording sheet.

Suggestion: Have students record the height of the probe in a different color on the recording sheet for each column on the box. Then, after they complete sampling all the holes in a single column, they can connect all the dots with that one color. This allows them to build a contour map of the objects as they are situated on the floor of the box.

EXPLAIN
Invite students to share their images and describe what they think is in the box or sketch the "terrain" on the bottom of the box. After looking at the 2-dimensional image, open the box and compare the image to the object. What characteristics of the object were not picked up by the point sampling process? (It isn't possible to image the underside of the object with an atomic force microscope or probe the underside of the object in the box).

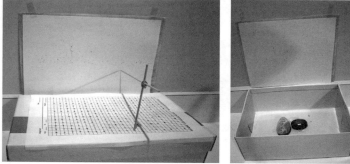

Example of a Shoebox With Graph Paper

Explain how the process is similar to the way an Atomic Force Microscope works, except that instead of making pen marks on paper a laser would pick up undulations in the movement of the tip of the probe. The tip movements are recorded and the computer uses these series of points to produce a three-dimensional drawing of the object.

EXTEND
- Discuss how the probe can be used to both image and manipulate objects. Ask students to think about the difficulties involved in building with a probe—where they cannot directly use their hands.
- Using the internet, books, and magazines, have students research new applications of nanotechnology and discoveries made with the Atomic Force Microscope.
- Explore the different ways that tips are made for the microscope.
- Investigate dip pen lithography and potential uses for this technology.

EVALUATE

To assess students' understandings you may ask your students:

- Make a drawing that explains how an Atomic Force Microscope works.
- What makes an Atomic Force Microscope different from a light microscope?
- How are samples different for light microscopes and an Atomic Force Microscope?
- What are the benefits and limitations of imaging with an Atomic Force Microscope?

Name _____

Images From Probes: Modeling an Atomic Force Microscope

Materials

Each group will need:

- 2 wooden barbeque skewers (snip off tips of skewers)
- Metal twist tie
- White paper (11 x 14 inches is ideal but any size as large as a shoebox top will work)
- Pen
- Shoebox with unknown object taped to the floor of the box. Box should be taped closed.
- Graph paper
- Tape

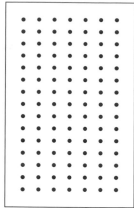

Graph Paper

Procedures

Prepare the Model Microscope:

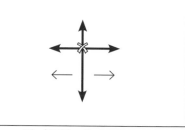

Skewers Tied With a Twist Tie

The Box

Tape a sheet of graph paper over the lid of the shoebox such that the graph covers most of the lid. Punch holes at each intersection of the lines on the graph so that you end up with rows and columns of holes. The holes should be large enough to allow a wooden skewer to move through the lid. Holes can be punched with a compass, ice pick, dental tool, or small scissors. Once the holes are punched give your box to your teacher or another team so they can tape one or two unknown objects in your box and seal the lid of the box to the bottom.

The Probe

Make a probing tip by connecting two skewers at right angles to each other with a metal twist tie. Allow the horizontal skewer to move forward and backward. The vertical skewer will serve as the probe in your model microscope and will be inserted into the holes in your box. The horizontal skewer will serve as a pointer allowing you to record the height of the sample in your box.

Recording Data

Tape a sheet of large white paper on a wall behind a table or desk. This is where you will record your data. Place your box against the wall just next to the paper. Begin sampling with each point on your graph paper by inserting the pointer into the box until the skewer hits either the sample or the bottom of the box. Make sure the horizontal skewer is straight and line it up so that the point just touches the paper. Mark the height of the skewer with a dot. Continue to sample each hole and mark the height on the paper. (To help you visualize the distance from the wall you may want to make each row a different color of ink or use a different symbol (stars, triangles, dots, etc.). After the first row is completed continue with the second row. Once all the holes have been sampled, look closely at the data you have recorded on the wall. Can you infer from the data the topography of the samples inside your box? Discuss your ideas with your group and check your inferences with the data that you collected.

Drawing:
In the space below, draw what you think the objects look like inside the box. Sketch the location of the objects in the bottom of the box.

Now you may open the box to see how accurate you were in your investigation of the unknown objects.

Questions for Discussion

1. What were the limitations of this method of sampling?

2. How could you redesign the tools to make them more accurate without looking at the objects in the box?

3. What were some possible sources of experimental error in your technique?

4. How is this modeling activity different from the workings of an Atomic Force Microscope?

PART III

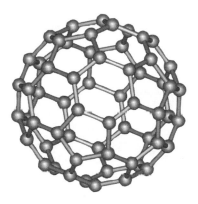

UNIQUE PROPERTIES
AND BEHAVIORS

CHAPTER 9

IT'S A SMALL WORLD AFTER ALL: NANOFABRIC

OVERVIEW

Nanotechnology is producing a variety of new materials we use in our everyday lives. One such development is the latest stain-resistant fabric. This inquiry activity gives students the opportunity to explore and discover unique nanoscale properties of this specially engineered fabric.

OBJECTIVES

- To develop an understanding of the unique properties of nano-technology-engineered fabric.
- To apply concepts of adhesion and cohesion.

Process Skills
- Predicting
- Observing
- Analyzing Data
- Controlling Variables
- Testing Hypotheses

Activity Duration
60 minutes

BACKGROUND

How big is a nanometer?
Like outer space, nanoscale science has only recently become explorable. However, the nanoscale is at the opposite end of the spectrum from the large scales of space exploration. A nanometer is so small that it takes one billion nanometers to equal one meter. That is very, very small. It would take 50,000 nanometers to equal the thickness of a hair on your head. Things like viruses, atoms, and molecules are typically measured at the nanometer size.

HOW DOES THE FABRIC WORK?

A cotton fiber is a round cylinder. Imagine that each cotton fiber is the size of a tree trunk. Also, imagine there are little hairs attached to the tree trunk. It is these nanowhiskers that give the fabric stain resistance. The nanowhiskers are placed onto the cotton fibers when the fabric is dipped into a secret industrial solution. The whiskers land on the surface of each fiber and point in the same direction—outward from the fiber. This physical arrangement allows liquids to sit on the whiskers without penetrating the fabric. In addition, the whiskers are chemically treated, giving the fabric a negative charge. Acid-containing foods (like mustard) tend to cling to the negatively charged fabric surface. Basic foods (such as milk) are typically repelled from the treated fabric.

INVESTIGATION

In this investigation students explore properties of nano-treated stain resistant-fabric. Students consider what types of materials stain and which do not. Are there differences in liquids and solids? Are there common properties of materials that do stain the treated fabric?

MATERIALS

Each group will need:

- 10 cm × 15 cm piece of nano-fabric*
- 10 cm × 15 cm piece of un-treated fabric
- Apron or old shirt
- 7 small cups
- 6 droppers
- Paper towels
- 2 small craft sticks
- Permanent marker
- Timer
- Student Sheet 1

*Note: Nanofabric can be obtained from a number of commercially sold manufacturers. Clothing made with nano-treated fabrics can often be purchased inexpensively at end of season sales. Look for labels such as Nanocare or Nanotex.

Staining Agents:

- Grape juice
- Orange juice
- Ketchup
- Mustard
- Oil
- Milk
- Cream

PROCEDURES

Prior to Lab:

1. Cut the treated and untreated fabric into 10 cm × 15 cm pieces. The students will label the pieces of fabric during the activity. Give each group one piece of treated fabric and one piece of untreated fabric.
2. Gather the staining agents and place small amounts of each into small cups. You may want to place these on a tray in case of spills. Droppers should be used to place staining agents on the fabric.
3. Make copies of Student Sheet 1.

ENGAGE

Open by asking: How many of you have to do laundry? Who would like to reduce the amount of laundry you have to do? Explain that you have purchased some fabric that has been treated through a secret process to make it stain resistant. You want to find out if it really works. Discuss with them that in order to have a controlled scientific experiment you must have a control variable. The control variable is a piece of untreated regular fabric. Explain that they are going to work in groups to test the fabrics using the staining agents and to see if they can predict which materials stain and which do not.

EXPLORE

*Safety: Students should wear safety goggles and a lab apron over their clothes.

Students should work in groups of four. Pass out the Student Sheet 1 to each group of students. Before testing the fabric the students should make a prediction of what they think will happen with a written hypothesis on Student Sheet 1. Instruct the students to follow the procedures on the Student Sheet. They should record their observations in Table 1. Once the students have made observations they should analyze their observations and complete the Conclusions section of the lab.

Discuss the results as a class. For more discussion you could ask the following questions: How many times did you repeat your experiment? Do you think you would get different results if you tried again? Would you buy fabric treated with nanotechnology? Why or why not?

EXPLAIN

Refer to the background section in the teacher notes to explain nanotechnology and how this fabric works. You could design a model of cotton fiber with the nanowhiskers attached. Model a cotton fiber by cutting a pool noodle so that it is about one foot long. Create the nanowhiskers by wrapping pipe cleaners around a pencil or other round object so that they appear to be coiled. Insert the nanowhiskers into the cotton fiber so that they cover the entire cotton fiber. You could demonstrate that the nanowhiskers attach to cotton fibers by actually assembling the model in class. A blown-up balloon or ball could represent a water molecule. Place the balloon or ball up to the nanowhiskers to show that there is very little contact between the surface of the water molecule and the nanowhiskers. This reduces friction between the two surfaces allowing liquids to roll off the surface. It also prevents the liquids from coming into contact with the actual cotton fiber. The liquid sits on the nanowhiskers. Explain to the students that the model is not to scale.

EXTEND

Have students brainstorm other ways to test the fabric. What might reduce the effectiveness of the treated fabric? Some students may suggest rubbing it with sandpaper, washing the fabric with soap, or drying it in a dryer. Are there other staining agents they would like to test? Students may suggest grass, mud, or dye. Have supplies ready for students to test their questions.

Have students present their experiments and results to the class. After hearing the various results, discuss as a whole class their thoughts on the effectiveness of the fabric.

EVALUATE

Check for understanding:

1. In your own words describe the structure of a cotton fiber that has been treated with nanotechnology to make it stain resistant.
2. How does this structure prevent some staining agents from staining the fabric?
3. Why did some of the staining agents we tested actually stain the fabric?
4. Why is this treated fabric beneficial?
5. From the results you have seen of the various experiments what are your ideas on how the structure of the treated cotton fiber could be modified to improve effectiveness?
6. Can you think of other useful ways this concept could be applied?

References

National Research Council (NRC). 1996. *National science education standards.* Washington, DC: National Academy Press.

Tretter, T., and M. G. Jones. 2003. A sense of scale. *Science Teacher, 70* (1): 22–25.

Note: This investigation is modified from Jones, M. G., B. Broadwell, M. Falvo, J. Minogue, and T. Oppewal. 2005. It's a small world after all: Exploring nanotechnology in our clothes. *Science and Children 43* (2): 44–46.

Name _____

Fabric Comparison Test

Problem Question: Does fabric treated with nanotechnology resist stains from the following staining agents: mustard, ketchup, grape juice, orange juice, oil, milk, and cream?

Write a hypothesis of what you think will happen:

_____

_____

_____

_____

_____

_____

_____

_____

_____

_____

Materials
- 10 cm × 15 cm piece of nanofabric
- 10 cm × 15 cm piece of untreated fabric
- Apron or old shirt
- 7 Small cups
- 6 droppers
- Paper towels
- 2 small craft sticks
- Permanent marker
- Timer

Staining Agents
- Grape juice
- Orange juice
- Ketchup
- Mustard
- Oil
- Milk
- Cream

Procedure

1. Put on an old shirt or lab coat to protect your own clothes.

2. Divide into groups of 4 students.

3. Place your two pieces of fabric flat on your desk. Label each with a marker so you don't get them confused in your data collection. The untreated fabric should be labeled "UF" and the treated fabric should be labeled "TF."

Label the fabric with the following abbreviations. Leave enough space between them to place the staining agents on the fabric above each label.

GJ = Grape Juice
OJ = Orange Juice
K = Ketchup
Mu = Mustard
O = Oil
Mi = Milk
C = Cream

4. Put the staining agents in the cups on your desk.

5. Place two drops of grape juice on each piece of fabric above the GJ label. Do the same with the other staining agents so that they correspond with the correct label.

6. Let the staining agents sit for five minutes.

7. When the time is up, remove the staining agents with a damp paper towel.

8. Make observations of what you see on each piece of fabric and record those observations in your data table.

Table 1. Data/Results.

	Fabric	
Staining Agents	**Untreated Fabric (control)**	**Treated Fabric (experimental)**
Grape Juice (GJ)		
Orange Juice (OJ)		
Ketchup (K)		
Mustard (Mu)		
Milk (Mi)		
Oil (O)		
Cream (C)		

Conclusion

1. Was your hypothesis proven or disproven? Explain.

_____

_____

_____

_____

2. What would you do to make this experiment better?

_____

_____

_____

_____

3. Would you buy fabric treated with nanotechnology? Why or why not?

_____

_____

_____

_____

4. How do you think nanotechnology-treated fabric works? You may draw a diagram to explain your ideas.

_____

_____

_____

_____

5. Are there other experiments you could try with nanofabric? What are they?

_____

_____

_____

_____

CHAPTER 10

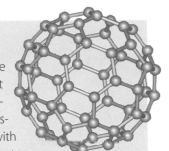

BIOMIMICRY:
THE MYSTERY OF THE LOTUS EFFECT

OVERVIEW

One of the most interesting applications of nanoscale science involves nanomimicry—or technology that mimics the unique structures of biomaterials. This activity uses the forensics approach to have students investigate various plant surfaces and their interactions with substances to explore the phenomena of the lotus effect.

OBJECTIVES

- To develop skills in observation.
- To use observations to make inferences about physical properties of leaves.

Process Skills

- Observing
- Predicting
- Compare and Contrast
- Collecting Data
- Analyzing Data

Activity Duration

90 minutes

BACKGROUND

For hundreds of years, humans have looked to nature for ideas about concepts that can be applied to the human world. The flight of birds inspired the Wright brothers to build a flying machine, Velcro mimics the cocklebur, and thousands of medications based on botanical compounds are now over-the-counter drugs. What better model than nature for us to learn from? The recent development of new tools permits scientists to manipulate matter at the nanoscale, allowing engineers to design new materials. Scientists are now mimicking nature at the nanoscale in an area of study known as biomimicry.

You may have noticed in the grocery store that water beads up and easily rolls off some plants, such as mustard greens and broccoli. These plants have a property known as the lotus effect named for the Asiatic Lotus, a culturally important plant that represents purity in some Asian countries. If you were to look at the surface of a lotus leaf with a microscope you would find the surface is covered in tiny wax particles (as small as a thousandth of a millimeter) making the surface appear very rough. This roughness, along with the hydrophobic nature of the waxy material, causes the leaf surface to be superhydrophobic because of the reduced contact area between the water and the solid leaf surface. What's more, the droplets pick up small particles of

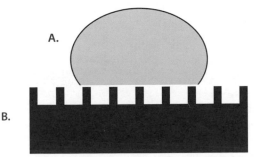

The water droplet (A) sits above the rough surface of the leaf (B). Water droplets roll across the leaf picking up particles (C) and washes them away due to the lotus effect.

dirt as they roll around; giving the lotus leaves a self-cleaning mechanism. It is believed that plants evolved this adaptation as a way to cleanse the surface of debris and spores, as well as to keep it dry. This effect is also observed on insect wings and is believed to serve the same purposes. Now scientists are taking this property and applying it to everyday products, resulting in "self-cleaning" windows and toilets. By mimicking the lotus effect seen in nature we can create materials with new properties and characteristics.

Create a crime scene either on poster board or a PowerPoint slide to show how blood splattered everywhere but did not adhere to the mystery plant.

Plants that exhibit lotus effect	Plants that do not exhibit lotus effect
Lotus (*Nelumbo sp.*)	**Ivy** (*Hedera sp.*)
Mustard plants: Mustard Collards Cabbage (From the family Cruciferae)	**Beech** (*Fagus grandiflora*)
	Magnolia (*Magnolia grandiflora*)
Taro or Elephant Ear (*Colocasia esculenta*)	**Maples** (From the family Aceraceae)

··MATERIALS··

Each group will need:
- 5 water droppers
- 5 small cups/beakers
- Corn syrup
- Liquid glue
- 1 tube of powdered graphite
- Chalk powder
- Dropper bottle with fake blood*
- Sample of the mystery plant (Elephant ear or Lotus leaf)
- Sample of each leaf
- Water
- Copy of case 728-1971
- Student Sheet 1

*Fake blood recipes can be found on the internet and usually consist of corn starch, food coloring, and vegetable oil.

Note: Various leaves for lotus and non-lotus effect can be found in the table on this page. Dividing the leaves up into labeled baggies that correspond to the data table works efficiently.

PROCEDURES

ENGAGE Have a student read the case study for the crime scene aloud. While students are reading the case study, ask them to take notes and sketch the crime scene. Alternatively, you can either create your own crime scene or draw a small version on poster board. Ask the students to summarize the important facts in the case study.

Tell the students that each lab group is a team working for Ms. Nan O'Meter to investigate the crime scene. Students should use Student Sheet 1 to guide them through this activity.

EXPLORE Once students are in the lab groups, they will first answer the question, *Why was the mystery plant not covered in blood?* Have the students find the baggie with a sample of the mystery plant and explore the interaction between the leaf and 2–3 drops of "blood." Ask the students what happens when they drop the fake blood on the leaf and tell them to record their observations on their sheet.

Ask them to answer the question, *Could blood have splattered, but not adhered to the plant?* They should explain their answer on their own paper and brainstorm why they think the "blood" did not adhere to the plant.

Tell the students to remember what they observed with the mystery plant while they investigate interactions other types of leaves in the baggies have with various substances listed on their data table. Note: Emphasize that when they are testing a solid substance, such as powdered graphite, that they should put a small amount on the leaf and rinse with 3–5 drops of water and observe the interactions.

As the students are testing the substances on the different leaves they should record their observations on the data table. Once the data is collected, the lab groups should answer the questions and write the conclusion as to whether or not is was possible for the mystery plant to be present during the murder.

Have lab groups share their conclusions with the class as part of evaluating their understanding. The leaves that exhibit the lotus effect will cause liquid substances to bead up on the surface while the non-lotus effect leaves will not display this effect.

EXPLAIN Once all groups agree that it is indeed possible for the mystery plant to be present during the murder because the substances "roll" off the surface of the plant, explain the phenomena called the lotus effect. Some plants exhibit the lotus effect and some do not. For more information on the lotus effect see the following references:

Barthlott, W., and C. Neinhuis. 1997. Purity of the sacred lotus, or escape from contamination in biological surfaces. *Planta* 202: 1–8.
Benyus, J. 1997. Biomimicry: Innovation inspired by nature. Available online at *www.biomimicry.net/intro.html*
Bonn University Department of Botany. Lotus effect. Available online at *www.lotus-effekt.de/*. (Choose the English version of the page in the lower right corner.)

EXTEND As a class, discuss the following questions: *What new products can you imagine? Contact lenses that never get dirty? Underwear that stays clean? A spoon that repels honey? Airplanes that never ice up?* Allow students time to think about how the use of self-cleaning surfaces in homes and work would impact the economy (reduce sales of cleansers) and the environment (less pollution due to detergent). After brainstorming about new self-cleaning products, have students write a few paragraphs about how the lotus effect could be used to benefit society as well as how it would impact it. Have students share the paragraphs about the lotus effect and society with the class.

EVALUATE Check for understanding:
1. What is the lotus effect?
2. Why do you think some plants exhibit the lotus effect and others do not?
3. What is biomimicry?
4. Name three products that could utilize the lotus effect.

Scanning Electron Micrograph of an Elephant Ear Plant Leaf

BIOMIMICRY

Name _____

Background
Case 728-1971

On the morning of November 10, jewelry store manager Ms. Ruby entered the store to find the horrific site of a ransacked office, stolen money and jewels, and her beloved security guard Mr. Locke shot. She found him lying by the plants near the entrance. After getting him medical help she called the police, explaining what she had observed. A rookie named Officer Maladroit was first on the scene and he called the shots until his boss, Detective Meticulous, arrived one hour later. Detective Meticulous was agitated when he observed that the crime scene appeared to have been tampered with and he immediately began pointing fingers at Officer Maladroit. It appeared that someone had placed a plant in the middle of the crime scene. Officer Maladroit emphatically denied tampering with the scene. If Maladroit did not bring in the plant after the shooting, then why were some plants covered in blood and not the mystery plant? Detective Meticulous called his crime scene investigator, Ms. Nan O'Meter, and her team to determine the reason it was not covered in blood like the rest of the crime scene.

Take notes about the crime scene below:

Back at the CSI laboratory, as part of Ms. Nan O'Meter's team, you are to investigate surface properties of plants to determine why the mystery plant was clean, unlike its surroundings.

Investigation at the lab
Why was the mystery plant not covered in blood? Place 3–4 drops of "blood" on the surface of a leaf from the mystery plant. Record your observations below:

Drop of water on surface of Elephant Ear leaf

Could blood have splattered, but not adhered to the plant? Support your answer.

Further investigation

Do all substances behave the same on all types of plants? In your lab group, you will test the interaction of plant surfaces with various substances listed in Table 1 and record your observations.

1. You have been supplied with several types of leaves. You should have several leaves of each type.

2. Place 3–4 drops of the liquid substances (glue, corn syrup, and water) on the surface of each leaf and record observations in Table 1.

3. Lightly sprinkle solid substances (graphite and chalk powder) on the surface of leaves and rinse with 3–4 drops of water. Record the observations in Table 1.

Analysis

1. Did all substances behave the same? If not, *how* were they different?

2. Why do you think some plants interacted differently than others?

3. Which plant samples behaved similarly to the mystery plant? Why?

Conclusion

Is it possible that the mystery plant was present during the murder? Support your answer using the data you collected.

TABLE 1. ···

Directions:

Record observations of substances interacting on the leaf surfaces in table below.

Test Substances Observations*					
Plant	Water	Corn syrup	Graphite	Glue	Chalk powder
A					
B					
C					
D					
E					
Mystery plant					

* Remember to sprinkle solid substances (graphite and chalk powder) lightly on the leaf surface and rinse with 3–5 drops of water and observe.

CHAPTER 11

HOW NATURE BUILDS ITSELF: SELF-ASSEMBLY

OVERVIEW

By designing and building models with Legos and placing them in a reaction chamber, students will simulate the process of molecular self-assembly. This activity provides a basis for understanding that thermal energy at the nanometer scale is a determining factor for whether or not self-assembly occurs.

OBJECTIVES

• To build an understanding of the effects of thermal energy at the nanoscale.
• To build an understanding of self-assembly.

Process Skills
• Observing
• Predicting
• Modeling

Activity Duration
90 minutes

Nanoscale…It's So Small

In order to understand molecular self-assembly, students need to understand just how small the world is at the nanoscale. A nanometer is one-billionth the size of a meter. The thickness of a single hair is 50,000 nanometers. Students have a difficult time conceptualizing a scale this small. Begin by having students complete the investigation *One in a Billion* and *It's Huge!* to gain an understanding of nanometers.

BACKGROUND

Self-Assembly: How Nature Builds

Self-assembly or spontaneous assembly is a process by which materials build themselves without assistance (Goodsell 2000). This is how nature builds its own structures and material, such as viruses, cells, and bone. The principles of self-assembly also inform how specific binding events occur in nature: how a virus binds to a cell or how a drug finds its target. They also inform the development of materials that build themselves. These advances in materials science can lead to new drug delivery and biomedical diagnostic technologies.

A WHOLE LOT OF SHAKING GOING ON

There are two major underlying principles of self-assembly: shakiness and stickiness. On the nanometer scale everything is shaking and bumping around very quickly due to thermal energy. The higher the temperature, the bumpier and shakier things are.

Everything sticks together on the nanoscale through *intermolecular* bonds. These bonds between molecules, sometimes called *physical* bonds, are much weaker than chemical bonds (covalent, ionic, metallic). Intermolecular bonds are so weak, in fact, that individual bonds between molecules are very likely to dissociate spontaneously at a very high rate. Hydrogen bonds between water molecules are such bonds. They are being made and broken continuously. Besides hydrogen bonding, other types of intermolecular bonding include van der Waals bonding and hydrophobic/hydrophilic interactions. The origin of these and other intermolecular bonds also resides in the polar or polarizable nature of molecules. It's important to understand that some form of attractive intermolecular bonding will occur between any two atoms or molecules (though it can be quite weak). The weak nature of these bonds is crucial to their ability to drive self-assembly.

But if everything sticks, how do the specific structures self-assemble instead of resulting in random blobs? Instead of one very strong bond sticking pieces together, nature utilizes several weak bonds in parallel. When the pieces fit properly, all of these bonds work together like many hands joining together. If only one bond exists, structures are not strong enough to stay together with all of the shaking. This occurrence serves as an error correction mechanism. Geometrical compatibility also plays an important role in the self-assembly. The pieces fit together like puzzle pieces such that the multiple weak bonds only come together when the pieces fit in the right way.

····MATERIALS····
• Boxes with lids
• Superglue
• Legos
• Drawing paper
• Small magnets

Teacher Tips

• Use Velcro and magnets in clever combinations to create more unique bonds.
• Extend this to include other materials besides Legos: For example, cardboard, Tinker Toys, or Styrofoam balls.
• If pieces are bonding too strongly with the magnets, place pieces of tape on the magnets' surface to adjust the force (by separating the magnets).

ENGAGE Put the Teacher Transparency on the overhead and ask the students, *What do all these objects have in common?* It is unlikely that anybody will say "They self-assemble." After hearing a few comments, you may lead them by asking, *How are these objects made?*

After a few responses explain to the students that these things make or build themselves through a process called self-assembly. Refer to the background section to define self-assembly. Explain to the class that self-assembly occurs at the nanoscale and the environment at this small scale is very different than the macroscale. Tell the students they are going to design their own molecular models that will be able to self-assemble using magnets and Legos.

EXPLORE

BUILDING A SELF-ASSEMBLY MODEL

Within this activity students design a self-assembling model. Several parts (2, 3, 4, or more) are designed to come together in a specific way (like puzzle pieces). On each of the pieces, magnets or Velcro strips are attached with glue or tape in such a way that the pieces will fit together in a specific pattern. The goal is to make the pieces fit together in only one unique pattern.

1. **Model Design**: Begin by having the students to design a model—it could be a molecular model or simply an abstract geometric model (see figure at right). Have students draw out plans for their model and work out the logic of their bonding schemes. You could even cut out pieces of paper with shapes and bonds represented to determine if the pieces will fit and bond the way you intended (and to make sure that pieces you do not want to bond strongly will not do so). Many mistakes

Model A:

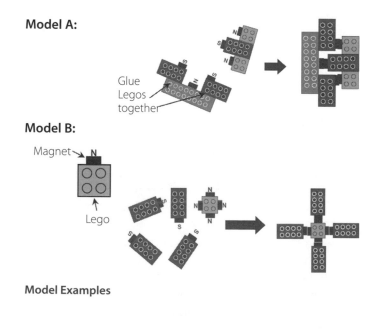

Glue Legos together

Model B:

Magnet

Lego

Model Examples

and false starts can be prevented at this stage. Encourage your students to use clever combinations of bonds (multiple weak bonds) and the lock and key strategy to allow several pieces to come together in a unique predetermined way.

2. **Model Construction**: The next step is to glue or tape your magnets onto your Lego pieces. The students found that superglue works best to withstand breaking from all the shaking that will occur. When applying magnets, remind the students that magnets have two sides: a north and a south (like poles repel, while opposite poles attract). Simply choose one side of a magnet as your reference to continue properly constructing you model. (See Figure 11.1 for model examples)

3. **Reaction Chamber**: Have students bring in shoeboxes with lids or small boxes that can be closed on all sides to serve as the reaction chambers. For the simplest self-assembly models you should use "2-D" shaking (side to side) in which the pieces are placed in the box (separated and randomly arranged). We discovered a simple way to enforce "2-D" shaking: Place the box on a desk or the floor and slide it back and forth in random directions. Be sure the top of the box is open so that students can observe the action inside the box. Adjust your "temperature" to break undesired bonding. That is, shake more vigorously if pieces that aren't supposed to come together stick. If their models are well designed, any such undesired bonds will be relatively weak. The students might find it takes several times for the model to work. If it works one out of five times, the student has made a pretty good model. (See figure below for additional explanations)

STEPS TO SUCCESSFUL ASSEMBLY

1. Select a reaction chamber.　　2. Place pieces in the chamber.　　3. Shake! You may leave the box open to observe the assembly.　　4. Successful Self-Assembly

   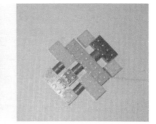

EXPLAIN
Ask the students the following questions throughout the activity or at the end of the activity.

1. What do the Legos represent?
   Answer: Molecules

2. What do the magnets represent?
   Answer: Receptor sites on the molecules

3. What does the reaction chamber represent?
   Answer: The environment where the reaction is occurring

4. What does the shaking of the reaction chamber represent?
   Answer: There are two major underlying principles of self-assembly: shakiness and stickiness. On the nanometer scale everything is shaking and bumping around very quickly due to thermal energy. The higher the temperature, the more bumping and shaking that takes place. Therefore, the shaking of the reaction chamber represents the temperature.

5. Why did some of the models not immediately self-assemble?
   Answer: Instead of one very strong bond sticking pieces together, nature uses several weak bonds used in parallel. When the pieces fit properly, all of these bonds work together like many hands joining together. If only one, it is not strong enough to stay together with all of the shaking. This serves as an error correction mechanism. Also, the environmental elements must be perfect for the self-assembly to occur. For example, the temperature must be at the correct level to cause

the needed amount of movement for correct self-assembly. If the temperature is too high then there may be too much movement and the bonds will break.

EXTEND

- If students feel ambitious—and they usually do with this activity—have them try "3-D" shaking (up, down, and side to side). Don't forget to have them put a lid on the box. This will take longer and require that the pieces can take a beating without losing magnets or breaking.
- Challenge the students to model protein folding. Use rubber tubing and a strip of cloth, paper, or duct tape folded to embed the magnets. Design the interactions such that when the strip is shaken, it folds into a predetermined shape (challenging!).
- There exist many simple and complex molecular structures that are difficult to conceptualize by words only. For additional ideas on demonstrating molecular structures using Legos, visit the website of The University of Wisconsin-Madison Materials Research Science and Engineering Center (MRSEC) Interdisciplinary Education Group (IEG) at *http://mrsec.wisc. edu/Edetc/LEGO/index.html*.

EVALUATE
As a formative assessment, ask students to share their models and explain the self-assembly process. Students can draw their design on an overhead for the entire class to see. Have students discuss why they think their model did or did not work. Encourage them to apply the new concepts of weak bonds and geometrical compatibility in their explanations. Give them the opportunity to redesign their models. For a hands-on assessment, create several models—some that would work and some that would not. Have the students predict which models would and would not self-assemble along with explanations. Then prompt students to test their predictions.

Reference

Campbell, D., E. Freidinger, and M. K. Querns. 2001. Spontaneous assembly of magnetic Lego bricks. *Chemistry Educator* 6:321–323.
Goodsell, D. 2000. Biomolecules and nanotechnology. *American Scientist* 88 (3): 230–237.

What do these items have in common?

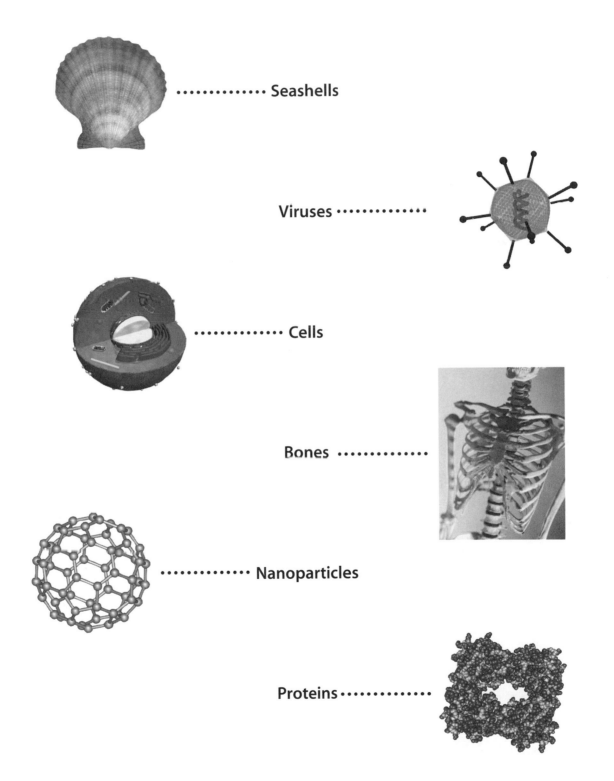

Seashells

Viruses

Cells

Bones

Nanoparticles

Proteins

PHYSICS CHANGES WITH SCALE

OVERVIEW

At the nanoscale, a completely different set of forces and interactions are experienced by molecules and atoms than we experience at the human scale. How do properties change with scale? Why is gravity so important to our daily lives but relatively unimportant to a molecule or a virus in our body? This exercise introduces the concept of scale-dependent properties to students as they explore how the sizes of materials change their behavior.

OBJECTIVES

- To describe scale-dependent properties.

Process Skills
- Observing
- Measuring
- Predicting

Activity Duration
60 minutes

BACKGROUND

One of the most fascinating aspects of the nanoscale is that properties that we don't typically think of as size-dependent, like color or magnetism, become size dependent as objects approach this tiny scale. Also, forces that are not apparent to us at the human scale (like hydrogen-bonding forces) are much more important than familiar forces like gravity. In other words there is a changeover in the dominance of one force over another. For example, as we approach the molecular scale, the stickiness of intermolecular bonding begins to completely overwhelm any influence of gravity. In this exercise, students are given a concrete example of a switch in dominance between two competing properties (inertia and wind resistance) with the changing size of an object. This exercise also provides a very clear example of the importance of understanding the relative scaling of surface to volume as things get smaller or larger.

MATERIALS

Each group will need:
- Set of 4 or 5 Styrofoam balls of diameters: ½", 1", 2", 3", and 4". These particular diameters are not important as long as there are some down at 1" and below (the smaller the better), some above 3", and some in between.
- Ruler
- Balance
- Clear area to throw balls across the room. This is preferably done indoors to avoid effects of wind outside. A school hallway or gym would be ideal.
- Student Sheets 1 and 2

PROCEDURES

ENGAGE Divide students into groups of 2 or 3 and provide each group with a set of Styrofoam balls. Have the students determine the density of each ball. The density of the balls should be close to the same (within 10–20%). Density can be determined by measuring the mass of each ball and dividing by the volume. This verification indicates that though the balls are of different sizes, they are the same otherwise (same material, same density). Density of Styrofoam should fall in the range of 0.01 g/cm³ to 0.03 g/cm³.

Surface Area:

$$a = 4\pi r^2$$

Volume:

$$v = \frac{4\pi r^3}{3}$$

Helpful Hint: The density of the Styrofoam used to test this exercise was roughly 0.03 g/cm³.

The students will then move to a clear area to throw the balls horizontally. They should predict which ball will travel the farthest. After predicting, ask students to observe whether they see obvious deceleration due to wind resistance. This will be most obvious with the smallest ball, especially if it is smaller than 1" in diameter. Most strikingly, students will not be able to throw the balls very far. The students should make observations to determine where they see the most pronounced indication of wind resistance. One way to clearly contrast the behavior of each ball is to put 2 or more of the balls of different sizes in the hand and throw them simultaneously (probably best underhand). In this case, all balls start out with the same initial velocity and you can see the contrast of the effect of air resistance. Keep in mind that in the absence of the effect of air resistance, all balls should travel just as far (and fast) given the same initial throw.

EXPLAIN

Though the exercise is an analogy to help students understand the properties of the nanoscale, the essence of the effect explored in the investigation has to do with surface-to-volume scaling and is the same argument that would be used for competing forces at the nanoscale.

The mass of an object is proportional to its volume (mass equals density multiplied by volume). The force of gravity on an object, or its *weight*, is proportional to mass and therefore proportional to its volume. Remember also that mass is also a measure of an object's *inertia*: its resistance to change velocity under external forces. Drag forces on a ball or any object when they are thrown or fall through the air are proportional to the *surface area* of the object. So when a ball is thrown through the air there are two competing effects: the *drag force*, which is proportional to the object's area, is slowing the object down, and the *inertia*, which is proportional to volume, resists changes in velocity. How quickly an object slows down (its deceleration) is given simply by the ratio of the drag force to the inertia (mass):

$$\text{Deceleration} = \text{Drag force/Inertia} = (C \times \text{Area} \times \text{Velocity})/(\text{Density} \times \text{Volume})$$

C is a coefficient that depends on the fluid the object is moving through and the particular shape of the object. For this exercise, all Styrofoam balls are roughly the same shape and are moving through the same fluid (air), so this coefficient will be the same for all. It should also be noted that drag forces become proportional to the square of the velocity at higher velocities (for a car moving at 60mph or a skydiver in free fall for example).

Styrofoam is of the correct density such that we can observe a crossover of the dominance of inertia (for larger balls 3" or 4" in diameter) to the dominance of viscous drag or air resistance (for balls of well below 1" in diameter). For very small pieces of styrofoam (< ¼") we will see a complete dominance of viscous drag.

EXTEND

Have students complete Student Sheet 2 for an extension activity. The deceleration of an object thrown at a particular velocity will be proportional to the ratio of area to volume. For objects made of the same material (like Styrofoam) the smaller the object, the larger the deceleration. The ratio of deceleration of ball one to ball two will be inverse ratio of their respective radii:

$$\frac{\text{Deceleration Ball 1}}{\text{Deceleration Ball 2}} = \frac{\text{Radius Ball 2}}{\text{Radius Ball 1}}$$

Put simply, what we see in this exercise is that the laws of physics that are most important to a particular system depend on the *size* of that system. Especially when one important property or force depends on volume (like mass or inertia) and another property depends on surface area (like wind resistance).

At the nanoscale, almost all interactions are mediated by surface effects. So forces between objects are often proportional to their surface area. This is why surface-related forces that bond molecules and nano-objects together—such as chemical and intermolecular bonds—are so much more important than gravity. Because the ratio of surface area to volume is dramatically higher (up to a billion times higher) for nano-objects than for human-scale objects, the surface-related effects dominate.

STUDENT SHEET 1

PHYSICS CHANGES WITH SCALE

Name _____

Problem
How far can you throw Styrofoam balls of different sizes? How fast can you throw them? Is there a difference in behavior between big and small balls? Why?

Prediction
- I predict that I will be able to throw the _____ ball the furthest.
- I predict that I will be able to throw the _____ ball the fastest.

Materials
Styrofoam Balls (½", 1", 2", 3", and 4" sizes)

Calculations
Determine the mass, volume, and density.
Record your calculations in Table 1.

Process
Predict which ball will travel the furthest.
Prediction:

TABLE 1●●●
TOSS EACH BALL THREE TIMES AND RECORD THE DISTANCE TRAVELED. DISCUSS
YOUR RESULTS WITH YOUR GROUP IN LIGHT OF YOUR PREDICTION.

Ball Size (diameter)	Mass	Volume	Density	Original Prediction (Which will go farthest?)	Toss 1 Distance	Toss 2 Distance	Toss 3 Distance
½ inch							
1 inch							
2 inches							
3 inches							
4 inches							

Conclusions

1. Which was the largest ball where you saw a clear effect of wind resistance?

2. Is the reason that the small ball slows down more (has larger deceleration) because it experiences larger wind resistance?

3. How would this exercise be different if we used the same sized objects but made of stone? Would you see the effect of wind resistance? Why?

PHYSICS CHANGES WITH SCALE

Name _____

Challenge Problem

If you have two Styrofoam balls, one 5 inches in diameter and the other 1 inch in diameter, answer the following questions.

1. What is the ratio of the masses of the two balls (mass of large ball over mass of small ball)?

2. If you throw them both at the same speed, which ball experiences higher air resistance? Why? What is the ratio of air resistance experienced by the large ball to the small ball?

3. Which decelerates more? Why? What is the ratio of deceleration of the large ball to the small ball?

Hints
- Air resistance is proportional to the surface area of an object.
- Deceleration of an object is proportional to the ratio of the air resistance to the mass of the object.

SHRINKING CUPS: CHANGES IN THE BEHAVIOR OF MATERIALS AT THE NANOSCALE

OVERVIEW

What if you were only one inch tall? This activity explores the behavior of liquids in different sizes and shapes of drinking containers. Students explore how the size of the cup determines if the liquid will pour out of the cup. This activity models at the macroscale similar types of changes in the behavior of materials that occur at the nanoscale. This investigation helps students imagine a very different nanoscale world.

OBJECTIVE

- To develop inquiry skills through exploration of how materials behave differently at smaller scales.

Process Skills
- Observing
- Predicting
- Inferring
- Collecting Data

Activity Duration
90 minutes

MATERIALS ....

Each group will need:
- Miniature cup (opening 1 cm or less)
- Normal sized cup
- Water dropper
- One piece of modeling clay (golf ball size or bigger and non-water soluble)
- Plastic tray or plate to control spills
- Pencils, dowels, toothpicks, and other tools to shape clay
- Student Sheets 1 and 2

Note: Miniature cups (diameter of pencil or smaller) can be found at craft stores where dollhouse accessories are sold.

Possible materials for extension activity:
- Ice water and hot water
- Salt water
- Syrup/honey
- Vinegar
- Cooking oil
- Other liquids students might want to explore

BACKGROUND

Most of us go about our everyday activities like drinking from a cup without contemplating the material properties and physical forces involved. What would happen if you were much smaller, only inches tall? What challenges would you face if you had to design a cup to drink from if you were 6–12 inches tall? Would we have to consider any aspects other than size? Scientists have learned that size can affect the way living things grow and the way materials behave.

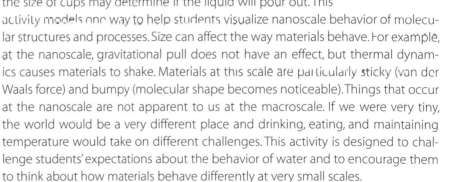

In this activity, students will explore how materials behave differently at smaller scales. Students observe how changes in the size of cups may determine if the liquid will pour out. This activity models one way to help students visualize nanoscale behavior of molecular structures and processes. Size can affect the way materials behave. For example, at the nanoscale, gravitational pull does not have an effect, but thermal dynamics causes materials to shake. Materials at this scale are particularly sticky (van der Waals force) and bumpy (molecular shape becomes noticeable). Things that occur at the nanoscale are not apparent to us at the macroscale. If we were very tiny, the world would be a very different place and drinking, eating, and maintaining temperature would take on different challenges. This activity is designed to challenge students' expectations about the behavior of water and to encourage them to think about how materials behave differently at very small scales.

PROCEDURES

ENGAGE Consider reading the Shel Silverstein poem, "One Inch Tall," from the children's book *Where the Sidewalk Ends*, to your students. Ask the class to consider what life would be like and how things would behave at that scale.

Ask the students to study the miniature cup provided in their lab materials and to predict what they think will happen when the tiny cup is filled with water and then tipped to drink.

Have the students record their prediction on Student Sheet 1. Predictions may vary. After students have recorded their prediction, each student should test their prediction using the tiny cup and water dropper. Observations should be recorded on the student sheet. Ask the students to describe what they saw and to suggest reasons for the water not coming out of the tiny cup when tipped.

EXPLORE
Explain to the students that they will be working in groups of four to use clay to design their own cups and explore why the water did not come out of the cup. Encourage them to design the cups with different depths, shapes, or sizes to see if these changes affect the behavior of the water in the cups. Suggest using toothpicks to observe what would happen if they put holes in their clay cups.

For each cup design, have the students sketch, describe, and record the observations as they try to pour the water out of each cup. When exploration is coming to an end, have your students compete in a Design Challenge to see which group can make a cup that can hold the largest amount of water without it pouring out when tipped. (Hint: Think about how a child's sippy cup works.)

Once the challenge is over and a winner has been named, have the student groups discuss their findings with the rest of the class.

EXPLAIN
Ask the students to brainstorm why water behaves as it did in different sizes and shapes of cups. Students should notice that water does not easily pour out of the very small cups they designed. Why do the tiny cups not work like normal-sized cups? Gravity comes into play when tipping most cups. Does it have to do with the design of the cup? The size of the cup? The properties of liquids?

Explain the properties of water such as adhesion, cohesion, polarity, and surface tension. Information on the properties of water can be found at: *http://ga.water.usgs.gov/edu/mwater.html*.

Ask the students to make connections between the properties of water and their observations of the behavior of the water in the different size and shape cups they made with clay.

The previous investigations used water at room temperature. Ask the students to suggest other common liquids like soft drinks or cooking oil that they would like to investigate with the tiny cups. They could also explore the liquids at either hot or cold temperatures.

Tell the students to work with their lab groups for the Design Your Own Inquiry activity. In their lab groups, the students should design an experiment to explore the use of other liquids and/or different temperatures of the liquids. Student Sheet 2 can be used to guide their inquiry.

Once you approve of their experiment, allow students to begin their inquiry. The inquiry should include a problem, predictions, data collection, and conclusions. Have the student groups present their findings to the rest of the class.

EXTEND
Show several movie clips or segments from books about experiences of living things at a tiny scale. For example, you could show the clip from the movie, *Honey, I Shrunk the Kids*, where the shrunken children are lost in their backyard. It shows several things that we take for granted at our large size, such as watering the lawn and tiny insects. Other movie clips include: *A Bug's Life, The Incredible Shrinking Man*, or *Innerspace*. Or perhaps you could read a passage from Jonathan Swift's *Gulliver's Travels: A Voyage to Lilliput*. During Gulliver's travels he is shipwrecked and finds himself a prisoner of people who are 15 centimeters high. Later, Gulliver is found by a farmer who is 22 meters tall (a scale of 12 to 1 compared to Lilliput people).

After viewing the clips or reading passages, have the students imagine they are that small and how things would appear from that perspective. Have students write a short story about their experiences being two inches tall. In their story they should describe how things would appear and how they would survive in a world where things behave differently.

EVALUATE
Lastly, ask the students to summarize what happened during their inquiries with cup sizes and the pouring of liquids. Particularly emphasize how not only the properties of water (adhesion and cohesion) affect their outcomes, but also how size (scale of an object) affects the behavior of materials.

The Exploratorium in San Francisco has an interesting exhibit where visitors can explore this phenomena with a doll hand and doll sink with dripping water. For further information on how materials behave differently at the nanoscale, have students conduct further research. Information can be found on websites such as: *www.strangematterexhibit.com*.

Appreciation extended to Dr. Tom Oppewal for his contributions to an earlier version of this activity.

STUDENT SHEET 1

SHRINKING CUPS

Name _____

Observations

Observe the tiny plastic cups and make a prediction about
what would happen if the tiny cup was filled with water and tipped to drink.

Record observations here:

_____

_____

_____

_____

Prediction

Predict what you think will happen if you filled the tiny cup with water and tried to pour it out. Write prediction below:

_____

_____

_____

_____

Test your prediction and record observations:

_____

_____

_____

_____

Materials
- Miniature cup
- Normal sized cup
- Water dropper
- One piece of modeling clay
- Plastic tray or plate to control spills
- Pencils, dowels, toothpicks, and other tools to shape clay

Procedure
1. Using the clay and provided tools, design your own cups with different shapes and sizes. Explore the reasons why the water did not come out of the tiny cup.

2. Sketch, describe, and record the observations of water of each cup designed below or on blank paper:

Design Challenge

Can you make a cup that can hold the largest amount of water without it pouring out when tipped? Describe your group's design below:

Conclusion

Explain what you have observed about how sizes and shapes affect whether or not liquids pour from tiny containers.

SHRINKING CUPS

Name _____

Design Your Own Inquiry
In your lab groups, design an experiment to explore the use
of other liquids and/or different temperature liquids. (Have your teacher approve the design before
you proceed.)

First, decide which liquids and what variables you are testing.

Materials needed:

_____
_____
_____
_____
_____

State your hypothesis:

_____
_____
_____
_____
_____
_____

Procedure
Write your procedures below:

_____
_____
_____
_____
_____
_____
_____
_____
_____
_____

Test your hypothesis and record observations in a data table you design.

Student Sheet 2 (cont.)

Shrinking Cups

Put your data table here:

State your conclusion and be ready to share your results:

CHAPTER 14

LIMITS TO SIZE:
COULD KING KONG EXIST?

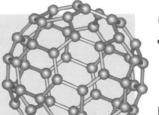

OVERVIEW

Why can't spiders be ten feet tall? Can an ape grow to the size of King Kong? Surface area-to-volume relationships help shed light on the question of the size limits of organisms. At the nanoscale, things are so small that surface area effects impact the behavior of materials. For example, things tend to stick together and gravity plays a minor role. This activity gives students the opportunity to explore the sizes of things and scale as they investigate questions like "Could an egg ever grow to be the size of a beach ball?"

OBJECTIVES

• To be able to describe how surface area-to-volume ratio affects the activities of a cell.

Process Skills
• Observing
• Predicting
• Manipulating ratios
• Applying Data

Activity Duration
60 minutes

BACKGROUND

Could giant creatures exist?

Our fascination with the idea of giant insects, reptiles, and other creatures is evident in our love of monster movies. The thought of a spider as big as a building is clearly fantasy, but is it biologically possible? Would such a giant creature be huge because it is comprised of huge cells or does it have a larger number of cells than a "normal" version of that creature? In order for that creature to survive, would it have bigger cells or more cells? Cells have microscopic lives that involve growing, dividing, acquiring nourishment, and getting rid of wastes. These processes are influenced by surface area-to-volume relationships. A cell has a size limit due to the

fact that at some point it would get too large to acquire enough nourishment or rid itself of toxic wastes. The surface area must be great enough to provide nutrients to the organelles within the cell's volume in order to keep the cell healthy. If the cell grows to the point where the requirements of the cell's volume outstrip the capacity of the surface to provide nutrient intake and waste outflow, then the cell either must divide or die!

Aside from cell size considerations, other surface and volume concepts relate to the ultimate size of animals. Some of the same arguments made for the cell can be made for the whole organism. In order to regulate body temperature, an animal must transfer heat to the environment. It does this through its outermost layer (for mammals this is the dermal or skin layer). If an animal is too large or too small, heat generated or lost within the volume of the body, cannot be compensated quickly enough through surface mediated heat transfer. The load of an animal's mass on its bones is another consideration. It turns out that the structural supports that hold our bodies together (bones) cannot simply be scaled up to skyscraper size and still be expected to work. To help illustrate a simple example: If you take a meterstick and hold one end down on the edge of a desk, it will remain almost straight bending only very slightly by its own weight even if cantilevered out over most of its length. If we simply scale a meterstick up 100 times so that it is 100 m long and perhaps 0.5 m in thickness, this scaled up version will break (or at least bend significantly) under its own weight if most of its length were cantilevered and unsupported. Simply put, the larger we make mechanical supports, the more they deform under their own weight even if scaled proportionally. So our skeletons, if scaled to large enough size, would simply break under our weight. This is why the larger the land animal, the proportionally thicker its leg and arm bones are to its body size. There is a certain body size above which bones become too weak to support the body. Sauropods are thought to be the largest land animal to ever to walk the Earth. What did its leg bones look like compared to ours?

SURFACE AREA-TO-VOLUME RATIO

Cells have a plasma membrane that acts as a protective barrier from the surrounding environment. This membrane forms the surface of the cell and serves as a gateway for the movement of nutrients or wastes through diffusion and active transport. The total area of the cell surface therefore determines the maximum rate at which the cell can uptake nutrients or release waste. The cytoplasm and cell organelles found inside comprise the volume of the cell and are constantly taking in nutrients and releasing by-products. The volume of the cell then determines the total nutrient uptake and waste release requirements of the cell. In this investigation students explore surface area-to-volume relationships through examining how when a cube gets larger, the volume grows more dramatically than the surface area. So in the context of cells, there is a maximum possible cell size, above which the needs of the volume of the cell (cytoplasm) outstrip the capabilities of the cell membrane to pass nutrients and waste. In order for students to understand and calculate the concept of surface area-to-volume ratio, cubes will serve as a model of a cell. To calculate the total surface area of a cube, multiply the surface area by six.

For example:

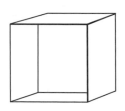

Surface Area equation: Length × Width × 6 (# of faces of cube)
Surface Area = 2 cm × 2 cm × 6 = 24 cm^2

Volume equation: Length × Width × Height
Volume = 2 cm × 2 cm × 2 cm = 8 cm^3

2 cm

In this investigation students explore the relationship between surface area to volume and the effect it has on living cells. Students consider what surface and volume ratios are most beneficial to cells to carry out processes necessary for life by modeling different sized cells with paper cubes. Could a spider the size of a car really exist?

PROCEDURES

ENGAGE Ask the students to brainstorm what they think are the largest and smallest organisms on Earth. Get the students thinking about the following:

1. Why are populations of giant organisms not very large?
2. What types of cells can be found in giant organisms?
3. Are the cellular processes, such as diffusion, the same in all organisms?

If time permits your could even show a montage of movie clips or posters with giant organisms and discuss the likelihood that those scenarios could ever exist, for example, *Godzilla, King Kong, Mothra*, and *Incredible Shrinking Man*.

MATERIALS

Each group will need:
- Goggles
- Triple beam or electronic balance
- Tape
- Sand, sugar, or salt
- Paper cube templates
- Scissors
- Student Sheets 1 and 2

EXPLORE Once you feel comfortable that the students understand that there are limits to size (including cells), discuss with the students the definitions of surface area and volume. Use any objects as examples but use cubes when calculating surface area-to-volume ratios. Help the students to determine the area of one face of a cube and to calculate the total surface area and volume of a cube. The students should record the formulas on Student Sheet 1.

Explain to the students that they will be working in groups of three to explore how surface area and volume contribute to limits to size. Ask them to state their hypothesis about whether a giant creature is huge because it consists of huge cells or because it has larger number of cells than the "normal" version of that creature. They should write their hypothesis on the student sheet.

In their lab groups, the students should then cut out and fold the five cube cells and tape the tabs together to form cubes that have one open side.

PAPER CUBE TEMPLATES

1 cube

2 cubes

3 cubes

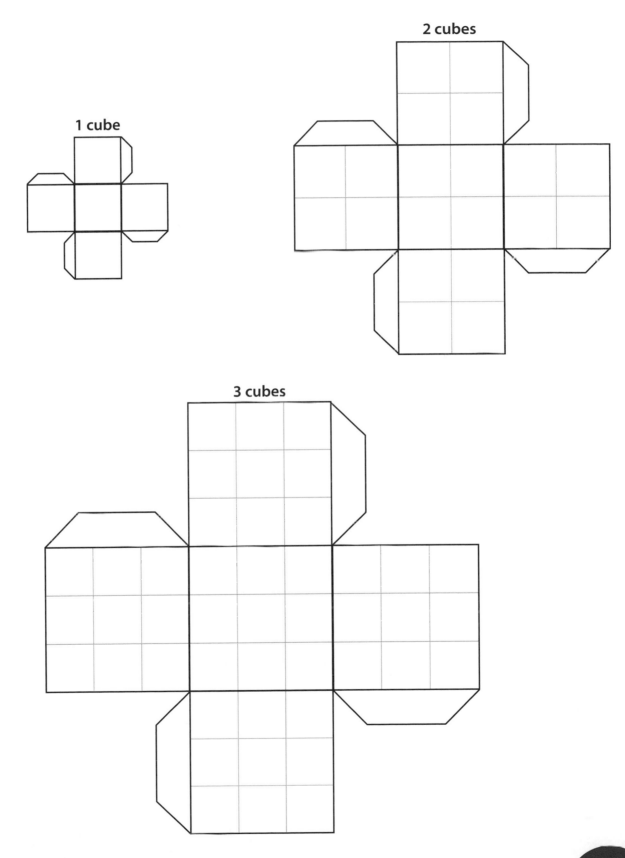

4 cubes

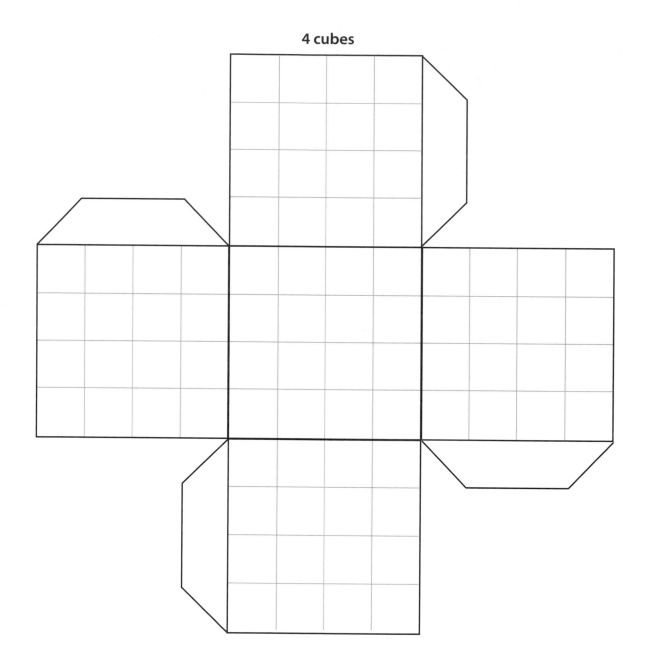

5 cubes

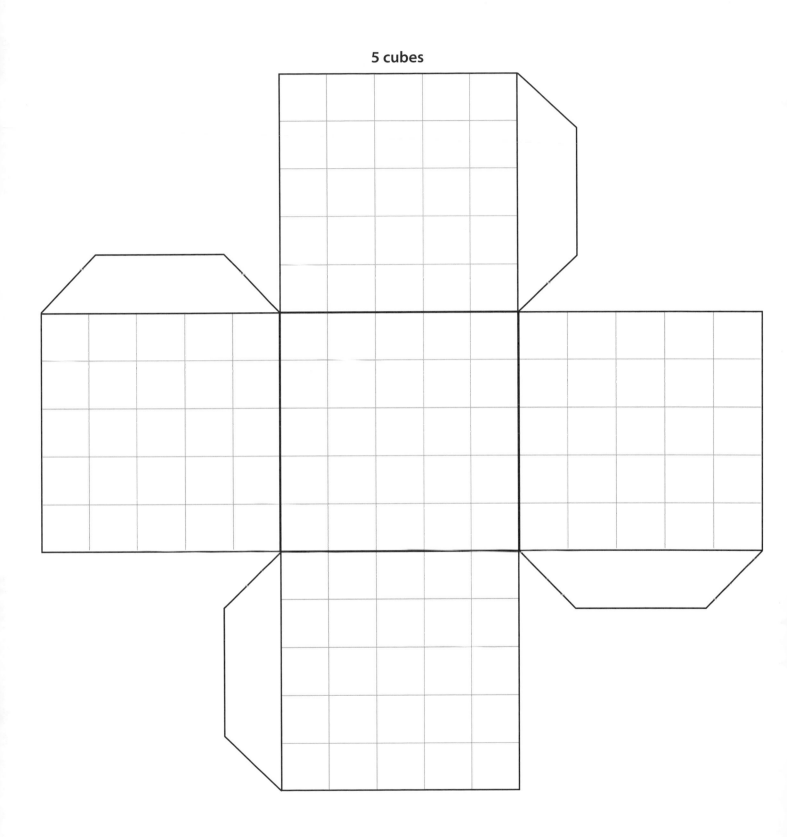

Once the five cubes have been constructed, the students should fill each cube with salt, sand, or sugar to the rim (whichever you have available) and find the mass in grams of each cube and record in data table on Student Sheet 1.

The students should then determine the area of one face of each cube and then calculate the total surface area and volume of each cube and record on the data table.

Once each group has finished completing the data table, they should discuss with their lab partners the answers to the analysis questions and write a conclusion about the relationship they see between surface area and volume and whether or not their hypothesis was correct.

EXPLAIN
Discuss the relationship between cell size and cell activities and how surface area and volume are the important limiting factors in this relationship. Explain how in relation to surface area, volume increases at a faster rate. At some point in cell growth, the volume of the cell gets too large for the surface area to support it. At that point the cell usually dies or divides because it cannot get enough nutrients into the cell and wastes out.

Use the example of different size eggs. Compare the size of an ostrich egg and a quail egg. There are pores in the eggshells that allow oxygen to enter. The surface area-to-volume ratio is much larger for the quail egg than the ostrich egg. Which egg would have a better rate of oxygen absorption? How could the volume of the egg affect the rate of absorption?

EXTEND
Give each student a type of cell (skin, brain, muscle, etc.) to research. Have them explore the cell functions that it must undergo for survival, parts of the cell, typical size of the cell, and how it divides.

Have students share their information with the class by creating posters or by discussion. Once students have investigated limits to size at the macroscale, have students apply their knowledge to nanoscale materials. What happens to surface area and volume as things get very small? How does having a high surface area affect the behavior of molecules at the nanoscale?

EVALUATE
Ask the students to tell you what they noticed about the surface area-to-volume ratio as cells increase in size. Based on their answers to the analysis questions, ask them to brainstorm all the challenges cells have as size increases.

Alternatively, ask students to describe how the surface area-to-volume ratio changes as things get smaller. How does the surface area of a virus (a nanometer-sized object) compare to a protozoan (a micrometer-sized object)?

STUDENT SHEET 1

Name _____

Surface Area and Volume Formulas

State the formula for calculating the following when the length of one side of a cell equals "s."

(a) Area of one face: _____

(b) Total surface area of a cell: _____

(c) Volume of a cell: _____

Hypothesis

State your hypothesis about whether a giant creature is huge because it consists of huge cells or because it has a larger number of cells than the "normal" version of that creature.

_____

_____

_____

_____

Materials

- Goggles
- Triple beam or electronic balance
- Tape
- Sand, sugar, or salt
- Paper cube templates
- Scissors

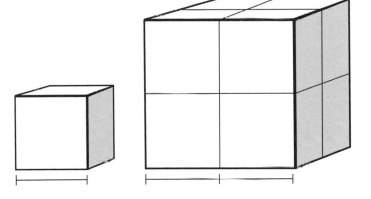

Investigation

1. Cut out and fold each of the five cube cells and tape ends together. One side should remain open.

2. Using the formulas above, calculate the surface area and volume data for each cell and record in the data table.

3. Fill each cube with salt, sugar, or sand (whichever your teacher has available).

4. Using a scale, record the mass (in grams) in your data table.

5. In your lab groups, discuss the data table and answer the analysis questions.

6. Finally, state whether your hypothesis was correct and write a conclusion paragraph.

LIMITS TO SIZE

Cell size (in "s" units)	Area of one face	Total surface area	Volume of cube cell	Mass (g) of cell when filled
1				
2				
3				
4				
5				

Note: The "s" represents the number of squares found in height of cube. For example, cell size 3 is three cubes high.

NATIONAL SCIENCE TEACHERS ASSOCIATION

Analysis Questions

1. Using the measurements from your data table, calculate the surface area-to-volume ratio and surface area-to-mass ratio for each cell and record below. Show your work.

Cell size (in "s" units)	Total surface area-to-volume ratio	Total surface area-to-mass ratio
1		
2		
3		
4		
5		

2. Substances that a cell takes in (food or oxygen), or expels (wastes such as carbon dioxide) must pass through the plasma membrane. Which measurement (mass, surface area, volume) best represents the amount of plasma membrane the cells have?

3. The cell organelles need the oxygen and food that passes through the plasma membrane and to be able to remove the waste products that are produced. Which two measurements represent the cell contents?

4. As the cell grows larger, does the total surface area-to-volume ratio increase, decrease, or stay the same?

5. As the cell grows larger, does the total surface area-to-mass ratio increase, decrease, or stay the same?

6. As the cell grows larger and acquires more content, will it need more or less plasma membrane to survive? Explain your answer.

7. Which cell has the greatest total surface area-to-volume ratio?

8. Which cell has the greatest chance of survival? Why?

9. Why can't cells survive when the total surface area-to-volume ratio becomes too small?

10. What can cells do to increase their total surface area-to-volume ratio?

11. How would the surface area-to-volume ratio of a nanometer-sized virus compare to a micrometer-sized cell?

12. Do you think giant creatures have huge cells? Why or why not?

13. Was your original hypothesis supported?

Conclusion

Write a conclusion about whether or not you believe that giant creatures could exist. Explain in detail your reasons.

PART IV

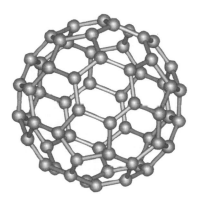

NANOTECHNOLOGY APPLICATIONS

NANOMATERIALS: MEMORY WIRE

OVERVIEW

Imagine metal eyeglasses frames that you can roll in a ball, only to watch them uncoil back to their original shape! How can an inanimate object, such as metal, do such a thing? There is a metal alloy that can do just that and it's one of the many discoveries coming from the field of nanotechnology. Students will explore the properties of memory metal and consider the many applications it might have today and in the future.

OBJECTIVES

- To explore the properties and behavior of memory wire.
- To apply knowledge of characteristics of memory wire to the design of new applications that could utilize an alloy that "remembers."

Process Skills

- Observing
- Predicting
- Inferring

Activity Duration

90 minutes

BACKGROUND

Say goodbye to bad hair days! What if you never had to style your hair again? Could memory wire be used to keep your hairstyle from going limp? What if the body of your parents' car was made of memory metal? Could it "cure" itself of dents? Currently products such as eyeglasses, medical stints, dental braces wires, brassieres underwire, and cell phones use the memory feature of one type of metal alloy called nickel titanium (NiTi). Materials scientists call this type of material a Shape Memory Alloy (SMA). These applications rely on this metal's ability to "remember" its original shape. For example, this wire can be kinked, flexed, or bent and it will return to its original shape without permanent damage. The shape change is temperature dependent. If the wire's shape is changed at its low temperature phase (room temperature), the original shape can be obtained by warming the wire to a higher temperature.

This metal has a unique phase change from solid-to-solid and consists of many single crystals called *grains* that are different sizes, shapes, and positions. When the metal is heated and "trained" into a shape, the atoms are repositioned and the metal "remembers" that position when cooled. When reheated, the atoms slide back into their original shape.

Memory wire is sometimes called Nitinol, named from the site of its discovery, Nickel Titanium Naval Ordnance Laboratory, in 1965. Like most every metal, it consists of tiny crystalline grains packed together. Within each crystalline grain, the atoms are ordered in a very specific way. In the case of Nitinol, different "phases"—patterns of ordered atoms of this crystal—are present at different temperatures. At room temperature, a phase called Martensite is present, and at higher temperatures a phase called Austenite is present. At room temperature, a wire made of Nitinol bends very much like a paper clip. You can bend it into different shapes and it will stay bent. The wire has been deformed "plastically" as opposed to elastically. What is very different about memory wire is how it accommodates the plastic deformation. In normal metals, when a wire is bent past its elastic range, planes of atoms slip long distances past each other in a process called "slip" or "dislocation motion." So after the bending of the wire, atoms near one of these "slip planes" have a completely different environment. They are in a completely different place relative to their original atomic neighbors. They have no "memory" of the original arrangement and therefore the material remains bent. In the case of Nitinol, the plastic deformation happens a completely different way. No slipping of crystalline planes occurs. All of the deformation is accommodated by local shifts in the crystal structure so that each atom has the same set of neighbors it had before, they have just shifted in their local arrangements. When the material is reheated, the atoms shift back to their original positions relative to their neighbors and the overall shape of the wire regains its original shape. In other words, in normal metals, plastic deformation results in nonlocal shifts in atomic position within the crystal,

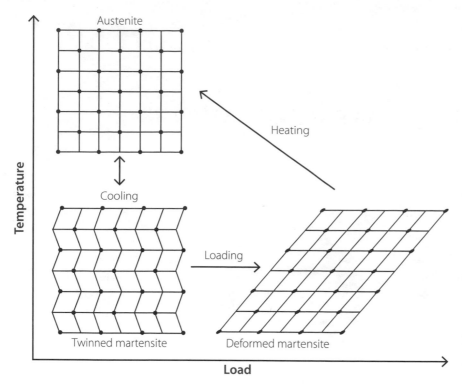

Austenite

Temperature

Heating

Cooling

Loading

Twinned martensite

Deformed martensite

Load

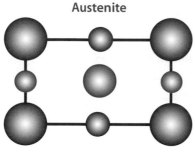

Austenite

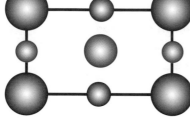

Martensite

while in the memory metal effect, the plastic deformation is completely local: Each atom retains its immediate neighbors and therefore can find its way back to its original position.

Shape Memory Alloys (SMA) have many exciting current and potential applications. In this activity students will brainstorm interesting ways in which this material might be used. Ask them to keep in mind that a convenient and useful way that the wire can be heated is through electrical current. In this way, the materials' motion can be controlled through electronic circuits and computers.

BIOMEDICAL APPLICATIONS

Within the context of biomedical technology, SMA can be used in a variety of contexts. A stent is a device that is typically tube shaped and is used to keep arteries open. It is placed within an artery and acts as an artificial wall to support a damaged or defective artery wall. Imagine a SMA stent that can be folded and compacted down to a very small volume and inserted into the artery with minimal surgery. Localized heating is then applied to the stent and it then unfolds in place to its full volume. Small surgical tools such as scalpels and forceps could also be compacted and introduced into small volumes of the body this way without the need for invasive surgery. There has also been progress made on the development of biocompatible shape memory polymers for use as sutures. Imagine a tiny loose suture knot that is placed over a targeted area then tightened with application of heat (for more information see Lendlein and Langer 2002). This would obviate the need for the surgeon to perform a lengthy, delicate, and invasive knot-tying procedure during a surgery.

CIVIL ENGINEERING APPLICATIONS

SMAs are currently being studied for their potential use as "smart" building materials. For example, engineers are exploring SMA use in earthquake proofing buildings. A few structural SMA members would be placed within the superstructure of the building. Along with the ability to "remember" the shape of the building's superstructure and being able to deform reversibly, SMAs dissipate (or absorb) a lot of energy in deformation, thereby acting as shock absorbers. The SMAs would be heated by running electrical current through them. They would be controlled dynamically by monitoring the motion of the building and applying the heating current when needed. Materials that can change their properties dynamically using input from the environment and sensors are known as "smart materials."

In this investigation students can explore the various properties of memory wire and ponder all of the interesting products that could come from such an unusual material. Students can see how changes at the nanolevel can been seen at the macroscopic level.

Reference

Lendlein, A., and R. Langer. 2002. Biodegradable, elastic shape-memory polymers for potential biomedical applications. *Science* 296: 1673.

PROCEDURES

ENGAGE

On the chalkboard or poster paper, have students brainstorm types of metals and products made of those metals. Ask the students, *Why in some cases is metal the best material rather than plastic, glass, or other materials?* Most likely the students would discuss factors such as strength and support.

Ask the students when it would be beneficial to have a very flexible metal. What type of products made of metal are sometimes ruined by bending?

Ask the students if they have ever heard of an alloy. Discuss with them the definitions of alloys. An alloy is a combination of two or more elements where at least one of the elements is a metal giving the alloy metallic properties. The properties of the alloy are usually more advantageous than either of the properties of the elements that make up the alloy. One example is that steel is stronger than iron, which is one of its components.

EXPLORE

Explain to the students that they will be working in groups to discover properties of different metals. One property allows the metal to be flexible and to change shape depending on its temperature.

The students will make observations of the different pieces of metal wire and investigate the property of memory wire. The students should complete the data table on Student Sheet 1 and answer the analysis questions in their lab groups. Make sure your students know how to calculate density using the formula:
Density = mass/volume.
You may also want to go over how to find the volume of a solid using a beaker, graduated cylinder, and water displacement.

EXPLAIN

After students have collected data on the four metals, you can discuss the chart and analysis questions. Explain that one of the metals was NiTi. Describe all of the unique properties that this metal alloy possesses including malleability, color, shape, and in particular the way it "remembers its shape."

See websites for more information:
- *www.ultimateniti.com/index.cfm*
- *www.memry.com*

EXTEND

After discussing the properties of NiTi, ask the students to work in pairs to design a product that could be made of NiTi. Challenge them to think about products that they could invent that make use of this unusual behavior. With their partner, they should draw the product and label where the alloy would be used on the product.

EVALUATE

Student pairs should present their product design and sketch to the rest of class. Have the students also answer, *Why would it be beneficial for this product to be made of this alloy?*

Student Sheet 1

Name _____

What is a metal?

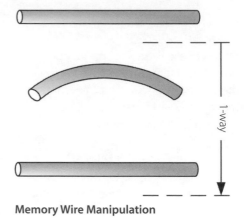

Memory Wire Manipulation

What is an alloy?

Materials
- 1 piece of memory wire
- 1 piece of copper wire
- 1 piece of brass
- 1 piece of steel
- Data table
- Hairdryer or access to hot water
- Tongs
- Beaker
- Graduated cylinder
- Balance
- Reference books about metals

Making observations
Complete the observation table for each metal:
(a)   Observe the color of the metal.

(b)   Using the balance, find the mass of the metal in grams.

(c)   Using a beaker and graduated cylinder, find the density of the metal.

(d)   Describe the original shape and length of the wire.

(e)   Coil the metal wire around a pencil. Holding the coiled metal with tongs, observe what
       happens when you place the coiled wire in hot water.

TABLE 1. OBSERVATIONS

Metal	Color	Mass (g)	Volume (ml or cm³)	Density (g/ml)	Original Shape	Shape After Bending	What happens when heated?
A							
B							
C							
D							

Analysis Questions

1. Which metals were similar in color?

2. Which metal has the largest mass?

3. Which metal had the greatest density?

4. Which metal was easiest to coil?

5. What happened to each metal when exposed to hot water?

6. What unusual property did you notice? Which metal had this property?

7. What do you think that metal is made of?

8. Name three ways you think that a metal with this unusual property could be of benefit in manufacturing a new product.

CHAPTER 16

NANOTECH, INC.

OVERVIEW

Socks that don't stink, graffiti-resistant paint, windows and sunscreen that reject UV rays… that's nanotechnology. Students will learn about some of the latest inventions using nanotechnology by exploring actual products of nanotechnology research.

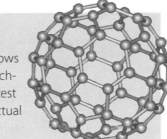

OBJECTIVES

- To learn about new and innovative products created through nanotechnology science.
- To develop an appreciation for nanotechnology as a problem-solving concept

Process Skills
- Observing
- Comparing
- Communicating
- Collecting Data
- Interpreting Data

Activity Duration
60–90 minutes

BACKGROUND

Nanotechnology is all the rage in the industrial world. It seems that there could be a possible solution to every problem when using nanotechnology. Do your feet stink? Does your food spoil? Do you have problems with graffiti in your community? Is your carpet fading in your home where the sun shines in the windows? These are all common problems that can be fixed with not-so-common products.

NANO-SILVER

In response to market demand researchers have developed everyday products that use nano-silver for its antimicrobial effects.

Silver has been used in medicine as an antimicrobial substance for centuries. Colloidal silver or small nanobits of silver have been traditionally used in these therapies as well as in other contexts. What has happened in recent decades with advances in materials science and imaging technologies is that nanotechnology researchers (chemists, physicists, materials scientists) have unprecedented control over the size and shape of these particles and can functionalize their surfaces with a wide range of chemical treatments. These new controls open up entire new avenues for potential materials and biomedical applications. Nanotechnology scientists have found ways to use nano-silver in fibers to enhance antimicrobial characteristics. Nano-silver is active against bacteria, yeasts, fungi, mold, and mildew. In the past it has been used mainly in the medical field in the fibers of items such as medical staff uniforms, ward linens, hand soap, surgical masks, the coating of catheters and endoscopic tubes, as well as in implants for soft tissues and tendon repairs. Nano-silver is now being used for many practical applications including socks and hosiery, theater curtains and gowns, grouting and tile fillers in bathrooms, and exterior paint that prevents mold and mildew growth on wood. One of the latest and most practical applications of nano-silver is in the plastic of food containers (example online at *www.nano-silver.net/eng/product_02.php*).

How does nano-silver work? Microbes that grow as a result of wet, dirty socks (for example) ingest the silver ions, which in effect interrupts the RNA replication, preventing the microbe from reproducing. Furthermore, silver ions are electrostatically attracted to the charged microbe cell wall, affecting the transport of materials in and out of the cell and essentially suppressing respiration and other cell metabolism. (JR Nanotech, *www.jrnanotech.com/antimicrobial.html*.) For more information on nano-silver visit *http://nano-silver.net/eng*.

GRAFFITI-RESISTANT PAINT

The writing is *off* the wall. Scientists have once again developed a solution to an age-old problem. The need for anti-graffiti paint seems to be growing in many communities. Anti-graffiti paint is applied to surfaces like regular paint and adds a barrier between the porous building material and any substance that could come in contact with the building surface. The nanotechnology here is in the advanced chemical treatment of the paint. When dry, the paint is hydrophobic and oleophobic, making any surface to which it is applied water and oil resistant, soil resistant, and paint resistant. It prevents water and solvent-based paints from entering the pores of the building material, whether it is brick or concrete. If graffiti is sprayed on a treated surface it can be easily removed with a cloth or brush and graffiti remover.

For a video clip demonstration that displays how anti-graffiti paint works, go to *www.protectosil.com/chemtrete/en/home. html* and click the link called "See how Protectosil Antigraffiti works."

UV-Protected Window Film

Many people complain about the Sun's damaging effect on their curtains, carpet, and hardwood floors. Over time, ultraviolet rays coming through windows can cause these items to fade. Not only can the Sun damage the fabrics of our homes, but the UVA and UVB rays passing through windows, including automotive glass, can cause skin damage as well. Nanotechnology researchers have developed a "nano-film" or coating for windows that reflects a significant amount of these damaging rays.

UV-Protected Sunscreen

Skin cancer is the most common cancer in the world today and is on the rise. Sun worshippers claim that they would wear sunscreen more often if the sunscreen rubbed into the skin more easily and did not give the skin a white tinge. Don't fret—nanotechnology to the rescue. Again, nanotechnology scientists have found a solution to an everyday problem through the application of nanoparticles.

Zinc oxide and titanium dioxide are broad-spectrum ultraviolet absorbers that have been used in sunscreens from the start. However, they do not rub in easily and leave a white film on the skin. By replacing traditional forms of zinc oxide (ZnO) and titanium dioxide (TiO_2) with nanoparticles of these substances, manufacturers can reduce the visibility of the cream.

One of the most common uses of nanotechnology in consumer products is the use of nanoparticles in sunscreen. There are well over 300 sunscreens on the market today that contain ZnO and TiO_2 nanoparticles. There is controversy about the effectiveness of these particles. Some researchers claim that these nanoparticles can induce free radical damage to cells, making it just as dangerous as exposure to ultraviolet rays.

What has made all of these new materials possible is the advances in fabrication methods in materials chemistry. Both the ability to control materials and evaluate the results through very powerful microscopes has provided scientists with unprecedented options for materials manufacture at the nanoscale.

Materials and Setup

The nanotechnology items listed in the Materials and Setup section can be obtained from manufacturers of the products. Call or e-mail these companies for samples of the products.

The Window film station and Sunscreen station could be set up by a window, but for best results these stations should be set up outside in the sunlight.

Copy the Directions and place a copy at each station.

For Graffiti Testing Station:
- Brick painted with anti-graffiti paint
- Brick not painted with anti-graffiti paint
- Permanent markers
- Water
- Several cloths and scrub brushes

Paint one brick with the anti-graffiti paint according to the manufacturers instructions. Label the painted brick as A and the unpainted brick as B. You may want to have several painted and unpainted bricks on hand to switch out after each class.

For Window Film Testing Station:
- Sample of nanotechnology-treated window film
- Sample of traditional window film
- UV probes

For Sunscreen Testing Station:
- Sunscreen with nanoparticle-sized zinc oxide
- Sunscreen with traditional-sized zinc oxide
- UV probes
- 2 pieces of clear glass, Plexiglas, or plastic
- Cloth to wipe off glass after each sunscreen application

For Food Container Testing Station:
- Nano-silver treated food container
- Regular food container
- Cherry tomatoes

You will need to set up the food containers with the food inside about two weeks prior to doing this activity to allow for molding and decay to occur.

For all students:
- Student Sheet 1 for recording observations
- Student Sheet 2 for writing a consumer report after the observations are completed

ENGAGE Ask the students to share examples of inventions that have solved everyday problems. You could mention dishwashers and handles on trash bags to get them started. Write their responses on the board. Ask the students to comment on whether the inventions have had positive or negative impacts on society.

Next, ask the students to list everyday problems that they face in which they *wish* someone would invent a solution to resolve. You could begin by giving the example of smelly socks. Write the student responses on the board.

Explain to students that one of the goals of nanotechnology is to find solutions for everyday problems. Before products are allowed to be sold to the public, they must be tested over and over by scientists and the FDA, as well as consumers.

EXPLORE Tell the students that they will be visiting Nanotech, Inc. today to test out some new inventions that their scientists have developed. The students will use the information they collect to write up a short consumer report after all the products have been observed for their effectiveness.

Put students into groups of 3–4 persons. The groups will rotate through each station. Each group should spend 3–5 minutes at each station. They should have enough time to investigate the products and record observations. They should read the directions at each station and follow the directions provided. They should then record their observations on their data sheets (Student Sheet 1).

As a class, discuss the results they found after they have made observations at all the stations. Ask them if they have any ideas about why some of the products were effective solutions to the stated problems. Probe them to think about what they have learned or know about nanotechnology and science concepts to answer this question. This should lead you into explaining the products and the concepts that make the products effective.

Results of testing the nano-film compared to using no film show that the nano-film is effective in blocking UVA and UVB rays (see example graphs below taken with Go Link! and Vernier probes).

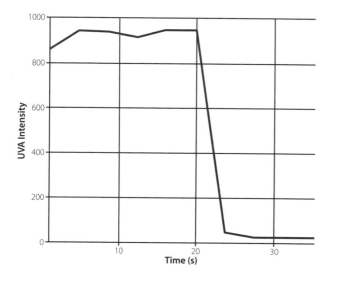

Left graph shows the UVA rays before using the film and the dramatic drop after placing the nano-film over the sensor.

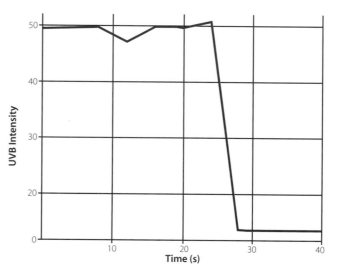

Right graph shows the UVB rays before using the film and the dramatic drop after placing the nano-film over the sensor.

EXPLAIN Examine how each product works:

Option 1: Refer to the background section of this activity and use the internet to create a PowerPoint slide show or a handout to explain the products.

Option 2: Have students do research on the internet to learn more about these products.

EXTEND Students should write a short consumer report for each product on Student Sheet 2. Each question should be addressed:
1. Was the product effective at solving the stated problem?
2. Support your answer to Question 1 by discussing your observations.
3. What is the purpose of this product?
4. How does this product work in terms of nanotechnology?

EVALUATE

As a class, go over questions 3 and 4 of their consumer reports. To finalize the activity ask students if they think the development of products to make our lives easier will have positive effects or negative effects on society. Also, ask if they think the products they observed will eventually become common household items.

GOING FURTHER

Have students look for items at home or in stores that have been developed through nanotechnology and report their findings back to the class.

DIRECTIONS

ANTI-GRAFFITI PAINT

Problem: Removing graffiti from public buildings.

Brick A: Painted with anti-graffiti paint
Brick B: Not painted with any substance

Using the marker, write on each brick. Using a wet cloth and/or brush attempt to remove the marker. Record observations in the data sheet.

PLASTIC CONTAINERS

Problem: Prolonging food freshness

Container A: Fresh Box Container
Container B: Conventional plastic container

This food has been inside of these containers for two weeks. Remove the lid and make observations. Remember to put the lid back on both containers…PEW!

SUNSCREEN

Problem: Protection from harmful UV rays

Dish A: Nanoparticle zinc oxide sunscreen
Dish B: Traditional zinc oxide sunscreen

Rub one piece of glass with sunscreen A and the other piece with sunscreen B. Be sure to apply the same amount of sunscreen to each piece so that one layer is not thicker than the other layer.

Use the UV probe to measure the amount of UV rays that are allowed to pass through the sunscreen and glass. Record your observations in the data sheet.

WINDOW FILM

Problem: Fading carpet, curtains, and dashboards from UV rays

Film A: Nanotechnology-treated window film
Film B: Traditional window film

Use the UV probe to measure the amount of UV rays that are allowed to pass through each film sample. Record your observations in the data sheet.

Be sure that you hold the sensor in the same position when testing the two films. If UVA and UVB probes are available, you may want to repeat the measurements to see if there are differences. Additional inquiries could include: comparing sunny to cloudy days, using clear glass and glass covered with the nanotechnology treated film.

NANOTECH, INC.

Name _____

Data Sheet

Products/Problems	Product A Observations	Product B Observations
Removing marker from brick		
Food freshness container		
UV rays rejected by sunscreen		
UV rays rejected by window film		

Name _____

Using the observations you made at the stations and the information you learned about each product, write up a brief consumer report for each product. You will need to answer the following questions in each report for the products:

1. Was the product effective?
2. Support your answer to question 1 by discussing your observations.
3. What is the purpose of this product?
4. How does this product work in terms of nanotechnology?

. . . .

Anti-graffiti paint:

. . . .

Fresh food container:

....

Nanoparticle sunscreen:

....

Window film:

CHAPTER 17

NanoMedicine

OVERVIEW

Nanotechnology has opened the door for medical applications that work at the molecular level to diagnose, treat, and prevent disease. This investigation models one approach to treating cancer that uses gold nanoshells to locate and destroy cancer. Students will also learn about different experimental approaches to medical treatments using nanoscale techniques.

OBJECTIVES

- To be able to describe nanoscale approaches to diagnosing and treating disease.
- To think critically about new potential treatments for cancer.

Process Skills
- Observing
- Prediction
- Measuring
- Collecting Data
- Analyzing Data
- Using Models

Activity Duration
60 minutes

NANOTECHNOLOGY TACKLES CANCER

Nanoscale medicine draws on many science domains through a focus on the raw materials—atoms and molecules, which are the building blocks of physics, chemistry, biology, and Earth science. In unprecedented ways scientists from different disciplines are collaborating in nanoscale research to explore science from multiple perspectives. Applications of nanotechnology in the biomedical arena fall into several broadly defined categories:

- **Diagnostics/Sensing.** Over the past 20 years or so, great advances in the ability to fabricate tiny mechanical devices and fluid-handling devices, as well as advances in materials synthesis have opened up a whole new arena of potential sensing technologies. Tiny fluidics devices containing even tinier mechanical and chemical sensors are able to detect very, very low levels of viruses, proteins, or drugs with very small sample sizes. In fact, in the laboratory, the ability to detect individual viruses (one virus landing on a sensor) has been demonstrated. Not only does this improve the overall capability of diagnostic sensing, it has improved the portability of state-of-the-art biochemical analysis for remote regions far from modern hospitals. In other words, simply shrinking current conventional diagnostic kits (for HIV testing, for example) to handheld fluidics devices would have dramatic impact on human health worldwide, especially in areas without modern biomedical infrastructure.
- **Drug Delivery.** Two of the most vexing problems in the administration of drugs and therapies are the problems of specifically targeting the problem areas in the body and regulating the concentration of drug levels in the bloodstream. When a person takes a drug, the side effects are typically caused by the fact that the drug acts on much more than the targeted problem and that the drug level in the bloodstream spikes immediately after taking the drug and then falls (the time-release problem). Scientists are now using clever engineering of nanoparticles as carriers for drugs that address both the specificity and time-release issue.
- **Tissue Engineering.** Another area of intense research focuses on nanomaterials techniques aimed at artificially synthesizing tissue. Researchers are intensively studying how biological systems make materials and attempting to apply what they learn to develop new materials for use in bone and muscle repair as well as improving biocompatibility of implanted devices and prostheses. In biological systems, materials such as shell and bone are made through very complex and still somewhat mysterious processes. Ultimately, these materials are built from the nanoscale up, and therefore efforts in the tissue-engineering area focus very heavily on nanomaterials research.

- **Nanoshells.** In the area of cancer treatment, there has been a lot of recent interest in the use of small nano-engineered particles called "nanoshells." Advances in nanomaterials synthesis procedures now provide scientists with the ability to make nanoparticles of tailored size and chemical functionality. Physicists are interested in the unusual electrical and optical properties of gold nanoshells. These tiny nanoparticles begin as tiny glass beads that are then covered with gold. The properties of the particle can be tuned by the choice of diameter and thickness of the gold shell.

Different-sized shells have different melting temperatures, different electrical conductivity behaviors, and even different colors. These properties make nanoshells an ideal tool for use in medical testing and treatment. The gold that coats the nanoshell is an inert metal that easily absorbs light, and the rate of absorption and reflection depends on the thickness of the gold layer. This means that the nanomaterials scientists making the shells can tune their optical properties such that they scatter light very effectively for use as a high contrast "dye" to see the cancerous cells with optical microscopy as well as for high absorbance of light energy from a laser to "burn up" cancer cells. Furthermore, the metal shell can be easily functionalized (chemically treated) with biologically active molecules (such as antibodies) that stick specifically to target cells. The antibodies stick only to a specific kind of cancer cell. When nanoshells are coated with antibodies and injected into the body, they are delivered by the bloodstream to the targeted cancer cells where antibodies on the nanoshell attach to antigens on cancer cells. The nanoshells now coat the cancerous cells and do not reside to a high degree on healthy cells. The optical tuning of the nanoshells is such that they scatter light very effectively in the near infrared (NIR) region of the electromagnetic spectrum. This is light that has wavelengths slightly longer than visible light. This is important because biological tissue is transparent to NIR light. Therefore, when NIR is shown on the suspected tissue in a microscope, only the nanoshells show up in the microscope and can be seen below the surface. Furthermore, when very intense NIR light (much stronger than for imaging) is shown on the cancerous area, the gold nanoshells heat up—essentially cooking the cancer while the surrounding healthy cells are unharmed because they do not absorb the NIR light. In this way, the cancer cells are located and destroyed without harming surrounding tissue. Keep in mind that most cancer treatments such as chemotherapy are very nonspecific in their targeting and damage healthy tissue, which in turn leads to harsh side effects. This is the motivation for therapies that are much more specific in their targeting of cancerous cells.

New Forms of Medical Treatment With Nanotechnology

With the new materials science and chemical techniques available to researchers, they are thinking very creatively about diagnosing, treating, and preventing disease with nanotechnology. As mentioned, much progress has been made in fabricating sensors with micro and nanoscale parts of mechanical and chemical functionality. These new forms of sensors involve detecting and tracking specific types of molecules. Sensing techniques range from providing tags that glow different colors in the presence of particular types of diseased or dysfunctional cells, to extremely small "lab on a chip" tests that sample minute amounts of tissues or fluids with handheld devices. One group of researchers is exploring the possibility of creating nanotags that could probe DNA and signal when an individual has a defect in their genome. This could be useful in predicting delayed-onset illnesses like Parkinson's disease and Alzheimer's disease. Imagine the day that you go to school and there is a sensor that can immediately detect whether or not you have been exposed to a cold or flu virus and could suggest you stay home and rest. Earlier detection of disease could greatly reduce the spread of infectious agents.

Complementing sensing and diagnostic applications of nanotechnology are techniques using nanotechnology for treatment of disease. Approaches for treatment include highly specific targeting of diseased tissue (like the gold nanoshells that heat up to kill cancer) or delivering very small amounts of chemicals that could destroy diseased areas. Techniques similar to gene therapy are also being explored where tiny viruslike capsules are used to deliver DNA to the defective cells and repair the dysfunctional DNA. This approach could be used to induce a cell to produce more of a hormone or insulin for a diabetic patient. Tiny capsules could also target specific areas that need repair and deliver materials to only that area. For example, if an individual had a small infection on the skin, the nanocapsules could deliver minute amounts of antibiotic that would travel only to the infected site. Other treatments include using nanoscale materials to improve artificial implants by eliminating impurities and building better bonding agents. For people who receive artificial hips or knees, providing materials that are more compatible with existing bones could decrease complications and healing time. Researchers are currently exploring the use of nanoengineered particles that could be inserted into broken bones and could provide better scaffolding for bone growth.

There is also potential to use nanomedicine to help keep healthy people healthy. Sensors could perform routine laboratory tests to monitor your cholesterol levels, kidney functioning, or stress hormone levels. For those with respiratory illness, nanotubes could deliver oxygen directly to tissues, supplementing circulating red blood cells.

The Unknowns

Nanomedicine seems like a wonderful solution to many medical problems but there is a lot that is unknown about nanoscale medicine. Will nanoparticles wander around the body—leaving the area that was targeted for treatment untouched? Will these particles cause harm? How will they be removed from the body? Is it possible that nanoparticles may interact with other medicines, cells, or tissues in harmful or unintended ways? The potential for good outcomes from these developments must be carefully balanced by research on side effects and unintended consequences.

Fry and Die: Modeling Nano Cancer Treatment

This investigation models how lasers are able to selectively heat and destroy cancerous tissues without harming surrounding healthy tissue. Students create a gold nanopacket surrounded by healthy tissue (gel). Using a heat lamp, the gold nanopacket melts, modeling the destruction of the diseased area (cancer) while the surrounding area (tissue) is left unharmed.

Preparation of Model Tissue and Cancer

Prepare one model for each student group.

..Materials ....

For the class:
Part 1: Artificial Tissue
- 10 Kool-Aid Gel cups (1 cup per 3 groups) in light color such as yellow, orange, or red
Note: Gel cups are available in most grocery stores and are used for this activity because they contain the gelling agent carrageenan, rather than gelatin. Carrageenan has a higher melting temperature, important in this activity.
- Student Sheet 2

Part 2:
The Nanoshells and Cancer
- 1 packet of unflavored gelatin
- 1.5 cups of hot water
- Gold or green food coloring (2–3 drops to make a contrast to the tissue gel color)

Part 3: Heating the Tissue
- 1–2 heat lamps

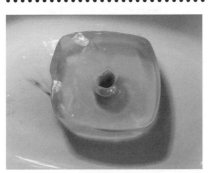

Gel Model of Tissue and Gold Nanoshell

Part 1: Artificial Tissue. Remove gel from container and make 2–3 slices (2 cm) across the gel. Each group gets one slice that represents the healthy tissue. Cut a hole from the center of the gel with a round cookie cutter or tube. The hole should be about 20% of the diameter of the gel.

Part 2: The Nanoshells and Cancer. Prepare the gelatin as directed on the package (reduce water to 1.5 cups per envelope of gelatin). Add 2–3 drops of food coloring to color the gel darker than the color of the Kool-Aid Gel. Pour gelatin into a square pan to a depth of at least 2 cm. Allow gelatin to cool and set. When firm, cut the gelatin with the same tube used to cut holes in the artificial tissue. Insert the column of gelatin into the hole in the Kool-Aid gel. Note: If the gelatin breaks up the investigation will still work. Simply fill the hole in the Kool-Aid Gel to the top of the gel slice.

Procedures

ENGAGE Read the traditional and nanomedical scenarios on the Student Sheet 1. Discuss the problems that are often encountered with traditional cancer treatments. Ask students how nanomedical treatment could be better than traditional treatment. (Be sure to note that at this stage these are experimental treatments and not yet available for people on a routine basis.)

EXPLORE Distribute Student Sheet 2 to the groups. Briefly describe how the model of the tissue and cancer was produced. Be sure to highlight that two different materials were used in the gel and the gelatin. The gel contains carrageenan and the gelatin contains gelatin.

Modeling the Cancer Treatment

Explain that students will investigate through the use of models how nanotechnology is used to treat cancer without harming the surrounding tissue.

Researchers are coating gold nanoshells with antibodies and injecting them into the body. The nanoshells circulate in the blood until they attach to antigens on cancer cells. When a laser is shown on the cancerous area, the gold nanoshells heat up—essentially cooking the cancer while the surrounding healthy cells are unharmed. This investigation uses gel and gelatin to model this process.

Directions: Place the tissue-cancer model approximately 20 cm under a heat lamp and observe. Within approximately 3–5 minutes students should see the gelatin melt while the surrounding gel is intact.

Targeting the "Nanoshell"

Melted "Nanoshell"

E X P L A I N Ask the students, *What happened to the gelatin and the gel? Why did the gelatin melt while the gel did not? Are they both made of the same ingredients?* (You may want to pass around the packages so students can see the ingredients).

Ask, *How does this process model nanoscale cancer treatment? What represented the laser? Why didn't the gel melt like the gelatin did?*

Explain that the gelatin has a lower melting point than the carrageenan. In nanotreatment, the laser would heat the metal nanoshells faster than the surrounding tissue thus killing the cancerous tissue while leaving the healthy tissue unharmed.

Ask, *Can you think of other ways we could target diseased tissues and eliminate them without surgery?*

E X T E N D Invite students to interview someone who is a cancer survivor about their experiences with cancer treatment. What were the greatest challenges that the person faced?

Place students into groups to brainstorm other creative ways that nanotechnology could be used to diagnose and treat diseases. Have the students share their ideas with the class.

E V A L U A T E Check for understanding:

1. Why must the nanoshell be metal in order to work properly?
   Answer: The metal absorbs the energy from the light or laser used in the treatment and heats up dramatically while the tissue and biological material is transparent to the light and therefore does not absorb the light energy.

2. Why isn't the healthy tissue destroyed?
   Answer: In these treatments, a certain wavelength of light is used for which tissue is transparent. This type of light is called *near infrared*. So it passes right through the tissue without being absorbed.

3. Are there environmental problems that could be solved using a similar process?
   Answer: Possibly oil spills could be broken up with nanoshells or toxic wastes incinerated by lasers and nanoshell tags.

Name _____

Medical Treatment, Today and Tomorrow

Today: Traditional Medical Treatment

"Sara" has just gone to the doctor and been told her symptoms suggest that she may have cancer. Sara's doctor orders a series of x-rays to try to detect the cancer. The x-rays have the potential to cause mutations in Sara's genes but she knows this is the first step in cancer diagnosis. The x-ray shows a suspicious mass and the next step is for Sara to have a biopsy. The biopsy involves having a surgeon stick a long needle into the mass and withdrawing small amounts of tissue to be sent to a histology lab. Sara and the physician must wait for the lab to examine the tissue. The lab confirms that Sara has an early stage of cancer and the surgeon recommends having the cancer removed. Sara proceeds and schedules the surgery for three weeks later. The surgery goes well and although the surgeon thinks he may have removed all the cancerous tissue he recommends radiation therapy to make sure there are no cancerous cells surviving. Sara now must endure the side effects of radiation, which include nausea and vomiting, as well as swelling and fluid retention. After the radiation therapy is complete, Sara is left with some damage to the tissue that was irradiated. The good news is that five years after the surgery Sara is still cancer free.

Tomorrow: NanoMedicine

Sara's character is fictional but the events surrounding cancer diagnosis and treatment are typical. New advances in nanotechnology suggest that a very different scenario may be possible in the near future for people who develop cancer. Imagine "Susan" goes to the doctor with suspicious symptoms and the doctor suggests a combination of tests and treatment that do not require surgery. Susan's doctor injects nanometer-sized gold shells into Susan's bloodstream. These minute shells are coated with antibodies that will bind only to antigens on cancer cells and will fluoresce, giving off a brilliant green light when the binding takes place. The nanoshells move through Susan's body and adhere to the cancer cells. The cancer cells are in a mass and when the nanoshells attach to the mass, Susan's doctor can see the spot of bright green light through her skin. The doctor shines a laser on the green area and because the nanoshells are gold metal—they heat up very quickly and in the process kill the cancer cells to which they are attached. The process simply fries the cancer cells. The surrounding cells are not metallic and do not heat up with the laser. The only tissue that is destroyed is the cancerous tissue. The process takes only a few minutes and Susan leaves the doctor's office feeling good knowing that the cancer cells have been eliminated. She has no need for surgery or radiation treatment. The nanoshells that have been injected into Susan will eventually be eliminated from Susan's body as part of the body's immune system.

Susan's nanotechnology medical treatment does not exist at this time but researchers are having success in using gold nanoshells to destroy cancer in experimental conditions. Other researchers have successfully identified tumors with nanoshells that fluoresce. These advances are happening very rapidly and there is widespread hope that nanotechnology will one day eliminate the need for painful surgery and follow-up chemo or radiation therapy.

Name _____

Fry and Die: Modeling Cancer Treatment

In this investigation you will make a model of the gold nanoshell treatment. Using gelatin and a flavored Kool-Aid Gel you will make artificial tissue and then embed a gold model nanoshell inside the tissue. The gelatin "shell" represents the gold nanoshells attached to the cancerous cells.

 You will place your tissue model under a heat lamp and observe what happens when the heat lamp heats up the gold capsule.

 The process models how lasers are able to selectively heat and destroy cancerous tissues without harming surrounding healthy tissues.

Materials
Each group will need:
Part 1: Artificial Tissue
• Kool-Aid Gel slice in light color such as yellow, orange, or red
Part 2: The Nanoshells and Cancer
• Block of unflavored gelatin with gold food coloring
Part 3: Heating the Tissue
• Heat lamp (1–2 for the class)

Procedures
Researchers are coating gold nanoshells with antibodies and injecting them into the body. The nanoshells circulate in the blood until they attach to antigens on cancer cells. When a laser is shown on the cancerous area, the gold nanoshells heat up—essentially cooking the cancer while the surrounding healthy cells are unharmed. This investigation uses Kool-Aid Gel and gelatin to model this process.

Directions
Predict what you think will happen when you place the tissue under the heat lamp.

_____

_____

_____

_____

_____

_____

_____

Place the tissue-cancer model approximately 20 cm under a heat lamp and observe every 30 seconds. Record your observations in the table.

Time	Observations
Starting time:_____	
At 30 seconds	
At 60 seconds	
At 90 seconds	
At 120 seconds	
At 150 seconds	
At 180 seconds	

Conclusions

1. Was your prediction accurate?

2. Explain what happened to the gelatin and Kool-Aid Gel.

3. Can you think of other contexts or applications where this process could be useful?

BUILDING SMALL: NANO INVENTIONS

OVERVIEW

Just as cells were discovered with early light micro-scopes and Saturn's rings by the first telescope, the nanoscale world has emerged due to new tools such as the Atomic Force Microscope (AFM). As a result of being able to build atom by atom a whole new world of inventions has evolved. Limited only by their imaginations, technologists are proposing nanobots, nanoscopic barcodes, and space elevators as the new inventions of tomorrow.

OBJECTIVE

- To be able to describe nanotech-nology applications in medicine, environment, and energy.

Process Skills
- Evaluating
- Synthesizing

Activity Duration
150 minutes or
two class periods

BACKGROUND

Small stuff equals BIG ideas

The ability to investigate and interact with the nanoworld is due to a large extent to technological advances in microscopy. Through use of these tools, scientists have been able to explore and manipulate materials at the atomic scale. In addition, scientists are able to investigate how the behavior of materi-als at that scale differs from the macroscale. By making these connections, ma-terials have been transformed into many products that are used today. More effective sunscreen, nonfading paint, antireflective glass, self-cleaning toilets, and stain-resistant clothes are just a few of the products of nanotechnology on the market today. Nanoscientists continue their endeavors to improve ef-ficiency in manufacturing, energy resources and utilizations, transportation medicinal products, communication, and food production.

What solutions could nanotechnology provide for society's problems? Nan-otechnology encompasses concepts from all science domains: physics, chem-istry, biology, and Earth science. Due to the interdisciplinary nature of this field of research, many opportunities arise to investigate various materials or appli-cations that could possibly remedy society's problems. The majority of nanoscience technology thus far consists of products that seem to make our lives a little easier. With continued research, the future holds a vast array of major discoveries that may not only make our lives easier but could be life-saving! Could a nanomachine exist that is can-cer seeking and cancer destroying? Could tiny probes and sensors seek and destroy pathogens or pollution in our air and water? Could there be more advanced ways of tissue regeneration? Imagine the possibilities!

Students of today, more than ever, need to understand the basics of nanotechnology. Major discoveries will occur during their lifetime. This investigation is designed to help students understand what discoveries have taken place, what inventions still lie ahead, as well as how those applications will impact human life. After an examination of the range of nanoscale advancements, students will apply their knowledge to their design of a nanotechnology applica-tion of their own creation.

PROCEDURES

ENGAGE
Discuss how nanotechnology has infiltrated just about every aspect of our lives, such as medicine, agriculture, transportation, communication, and energy sources. Give examples and pictures if possible.

Examples of nanotechnology inventions:
- More effective sunscreen
- Non-fading paint
- Anti-reflective glass
- Self-cleaning toilets
- Stain-resistant clothes
- "Never go flat" tennis balls
- Baseball bats made with carbon nanotubes that don't break

Other resources:
- www.zyvex.com/nanotech/nanotechAndMedicine.html
- www.nanotech-now.com
- www.smalltimes.com

MATERIALS

Each group will need:
- Student Sheet 1
- Access to research about nanotechnology (books, internet, magazines)
- Paper to create brochure
- Large post-it paper or poster board for brainstorming
- Color pencils, markers
- Rulers

Note: If you have access to computers, students could create their brochures electronically.

EXPLORE
Give each student the brainstorming chart on Student Sheet 1 and have students (in small groups) search for new inventions in the area that you assign them to research. Use the brainstorming chart as a guide. They can use books or the internet. Assign one the following areas of research to each group: medicine, environment, agriculture, communication, energy sources/utilization, transportation, and others that you choose. This portion of the activity could be given as homework or classwork, as long as they have sufficient time to find some examples.

EXPLAIN
After the students have gathered information about their assigned area of research in technology, conduct a classroom discussion involving the information the students found. Have each group share their information and have other groups take notes and ask questions.

By this point, students should be getting quite familiar with the types of nanotechnology inventions that exist. Stress the benefits and impacts of these inventions. One impact to consider is the economic impact. For example, if a product is made using nanotechnology, such as "never go flat" tennis balls, how will that impact the tennis ball manufacturing business?

In small groups, have the students come up with a list of possible inventions that they would like to see in the future. You may want to get them started with a few imaginative examples:

- No-chip fingernail polish
- Razor bots (nanomachines that shave hair at the nanoscale)
- Nano-sized pimple popper
- Memory wire hair weave (never style your hair again)
- Nano-sized flea-killing machines for dogs
- Nano-sized barcodes on agricultural crops

As each group shares their nano inventions, make sure they explain the benefits and impacts on humans and/or the environment.

EXTEND
Tell each group to pick one of their new nano inventions you just discussed and design a brochure describing the invention in detail. The students could either use color pencils and paper or computers to make brochures. Make brochure attractive, interesting, and organized.

Suggested items to include in brochure:

- Title
- Sketch of invention
- What is the purpose of the invention?
- In what area of research does this invention belong? (medicine, agriculture, communication)
- Why is it considered to be a nanotechonology invention?
- How was it discovered?
- What are the advantages and disadvantages of this invention?
- How does this invention impact society? (personally or economically)
- How likely is it that this invention will ever become a reality? Explain your answers.
- Who would buy this product?
- What company might sell this product?

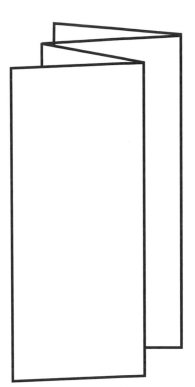

Nano Invention Brochure

EVALUATE Have the students share their nano invention brochures with the rest of the class. To check for understanding, ask:

1. Why are there so many new nano inventions?
2. How are many of these new inventions similar?
3. Which inventions are most likely to be used widely?

BUILDING SMALL

Name _____

Brainstorming Chart

1. Search for nano inventions found in the field of: _____.

2. List and describe inventions you find during your research:

3. What are the possible benefits of these inventions?

4. What are the possible negative side effects of these inventions?

PART V

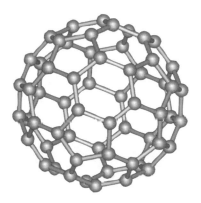

SOCIETAL
IMPLICATIONS

TOO LITTLE PRIVACY:
ETHICS OF NANOTECHNOLOGY

OVERVIEW

Advances in nanotechnology allow us to create unique and tiny labels for manufactured materials, create tiny sensors that can detect the presence of specific molecules, and make machines that are so small they can work invisibly. Through a series of scenarios students confront the potential threats to our privacy as well as the ethics of nanotechnology.

OBJECTIVES

- To be able to describe potential threats to privacy that can emerge with nanoscale technology.
- To be able to explain ethical uses of technology.

Process Skills
- Predicting
- Inferring
- Analyzing

Activity Duration
40–60 minutes

BACKGROUND

In 2003, the Gillette Company reported it was purchasing hundreds of millions of tiny NanoBlock circuits and putting them on its razors (Fitzgerald). These tiny circuits use radio waves to transmit information. The size of these tags is about the size of a dust mote (some NanoBlock circuits are as small as 70 microns across) and the tags transmit information reliably up to a distance of about three feet. The goal was for stores to use the tags to identify thieves stealing the razors, but customers were concerned that these types of tags could be used to invade their privacy. What if someone driving by your house could detect the tags? What if everything you bought could be detected and monitored by different stores? Would you care if your neighbors or the government knew which brands of toothpaste, clothing, or shoes you owned? What if these tiny tags were used to monitor more than things you buy and instead monitored your health, your diet, or the places you go during the day?

Recent advances in nanotechnology are resulting in smaller and smaller electronic devices, new forms of sensors, and the ability to add molecular nametags to products. These new technologies present us with ethical challenges in ways we have only imagined. Some futurists have argued that nanotechnology's greatest impact will be the loss of our privacy as a society. This investigation uses four scenarios to encourage students to think about the ethics and consequences of nanotechnology.

PROCEDURES

ENGAGE Invite your students to name significant technological advances that have occurred in human history. Generate a quick list of technological advances and record these on the board.

Using this list, ask them, *How have each of these technologies changed the lives of people?* Encourage students to share both positive and negative consequences of technology and record these on the board. Discuss how new technologies have removed our privacy. Already we live in a world where our food selections are monitored by grocery stores, our cars are tracked on highways with video monitors, our keys are electronically coded so that our employers know when we enter and leave the building, our conversations are monitored on city streets by police, and our movements are tracked as we shop in the mall.

Continue the discussion by asking students to think about the following:
- *How does this electronic surveillance make our lives safer?*
- *Are there times when this monitoring is not in our best interest but serves to help someone else make money?*

MATERIALS

Each group will need:
- Case scenarios (Student Sheet 1)

EXPLORE

Launch this lesson by sharing the news report that Gillette razors will be made with tiny radio wave transmitters embedded inside the razor. Ask your students to brainstorm the pros and cons of this new technology. Encourage them to think about the issues from the standpoint of the store, the razor company, the buyer, and the government. Do different people have different perspectives on the value and ethics of using these tiny tags?

Divide students into groups of 2–4 and provide each group with a scenario from Student Sheet 1 to discuss. Ask them to decide the following:

1. What aspects of our society are affected by this new nanoscale technology?
2. Who is affected by the use of the technology?
3. Who profits and who loses if this technology is adopted?
4. Who should decide if the technology is used or not?

You may want to use an ethical decision-making model to frame the discussion. The Jennings, Campbell, Donnelly, and Nolan (1990) framework invites students to identify the stakeholders, establish the relevant facts, identify unanswered questions, determine the values of each stakeholder, and consider possible solutions.

EXPLAIN

Discuss why these new technologies are now appearing, enabled by the development of new tools and techniques that miniaturize conventional surveillance and sensing technology down to the micro- and nanoscale. Define ethics for students, emphasizing the ideas of morality. Encourage students to think about all the "shades of gray" that may influence our decisions to use or not use new technology. For example, in the case of technology that enables tracking of individuals, we may not want to monitor the movement of all visitors to our country, but we may want to monitor a patient with Alzheimer's disease. Ask students to consider how attitudes toward a particular technology (especially those that may affect privacy) may differ for people living in a democratic society versus those that live under a dictatorship. What responsibilities do we have as citizens to participate in the decision-making process about uses of new technologies?

EXTEND

New applications of nanotechnology appear almost daily in the media, and these new products and materials can provide an ongoing discussion of ethics and privacy.

Invite a nanoscience researcher to come to your class (or visit virtually through web conferencing or e-mail) to share his or her research. This interaction can also stimulate students to think about new career opportunities in nanoscience. One interesting way to introduce the guest is to tell students that a mystery scientist is visiting, and they get 20 questions to figure out what the scientist does in his or her job. They can only ask yes or no questions until they are ready to guess the exact type of job. If they guess incorrectly, that student is no longer allowed to continue to ask questions of the guest. This approach to guest speakers makes the students think hard about the types of work that scientists do while also highlighting the diversity of different fields.

This investigation can be extended into thinking about futuristic potential applications of nanotechnology. Have students brainstorm and write about new ways nanotechnology could be used in our lives. Launch the lesson by sharing an idea developed by Robert Freitas (Institute for Molecular Manufacturing) for creating a programmable dermal display that would display health information directly on the hand. This display (a pixelbot) would be made of tiny robots that are implanted under the skin that detect information from an array of other medical robots that circulate in the body monitoring different components of health.

An interesting animation of this pixelbot can be found at *www.nanogirl.com/museumfuture/dermaldisplay.htm*.

EVALUATE

Check for understanding:

1. What makes nanotechnology different from other types of technology?
2. How are issues of privacy different for nanotechnology when compared to the technologies that are common in our world today?
3. In a democratic society, how should people decide which technologies should be used?

References

Butler, D. 2006. 2020 computing: Everything, everywhere. *Nature* 440: 402–405.

Chowning, J. 2005. How to have a successful science and ethics discussion. *The Science Teacher* 72 (9): 46–50.

Fitzgerald, M. 2003. Alien lands big Gillette deal, but privacy is not on razor's edge. *Small Times* (March 24). Available online at *www.small-times.com/document_ display.cfm?document_id=5363*

Jennings, B., C. Campbell, S. Donnelly, and K. Nolan. 1990. *New choices, new responsibilities: Ethical issues in the life sciences.* Briarcliff Manor, NY: Hastings Center.

TOO LITTLE PRIVACY

Name _____

Nanotechnology and Privacy Scenarios

Scenario 1: Nano Labels

Researchers are developing tiny nano-sized bar codes that can be used to invisibly tag almost anything that is manufactured. These tags have the potential to monitor sales, track sales by types of customers or geographic regions, indicate thefts, and signal inventories held by stores and warehouses.

- What do you think about this idea to label manufactured goods?
- Do you care if people know what brand of underwear you buy?
- What if the labels were put in bullets or explosives so that police could track and locate murderers or terrorists?
- If you could track food from the farm to your mouth, what are the advantages and disadvantages?
- Would it be a good idea to put nano tags in compact discs so that manufacturers could make sure CDs are legal? Are there any negative concerns about having the music industry track the music that you buy?
- If we could label and monitor money flow, how could this be used in beneficial and harmful ways?

Scenario 2: Nano Health

A growing area within nanotechnology is development of sensors that can be used to monitor your health. The goal is to produce tiny sensors that could be injected into your blood stream that can monitor a wide range of health indicators including your heart rate, blood pressure, blood glucose levels, cholesterol, as well as the presence of pathogenic viruses or bacteria.

- What are the advantages and disadvantages of nano-sized monitors that would be injected into your body?
- How could this type of monitoring system be useful to diabetics or people with a history of heart problems?
- What if the monitor could send an alarm if you ate high-fat foods like cookies or cake—would this be a useful tool to help you watch your nutrition?
- Would it be helpful to have a monitor that could signal if you haven't eaten enough protein or are missing essential vitamins?
- Are there groups of people that would benefit more from these types of monitors than others?
- If the monitors were expensive, would you be in favor of allowing wealthy people to purchase them if they were not available for the poor?
- If large numbers of monitors from different people could be networked, the data could be used to monitor large-scale health issues. What privacy issues might arise from this type of application? If it could signal a sudden rise in the flu or colds, would this change your view of this type of monitoring?

- Should visitors to the country be screened with these tiny monitors to ensure that they are not bringing new diseases to our country? What would be the implications of this type of policy?
- Should an individual ever be monitored against their will? What if the person was mentally handicapped and had difficulty taking critical life-saving drugs? Should this person be monitored without consent?

Scenario 3: Nano Environment

Environmental researchers are currently using remote sensors to monitor the health of water, soil, and air. Researchers are finding new ways to make these sensors smaller and smaller with a goal of creating invisible sensors that could be networked to provide data on the health of whole ecosystems.

- Would you want sensors in your watershed keeping track of pollutants, pH, and oxygen levels?
- If networks of sensors could be created, how would you feel about having the forest near your house filled with tiny sensors that could detect movement, changes in temperature, and the presence of pollutants?
- Would you want clouds of sensors released that could monitor global warming?
- Should we track endangered species by placing a sensor in each animal and monitoring its movement and health over its lifespan?
- Would you purchase building sensors that could monitor your house, apartment, or workplace to ensure that the air quality is good?

Scenario 4: Nano Travel

One idea that has been proposed is to create smart dust that could be put in paints, sidewalks, or ceilings that could monitor the movement of people. Already we monitor movement in stores, airports, train stations, streets, and hotels.

- Should we monitor the movement of people on a large-scale basis?
- If this monitoring allowed us to identify terrorists, would it be more ethical?
- Is it more acceptable to monitor the movement of children as a way to keep them safe?
- If your grandfather had Alzheimer's disease, would you want him monitored to make sure he didn't wander off into unsafe situations?
- Would you want this type of sensor put in your pet so that if the pet were lost or stolen it could be retrieved? (Some pet owners already put chips in their pets that can be detected by animal shelters so the owner can be notified. Other pet owners use radio collars on their dogs to be able to track them when the dog is running free.)
- What rules should be in place to ensure that people have safety, privacy, and freedom?
- When is monitoring people without their knowledge acceptable? Are there already situations where you are monitored without your explicit knowledge?

CHAPTER 20

PROMISE OR PERIL: NANOTECHNOLOGY AND THE ENVIRONMENT

OVERVIEW

Nanoscience research has made great strides in recent years in areas such as nanomaterials and drug delivery. This success has kindled hope for exciting technological breakthroughs in the near future in areas ranging from new cures for cancer therapies to new materials that gobble up toxic waste in the environment. The nano-sized particles utilized in these proposed technologies products have beneficial results, but at what cost? Do we really know the effect these particles have on our environment or even our health?

OBJECTIVES

- To explore the advantages and disadvantages of nanotechnology on the health of living things.
- To simulate the use of nanosensors in pollution remediation.

Process Skills
- Observing
- Predicting

Activity Duration
90 minutes

BACKGROUND

Nanoparticles naturally exist in our world. Viruses, pollen, sea spray, and ash are all tiny natural particles that affect our environment and our health. Now that nanoscience allows scientists to build products atom by atom, many human-made nano-sized particles are utilized in industry, laboratories, and medicine. Along with being engineered with specific chemical and biological functionality, nanoparticles are particularly reactive simply because of their size. Since they are so small, an ensemble of billions of nanoparticles has an enormous surface area exposed to the environment and they can diffuse quickly throughout a system into which they are introduced. The benefits of these new nano products are evident, but questions lie in the fate of these particles. Where will free particles such as nanosensors made for detecting contaminants in water end up after their job is done? Or what about decomposing products that consist of nano-sized particles? Where do those particles go? Because these particles behave in novel ways, their impact on the environment is an unanswered question. Proper management of these particles is necessary for the protection of environment and human health. To fully realize nanotechnology's promise, the risks must be weighed against the benefits.

Imagine cleaning a contaminated waterway with nanoparticles that can detect and destroy pollution or using tiny sensors to warn a soldier of potentially harmful chemicals. Wei-zian Zhang, a scientist at Lehigh University, has shown that iron nanoparticles from 100–200nm in size can be beneficial in cleaning toxic organic wastes such as trichloroethylene (TCE) in ground water. In a demonstration study in a manufacturing plant, the particles were shown to reduce TCE levels significantly and show real promise as a tool to clean up toxic contamination sites. Even with those benefits, many unknown risks are evident. One particular study investigated the harmful effects of the synthetically produced buckyballs on fish. This study found that these particles can destroy lipid cells, a major component of brain tissue.

In this activity, students will explore the advantages and disadvantages of nanotechnology. Students will also simulate the use of nanosensors to detect harmful materials in the environment.

·MATERIALS·

Each group will need:
- Small plastic container with tight-fitting lid (shoebox size)
- Sand to fill ¾ of plastic container
- 10 metal pellets (such as BBs)
- 10–15 small magnets
- Student Sheet 1

PROCEDURES

ENGAGE
Ask students to name different types of water pollutants. Make a list of contaminants on the board or overhead projector. Discuss with students the different causes of water pollution and why it is harmful to humans and the environment. Students may name oil spills, sewage spills, industrial spills, and so on. For more information on different types of pollution visit *www.epa.gov*.

Ask the students to pair up with a partner and brainstorm different methods of getting rid of pollution. Most students will probably name preventative methods such as preventing illegal dumping. Suggest that through new nanotechnology discoveries there might be a method in the near future to clean up polluted waters thought to be permanently contaminated. Give the example of nanoscientists trying to use nanoparticles to detect pollutants and destroy them.

You also want to make sure students understand that there are unknown risks of setting nanoparticles free into the environment that policy makers and scientists cannot ignore. Can these nanoparticles enter the bodies of organisms, and if so, do they affect one organ or all of them? Do possible toxic effects stem from one nanoparticle or only when they are clumped together in large numbers?

FURTHER READING

Berube, D. M. 2006. Nanohazards and nanotoxicology. In *Nano-hype: The truth behind the nanotechnology buzz*, 275–304. Amherst, NY: Prometheus Books.

Feder, B. J. 2004. Study raises concern about carbon particles. *New York Times*, March 29, 2004. *http://query.nytimes.com/gst/fullpage.html?sec=health&res= 9E06E7DD1E30F93AA15750C0A9629C8B63*.

Owen, R., and M. Depledge. 2005. Nanotechnology and the environment: Risks and rewards. *Marine Pollution Bulletin* 50: 609–612.

EXPLORE
Now that students are aware of sources of pollution and approaches that nanotechnologists are working on to remediate these problems, students will simulate what it would be like to try to detect contaminants in water or the air. Place students in groups of three and charge them with developing a strategy to "detect" pollution molecules with their nanosensors.

Each group will use the container of sand to represent their water sample. The BBs or other metal pellets represent the pollutants in the water sample. The magnets will represent the nanosensors designed to attach and possibly destroy the pollution particles. The students will drop the magnets into the container of sand and

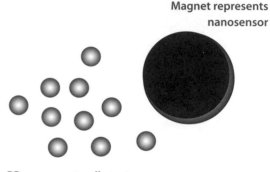

Magnet represents nanosensor

BBs represent pollutants

BBs. As students gently shake the container, the nanosensors (magnets) will "seek out" the pollutants (BBs) and attach. The shaking represents the natural occurrence of interaction of particles in a lake or river.

EXPLAIN
Explain to the students that this interaction of a nanosensor and harmful particle is similar to the antibody-antigen interaction that takes place in their bodies.

Use the analogy of a foreign particle in the human body that causes an immune response to kick in. That foreign particle has "unknown" risks and the body's systems detect this issue. How does this compare to scientists sending nanoparticles into the environment and the environment's response to those particles? The outcomes are still not fully known.

EXTEND
- Ask the students to consider the advantages and disadvantages of using nano-sized particles in our immediate surrounding.
- For an extension in this area, create a web quest for current research on the use of nanosensors to detect pollution and other harmful chemicals.

EVALUATE
Check for understanding:
1. What are the implications of using nanoparticles in our environment?
2. What are possible risks of releasing nanoparticles into the environment?
3. How could nanoparticles be gathered once they are released into a given space?

PROMISE OR PERIL

Name _____

Oil Droplet

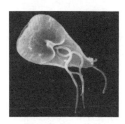

Giardia Lamblia

Problem

How could nanoscientists detect and destroy pathogens, pollutions, or other harmful particles in our environment?

Pros and Cons

Discuss with your lab group the pros and cons of trying to detect pathogens and pollution in our environment.

Materials

- Container of sand
- Metal pellets (BBs)
- Magnets

Process

1. Open the container of sand. The sand represents your environment (air, water, and so on).

2. Drop the BBs or metal pellets into the container of sand. What do the BBs represent in this simulation?

3. Drop the magnets into the container of sand and metal pellets. What do the magnets represent in this simulation?

4. Note the time: _____. Close the container and gently shake it. What does the shaking of the container represent in this simulation?

5. Check every few minutes until you see that the magnets have detected all the BBs and are attached.

6. Once you have all magnets and BBs attached to each other, note time: _____.

7. Once all the BBs are captured by the magnets, how can they be removed from the environment?

Conclusion

1. What are the advantages of using nanosensors to clean up oil spills or other types of pollution?

2. What are the possible disadvantages of using nanosensors to detect or clean up pollution?

3. Why is efficient clean-up time an issue in environmental disasters?

APPENDIX

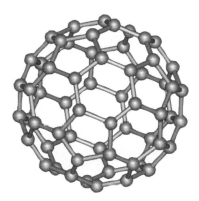

OTHER RESOURCES ABOUT NANOSCIENCE FOR TEACHERS

WEBSITES

The NanoScale Science Education Research Group at North Carolina State University
Information and resources for teachers about scale and scaling, haptics, viruses, and nanotechnology education.
http://ced.ncsu.edu/nanoscale

Comprehensive and Informative Nanotechnology Portal
Provides introduction to nanotechnology, general information, images, interviews, news, and events.
www.nanotech-now.com

Howstuffworks
"How Nanotechnology Will Work." Animated narrative shows how nanotechnology has the potential to change manufacturing, health care, and other fields.
www.howstuffworks.com/nanotechnology

The Exploration of Student Engagement and Understanding of Nanoscience and Technology
What knowledge, beliefs, and teaching practices do science teachers need to support student achievement of nanoscience learning goals?
http://hi-ce.org/projects/iopd/Nano.html

Powers of Ten
Explore powers of ten, from 10^{25} meters (one billion light years) to 10^{-18} meters (0.001 fermis)
http://powersof10.com

National Center for Teaching and Learning in Nanoscale Science (NCLT)
Focuses on how to support students—from middle school through college—in learning nanoscience ideas
http://nclt.us

The National Nanotechnology Initiative (NNI)
A federal research and development program established to coordinate the multiagency efforts in nanoscale science, engineering, and technology.
www.nano.gov/html/edu/home_edu.html

The National Nanotechnology Infrastructure Network (NNIN)
An integrated partnership of thirteen user facilities, supported by NSF, which provides support for nanoscience and nanotechnology research. The organization is developing an education site called the Nanotechnology Educational Resources and Activities for K–12 Teachers.
www.nnin.org/nnin_k12teachers.html

UNC-Chapel Hill Nanoscale Science Research Group

Exploring nanoscale science in biomotors, nanocontacts, cystic fibrosis, gene therapy, DNS, molecular motors, the nanoManipulator, and the 3-D Force Microscope.

www.cs.unc.edu/Research/nano/research.html

FIELDS OF NANOSCIENCE RESEARCH

Windows That Never Need Cleaning

www.chemsoc.org/chembytes/ezine/2002/ashton_jun02.htm

Molecular Memory

www.trnmag.com/Stories/071801/HP_maps_molecular_memory_071801.html

Nanoparticles in Sunscreen

www.csiro.au/csiro/content/file/ppf33.html

Nano Pants

www.csiro.au/csiro/content/standard/ps2d1.html

Building Computers With Nanoscale Components

www.trnmag.com/Stories/071801/HP_maps_molecular_memory_071801.html

JOURNAL ARTICLES

Alivisatos, A. P. 2001. Less is more in medicine: Sophisticated forms of nanotechnology will find some of their first real-world applications in biomedical research, disease diagnosis, and, possibly, therapy. *Scientific American* 285 (3), 66–73.

Bishop, D., P. Gammel, and R. C. Giles. 2001. The little machines that are making it big. *Physics Today* 54 (10): 38–44.

Freitas, R. 2005. Current status of nanomedicine and medical nanorobotics. *Journal of Computational and Theoretical Nanoscience* 2: 1–25.

Goodsell, D. S. 2000. Biomolecules and nanotechnology. *American Scientist* 88 (3): 230–237.

Jones, M. G., T. Andre, R. Superfine, and R. Taylor. 2003. Learning at the nanoscale: The impact of students' use of remote microscopy on concepts of viruses, scale, and microscopy. *Journal of Research in Science Teaching* 40: 303–322.

Kahn, J. 2006. Welcome to the world of nanotechnology. *National Geographic* 209 (6): 98–119.

Kunzig, R. 1997. A head for numbers. *Discover* 18 (7): 108–115.

Qian, L., and J. P. Hinestroza. 2004. Application of nanotechnology for high performance textiles. *Journal of Textile and Apparel Technology and Management* 4 (1): 1–7.

Stix, G. 2001. Nanotechnology is all the rage. But will it meet its ambitious goals? And what the heck is it? *Scientific American* 285 (3): 32–37.

Tretter, T. R., and M. G. Jones. 2003. A sense of scale: Studying how scale affects systems and organisms. *The Science Teacher* 70 (1): 22–25.

Tseng, G. Y., and J. C. Ellenbogen. 2001. Nanotechnology: Toward nanocomputers. *Science* 294 (5545): 1293–1294.

Whitesides, G. M. 2001. The once and future nanomachine: Biology outmatches futurists' most elaborate fantasies for molecular robots. *Scientific American* 285 (3): 78–83.

Whitesides, G. M., and B. Grzybowski. 2002. Self-assembly at all scales. *Science* 295 (5564): 2418–2421.

OTHER BOOKS AND JOURNALS OF INTEREST

Booker, R., and E. Boysen. 2005. *Nanotechnology for dummies*. Hoboken, NJ: Wiley Publishing.

Regis, E. 1995. *The emerging science of nanotechnology*. Boston: Bay Back Books.

The Small Times Magazine: Micro and nanotech manufacturing, tools, and materials. *www.smalltimes.com*

INDEX

Page numbers in **boldface** type refer to figures. A following "t" indicates a table.

Daily Skill Builders:
Fractions & Decimals

By
CINDY BARDEN AND SARA BIERLING

COPYRIGHT © 2008 Mark Twain Media, Inc.

ISBN 978-1-58037-444-6

Printing No. CD-404085

Mark Twain Media, Inc., Publishers
Distributed by Carson-Dellosa Publishing Company, Inc.

Table of Contents

Table of Contents (cont.)

Introduction to the Teacher

This edition of *Daily Skill Builders* is a powerful tool that will help you equip your students with a variety of important skills relating to fractions and decimals. Each half-page reproducible activity targets a specific skill, as shown in the Table of Contents. Tied to NCTM standards, these activities provide practice in basic calculations involving fractions and decimals.

The activities in this book will give your students daily practice with a variety of essential math skills. They are arranged so that each activity builds on the skills covered in the previous activities. You may use them in order, or use any section you need to reinforce your curriculum. Use the standards-correlation chart in the beginning of the book to locate problems on a specific skill.

When they complete the activities, students will be mastering skills such as adding and subtracting fractions with common denominators, mixed numbers, and without common denominators; multiplying and dividing fractions, mixed numbers, and improper fractions; comparing fractions and decimals; adding and subtracting whole numbers with decimals, and multiplying and dividing whole numbers with decimals.

We hope you and your students find these exercises both useful and engaging. Fractions and decimals are an integral part of performing higher math skills and achieving higher test scores. These *Daily Skill Builders* are designed to help your students hone their math skills to razor sharpness.

In short, use these *Daily Skill Builders* any and every way you can to make the most of all the tools packed inside. Expect your students' fraction and decimal skills to grow throughout the year!

NCTM Standards Matrix for Grades 3–8

This standards correlation chart is based on *Principles and Standards for School Mathematics* from the National Council of Teachers of Mathematics. The expectations listed here represent the part of the Number and Operations content standard for grades 3–8 that relate to fractions and decimals.

Understand numbers, ways of representing numbers, relationships among numbers, and number systems

Expectations	Activity Number
Understand the place-value structure of the base-ten number system and be able to represent and compare whole numbers and decimals	99, 100, 101, 102, 103
Develop understanding of fractions as parts of unit wholes, as parts of a collection, as locations on number lines, and as divisions of whole numbers	1, 2, 3, 4, 5, 6, 7, 8, 11, 12, 13, 15, 16, 20, 27, 28, 31, 33, 34, 35, 36, 37, 38, 53, 54, 60, 95
Use models, benchmarks, and equivalent forms to judge the size of fractions	8, 15, 16, 17, 18, 29, 30, 41, 42, 43, 44, 46, 53, 54
Recognize and generate equivalent forms of commonly used fractions, decimals, and percents	9, 10, 11, 14, 47, 48, 49, 50, 65, 66, 79, 97, 120, 121, 133, 134, 135, 136, 137, 138, 140, 147, 149, 150
Work flexibly with fractions, decimals, and percents to solve problems	15, 16, 21, 23, 24, 25, 26, 51, 52, 77, 78, 79, 80, 81, 82, 89, 90, 91, 92, 93, 98, 113, 115, 116, 117, 118, 129, 130, 131, 132, 145, 146, 151
Compare and order fractions, decimals, and percents efficiently and find their approximate locations on a number line	19, 20, 41, 42, 43, 44, 45, 46, 53, 54, 61, 62, 63, 64, 96, 103, 104, 105, 106, 107, 108, 147, 149, 150
Understand and use ratios and proportions to represent quantitative relationships	60
Use factors, multiples, prime factorization, and relatively prime numbers to solve problems	55, 56, 57, 58, 61, 62, 63, 64, 69, 70, 71, 72, 79, 80, 96, 97
Understand meanings of operations and how they relate to one another	
Understand various meanings of multiplication and division	33, 34, 35, 36, 38, 55, 56, 67, 68, 73, 74, 75, 76, 77, 78, 79, 80, 81, 82, 83, 84, 85, 86, 87, 88, 91, 92, 95, 98, 117, 127, 128, 129, 130, 131, 132, 141, 142, 143, 144, 145, 146, 152
Identify and use relationships between operations, such as division as the inverse of multiplication, to solve problems	81, 82, 83, 84, 85, 86, 87, 88, 91, 92, 94, 141, 142, 143, 144

NCTM Standards Matrix for Grades 3–8

Understand meanings of operations and how they relate to one another (cont.)	
Expectations	**Activity Number**
Understand the meaning and effects of arithmetic operations with fractions, decimals, and integers	33, 34, 35, 36, 38
Use the associative and commutative properties of addition and multiplication and the distributive property of multiplication over addition to simplify computations with integers, fractions, and decimals	70, 72, 77, 78, 91, 92, 117, 131, 132, 139, 145, 146
Understand and use the inverse relationships of addition and subtraction, multiplication and division, and squaring and finding square roots to simplify computations and solve problems	81, 82, 83, 84, 85, 86, 87, 88, 91, 92, 94, 141, 142, 143, 144
Compute fluently and make reasonable estimates	
Develop and use strategies to estimate computations involving fractions and decimals in situations relevant to students' experience	70, 71, 76, 86
Use visual models, benchmarks, and equivalent forms to add and subtract commonly used fractions and decimals	21, 22, 23, 24, 25, 26, 33, 34, 35, 36, 38, 39, 40, 55, 56, 59, 67, 68, 69, 70, 71, 72, 73, 74, 75, 76, 77, 78, 79, 80, 81, 82, 83, 84, 85, 86, 87, 88, 91, 92, 95, 98, 113, 114, 115, 116, 117, 120, 121, 123, 124, 125, 126, 127, 128, 129, 130, 131, 132, 140, 148, 141, 142, 143, 144, 145, 146, 151, 152
Select appropriate methods and tools for computing with fractions and decimals from among mental computation, estimation, calculators or computers, and paper and pencil, depending on the situation, and apply the selected methods	22, 36, 74, 76, 82, 86, 107, 114, 124, 126, 131, 132, 133, 137, 138, 142, 144
Develop and analyze algorithms for computing with fractions, decimals, and integers, and develop fluency in their use	21, 22, 23, 24, 25, 26, 33, 34, 35, 36, 38, 39, 40, 55, 56, 59, 67, 68, 69, 70, 71, 72, 73, 74, 75, 76, 77, 78, 79, 80, 81, 82, 83, 84, 85, 86, 87, 88, 91, 92, 95, 98, 113, 114, 115, 116, 117, 120, 121, 123, 124, 125, 126, 127, 128, 129, 130, 131, 132, 140, 141, 142, 143

ACTIVITY 1 Parts of a Whole

Name: _____

Date: _____

A **fraction** names equal parts of a whole.

1 of 2 equal parts of this circle is shaded.

One-half of this circle is shaded.

$\frac{1}{2}$ of this circle is shaded.

3 of 8 equal parts of this square are shaded.

Three-eighths of this square is shaded.

1. Write the fraction for the part of the square that is shaded. _____

2 of 3 parts of this triangle are shaded.

The shaded part is not $\frac{2}{3}$ of the triangle.

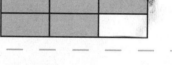

2. Why not? _____

3. What fraction of this rectangle is shaded? _____

- -

ACTIVITY 2 Parts of a Whole

Name: _____

Date: _____

Fractions are made up of two numbers. The top number is the **numerator**. It tells how many parts are being discussed. The bottom number is the **denominator**. It tells the number of equal parts all together. To help you remember, make up a two-word phrase, such as "Nothing Doing" or "Nine Donuts." The first word should begin with an "n." The second word should begin with a "d." When you want to remember which number is on top, think of your phrase.

1. _____ is the numerator. It tells how many parts of the circle are shaded.

2. _____ is the denominator. It tells the total number of equal parts in the circle.

Write the fractions to show the number of shaded parts for each shape.

3. _____   4. _____   5. _____   6. _____

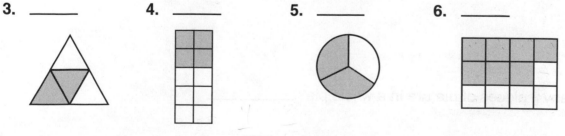

3

 **ACTIVITY 3** **Parts of a Whole**

Name:_____

Date:_____

1. Draw lines to show three different ways to divide the squares into halves.

2. Draw lines to show two different ways to divide the rectangles into sixths.

3. Color one-sixth of the first rectangle above red. Shade three-sixths of this rectangle gray.

4. Color two-sixths of the second rectangle above red. Shade two-sixths of this rectangle gray.

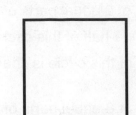 **ACTIVITY 4** **Parts of a Whole**

Name:_____

Date:_____

Draw a picture or diagram to show each fractional amount.

1. $\frac{1}{2}$ of a pie

2. $\frac{1}{3}$ of a glass of juice

3. $\frac{1}{4}$ of a cookie

4. $\frac{1}{2}$ of an apple

5. $\frac{3}{4}$ of a sandwich

6. $\frac{2}{3}$ of a bottle of water

7. How many $\frac{1}{6}$ pieces of pie are in a whole pie? _____

ACTIVITY 5   Parts of a Group

Name:_____

Date:_____

One of five balls in the group is striped.

One-fifth of the balls are striped.

$\frac{1}{5}$ = the number of balls with stripes

1. In the fraction, 1 is the _____. It tells the number of balls with stripes in the group.

2. In the fraction, 5 is the _____. It tells the total number of balls in the group.

3. How many triangles in this group are white? _____

4. What fraction of the triangles are white? _____

In a group of 11 children, 5 are girls and 6 are boys.

5. What fraction of the group are boys? _____

6. What fraction of the group are girls? _____

ACTIVITY 6   Parts of a Group

Name:_____

Date:_____

1. How many students are in your class? _____

2. What fraction of the class are girls? _____

3. What fraction of the class are boys? _____

Ms. Mason planted 18 tulip bulbs. $\frac{1}{3}$ were white. The rest were red.

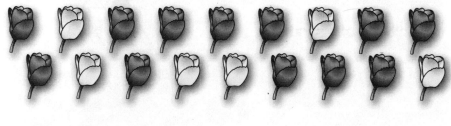

4. How many are white? _____

5. What fraction are red? _____

ACTIVITY 7 Parts of a Group/ Use a Table

Name: _____

Date: _____

Use the table to answer the questions.

Top Readers at Jefferson School	
Name	Books Read in January
Mary	⊬ //
Terry	⊬ ⊬ /
Sherry	⊬ ////
Larry	⊬ ///
Jerry	⊬ ⊬ ////
Barry	⊬ /

1. How many students were in the group of top readers at Jefferson School? _____

2. What fraction of the group read more than 10 books? _____

3. What fraction of the group read between 8 and 14 books? _____

4. What fraction of the group read fewer than 9 books? _____

5. How many books did the group read all together? _____

6. What fraction of the total number of books did Larry read? _____

7. What fraction of the total number of books did Mary and Sherry read? _____

ACTIVITY 8 Fractional Parts of a Whole and a Group

Name: _____

Date: _____

Write fractions for each shape.

1. Shaded part of the circle = _____

2. Part of the circle not shaded = _____

3. Shaded part of the triangle = _____

4. Part of the triangle not shaded = _____

5. Draw a shape. Color $\frac{3}{5}$ of it.

6. Draw a group of objects. Circle $\frac{2}{3}$ of the objects.

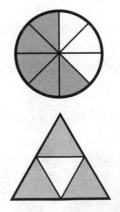

ACTIVITY 9 Fraction Words

Name:_____

Date:_____

Fractions can be written in numbers or words. When fractions are written in words, the words are joined by a hyphen.

Example: $\frac{1}{2}$ = one-half

Write the words for each fraction.

1. $\frac{3}{4}$ _____

2. $\frac{2}{7}$ _____

3. $\frac{7}{9}$ _____

4. $\frac{3}{10}$ _____

5. $\frac{2}{6}$ _____

6. $\frac{8}{11}$ _____

Write the fraction for the fraction words.

7. eleven-twentieths _____

8. four-hundredths _____

9. six-eighteenths _____

10. nine-thirty-seconds _____

ACTIVITY 10 Fraction Words

Name:_____

Date:_____

Write the number for the numerator of each fraction.

1. eleven-sixteenths _____

2. six-twelfths _____

Write the number for the denominator of each fraction.

3. seven-thirteenths _____

4. nineteen-twentieths _____

Write the fraction for the fraction words.

5. nine-elevenths _____

6. one-ninth _____

ACTIVITY 11 Review

Name: _____

Date: _____

1. Draw a shape. Color $\frac{7}{8}$ of it.

Write the fraction for the shaded portion of each shape.

2. _____   3. _____   4. _____

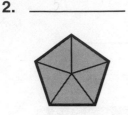   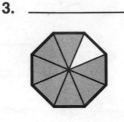   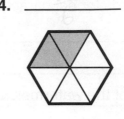

Write fractions equal to one using the denominator given.

5. $\frac{\square}{7} = 1$ 6. $\frac{\square}{14} = 1$ 7. $\frac{\square}{9} = 1$ 8. $\frac{\square}{100} = 1$

- -

ACTIVITY 12 Review

Name: _____

Date: _____

1. Draw a group of objects. Color $\frac{6}{15}$ of the objects.

2. Fraction of the stars that are shaded = _____

   Fraction of the stars that are not shaded = _____

3. A regular deck of playing cards contains 52 cards. If the dealer gives out five cards each to three players, what fraction of the cards have been dealt? _____

4. If 35 students sit on a bus that can hold 48 students, what fraction of the seats are full? _____

5. If you flip a coin, what fraction describes the chances of it landing on heads? _____

ACTIVITY 13 Review

Name:_____

Date:_____

Circle the numerator of each fraction.

1. $\frac{2}{5}$ 2. $\frac{12}{16}$ 3. $\frac{30}{90}$

Circle the denominator of each fraction.

4. $\frac{16}{32}$ 5. $\frac{4}{5}$ 6. $\frac{15}{100}$

7. Circle $\frac{1}{2}$ of the watermelon seeds.

- -

ACTIVITY 14 Review

Name:_____

Date:_____

1. $\frac{76}{92}$ of the seats on a plane are filled.

    How many total seats are on the plane? _____

2. How many passengers are on the plane? _____

Write the fractions using numerals.

3. three-fifteenths   _____   4. eleven-fourteenths   _____

5. two-hundredths   _____   6. two-thirds   _____

Write the fractions using words.

7. $\frac{1}{4}$ _____

8. $\frac{18}{30}$ _____

9. $\frac{5}{8}$ _____

10. $\frac{12}{100}$ _____

ACTIVITY 15 Everyday Math With Fractions

Name:_____

Date:_____

1. If you attend school Monday through Friday, what fraction of the week do you attend school? _____

2. If you have vacation during June, July, and August, what fraction of the year do you have vacation? _____

3. If you sleep 8 hours every night, what fraction of the day do you sleep? _____

4. If you sleep 8 hours every night and attend school for 6 hours, what fraction of the hours you are awake are spent in school? _____

5. December, January, and February are considered winter months. What fraction of all the months are winter months? _____

6. If you spend 30 minutes studying, what fraction of an hour did you study? _____

- -

ACTIVITY 16 Everyday Math With Fractions

Name:_____

Date:_____

1. If you ate 13 ounces of spinach, what fraction of a pound of spinach did you eat? (There are 16 ounces in 1 pound.) _____

2. Ramón worked Wednesday, May 1, and every other Wednesday during the month of May. What fraction of the month did he work? _____

3. A cookie recipe calls for equal amounts of chocolate chips, walnuts, pecans, raisins, and coconut. What fraction of the ingredients are nuts? _____

4. The annual bike race at Creston Middle School provided snacks including bananas, apples, granola bars, bagels, bottled water, yogurt, and grapes. What fraction of the snacks were fruit? _____

5. If you plant 14 bean seeds and only 9 grow, what fraction of the bean seeds did not grow? _____

6. If you drank $\frac{1}{2}$ of a cup of milk, how many ounces of milk did you drink? (There are 8 ounces in 1 cup.) _____

ACTIVITY 17 Estimate With Fractions

Name:_____

Date:_____

Circle the fraction that is closest to the amount in each container.

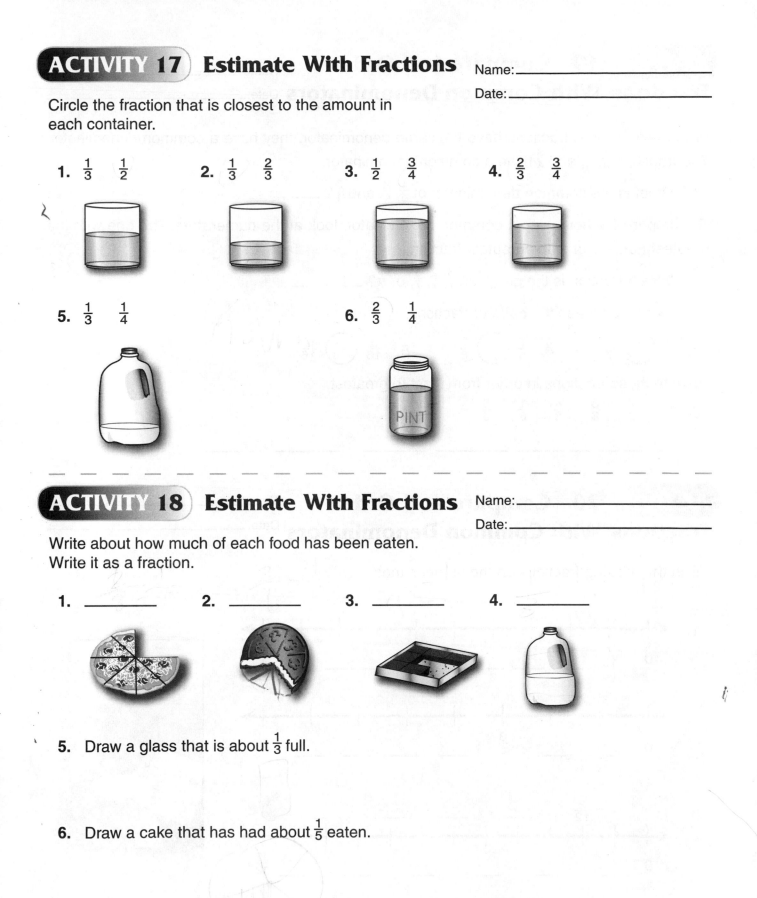

1. $\frac{1}{3}$ $\frac{1}{2}$ 2. $\frac{1}{3}$ $\frac{2}{3}$ 3. $\frac{1}{2}$ $\frac{3}{4}$ 4. $\frac{2}{3}$ $\frac{3}{4}$

5. $\frac{1}{3}$ $\frac{1}{4}$ 6. $\frac{2}{3}$ $\frac{1}{4}$

ACTIVITY 18 Estimate With Fractions

Name:_____

Date:_____

Write about how much of each food has been eaten.
Write it as a fraction.

1. _____   2. _____   3. _____   4. _____

5. Draw a glass that is about $\frac{1}{3}$ full.

6. Draw a cake that has had about $\frac{1}{5}$ eaten.

ACTIVITY 19 **Compare and Order**   Name:_____

Fractions With Common Denominators Date:_____

When two or more fractions have the same denominator, they have a common denominator. The fractions $\frac{1}{4}$, $\frac{2}{4}$, and $\frac{3}{4}$ have a common denominator.

1.   What is the common denominator of $\frac{1}{4}$, $\frac{2}{4}$, and $\frac{3}{4}$? _____

To compare fractions with a common denominator, look at the numerators. The one with the greatest numerator is the greatest fraction.

2.   Which fraction is the greatest: $\frac{3}{7}$, $\frac{2}{7}$, $\frac{6}{7}$, or $\frac{1}{7}$? _____

Write > or < between the pairs of fractions.

3. $\frac{5}{7}$ ◯ $\frac{6}{7}$ 4. $\frac{7}{8}$ ◯ $\frac{2}{8}$ 5. $\frac{9}{16}$ ◯ $\frac{7}{16}$

Rewrite these fractions in order from least to greatest.

6. $\frac{2}{8}$ $\frac{7}{8}$ $\frac{3}{8}$ $\frac{6}{8}$ $\frac{1}{8}$ $\frac{5}{8}$

_____ _____ _____ _____ _____ _____

- -

ACTIVITY 20 **Compare and Order**   Name:_____

Fractions With Common Denominators Date:_____

Fill in the missing fractions on the number lines.

1.

0    $\frac{1}{10}$ ___ ___ ___ ___ ___ ___ ___   1

2.

0   ___ ___ $\frac{3}{8}$ ___ ___ ___ ___   1

3. $\frac{2}{12}$ ___   ___   ___   ___

0   ___   ___   ___   ___   ___   ___ $\frac{12}{12}$

12

ACTIVITY 21 Add Fractions With Common Denominators

Name:_____

Date:_____

To add fractions with a common denominator, write the sum of the numerators over the common denominator.

Example: $\frac{3}{8} + \frac{4}{8} = \frac{7}{8}$

Find the sums.

1. $\frac{1}{5} + \frac{2}{5} =$ _____

2. $\frac{6}{100} + \frac{8}{100} =$ _____

3. $\frac{13}{24} + \frac{4}{24} =$ _____

4. $\frac{2}{7} + \frac{3}{7} =$ _____

5. Mitch pitched for $\frac{2}{9}$ of a 9-inning baseball game. Rich pitched $\frac{4}{9}$ of the game.

   Together, how many innings of the game did Mitch and Rich pitch? _____

ACTIVITY 22 Add Fractions With Common Denominators

Name:_____

Date:_____

Find the sums. Since these problems use small numbers, use mental math if you can.

1. $\frac{5}{6} + \frac{1}{6} =$ _____

2. $\frac{3}{8} + \frac{4}{8} =$ _____

3. $\frac{1}{5} + \frac{3}{5} =$ _____

4. $\frac{1}{4} + \frac{2}{4} =$ _____

5. $\frac{33}{99} + \frac{33}{99} =$ _____

6. $\frac{27}{40} + \frac{9}{40} =$ _____

7. $\frac{5}{20} + \frac{1}{20} =$ _____

8. $\frac{10}{12} + \frac{1}{12} =$ _____

9. $\frac{1}{3} + \frac{1}{3} =$ _____

10. $\frac{5}{9} + \frac{4}{9} =$ _____

ACTIVITY 23 Subtract Fractions With Common Denominators

Name:_____

Date:_____

To subtract fractions with common denominators, write the difference of the numerators over the common denominator.

Example: $\frac{7}{8} - \frac{2}{8} = \frac{5}{8}$

Subtract.

1. $\frac{9}{10} - \frac{4}{10} =$ _____

2. $\frac{11}{14} - \frac{7}{14} =$ _____

3. $\frac{81}{100} - \frac{41}{100} =$ _____

4. $\frac{9}{16} - \frac{5}{16} =$ _____

5. $\frac{27}{64} - \frac{12}{64} =$ _____

6. $\frac{17}{19} - \frac{13}{19} =$ _____

ACTIVITY 24 Subtract Fractions With Common Denominators

Name:_____

Date:_____

Solve using subtraction.

1. Sam ate $\frac{3}{16}$ of a bag of cookies. Pam ate $\frac{5}{16}$ of the cookies. What fraction of the cookies were left? _____

2. Six of the 24 students in one class joined the soccer team. What fraction of the students did not join the team? _____

3. Shannon worked for $\frac{4}{7}$ of the week. How many days did she not work during the week? _____

4. The train regularly made 8 stops on its way to Chicago. So far the train had made $\frac{3}{8}$ of its stops. What fraction of the stops were left? _____

5. Aidan brought home 12 fish from the school fair. Seven of the fish were goldfish. What fraction were not goldfish? _____

6. Michaela and her friends took $\frac{36}{98}$ of the clothing they collected to the thrift store. They took another $\frac{36}{98}$ to the homeless shelter. They kept the rest to give to needy kids at school. What fraction did they keep? _____

ACTIVITY 25 **Add and Subtract**   Name:_____

Fractions With Common Denominators Date:_____

Add or subtract. Pay attention to the math signs.

1. $\frac{11}{13} - \frac{5}{13} =$ _____

2. $\frac{4}{11} + \frac{6}{11} =$ _____

3. $\frac{31}{32} - \frac{17}{32} =$ _____

4. $\frac{6}{15} + \frac{3}{15} =$ _____

5. $\frac{72}{100} + \frac{11}{100} =$ _____

6. $\frac{26}{64} - \frac{9}{64} =$ _____

7. Harry worked in the garden for $\frac{35}{60}$ of an hour. Jerry worked for only the next $\frac{20}{60}$ of an hour.

   What fraction of an hour did the two boys work together? _____

8. How much longer did Harry work? Write your answer as a fraction. _____

9. How many minutes did Jerry work in the garden? _____

10. Together, they finished $\frac{7}{10}$ of the garden work. How much was left to finish? _____

- -

ACTIVITY 26 **Review**   Name:_____

          Date:_____

Circle *T* for true and *F* for false.

1. T F The numerator is the number below the line in a fraction.
2. T F A fraction is a number less than 1.
3. T F A fraction can only name parts of a group.
4. T F A fraction can name parts of a whole.
5. T F The denominator is the number below the line in a fraction.
6. T F If two fractions have a common denominator, they are equal.
7. T F Two fractions cannot be added together.
8. T F Fractions of a whole can be subtracted.
9. T F The fractions $\frac{3}{8}$ and $\frac{7}{8}$ have a common denominator.
10. T F Fractions can only be written in numbers, not words.
11. There are 15 cats and 17 dogs at the animal shelter. What fraction of the animals are cats? _____
12. Toby ate $\frac{1}{5}$ of a box of cereal for breakfast every morning. How many days did it take him to eat one box of cereal? _____

ACTIVITY 27 Measurement With Fractions

Name:_____

Date:_____

1. 4 inches is what fraction of a foot? _____

2. 5 ounces is what fraction of a cup? _____

3. 11 ounces is what fraction of a pound? _____

4. 16 inches is what fraction of a yard? _____

5. 7 is what fraction of a dozen? _____

6. $\frac{7}{12}$ of a foot equals how many inches? _____

7. $\frac{3}{8}$ of a cup equals how many ounces? _____

8. $\frac{21}{36}$ of a yard equals how many inches? _____

9. $\frac{3}{7}$ of a week equals how many days? _____

10. $\frac{3}{12}$ of a dozen eggs equals how many eggs? _____

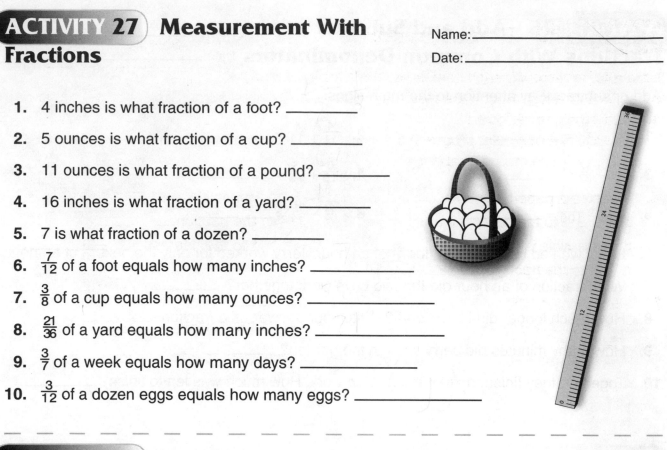

ACTIVITY 28 Measurement With Fractions

Name:_____

Date:_____

1. 1 cup is what fraction of a gallon? _____

2. 1 foot is what fraction of a yard? _____

3. 1 teaspoon is what fraction of a tablespoon? _____

4. 1 inch is what fraction of a foot? _____

5. 1 day is what fraction of a year? _____

6. 1 second is what fraction of an hour? _____

7. 10 cents is what fraction of a dollar? _____

8. 1 ounce is what fraction of a pound? _____

9. 2 quarts are what fraction of a gallon? _____

10. 1 week is what fraction of a year? _____

16

ACTIVITY 29 · Round Fractions

Name:_____

Date:_____

Use a ruler to measure each item listed. Write the answers as fractions of a foot. Round the measurements to the nearest inch: $\frac{1}{2}$ inch or more, round up; less than $\frac{1}{2}$ inch, round down.

Example: A computer mouse is $3\frac{3}{4}$ inches long. Round to the nearest inch = 4 inches. The mouse is about $\frac{4}{12}$ of a foot long.

1. Measure a paperback book.
   a. How long is it? _____
   b. Round to the nearest inch. _____
   c. Write the fraction. _____
   d. How wide is the book? _____
   e. Round to the nearest inch. _____
   f. Write the fraction. _____

2. Measure a pencil.   a. How long is it? _____
   b. Round to the nearest inch. _____
   c. Write the fraction. _____

3. Measure your hand from the tip of your thumb to the tip of your little finger.
   a. How long is it? _____
   b. Round to the nearest inch. _____
   c. Write the fraction. _____

ACTIVITY 30 · Estimate

Name:_____

Date:_____

Select three objects in the classroom that are shorter than one foot. Estimate the length of each item. Then measure the items with a ruler.

Item 1: _____

   a. Estimated length to the nearest inch _____
   b. Actual length rounded to the nearest inch _____
   c. Was your estimate high or low? _____

Item 2: _____

   a. Estimated length to the nearest inch _____
   b. Actual length rounded to the nearest inch _____
   c. Was your estimate high or low? _____

Item 3: _____

   a. Estimated length to the nearest inch _____
   b. Actual length rounded to the nearest inch _____
   c. Was your estimate high or low? _____

ACTIVITY 31 **Mixed Numbers**

Name:_____

Date:_____

A mixed number is a whole number and a fraction.

Examples: $1\frac{2}{3}$ $6\frac{5}{8}$ $9\frac{7}{16}$

Estimate the amount you see. Write the mixed number for each set of objects.

1. _____

2. _____

3. _____

4. _____

ACTIVITY 32 **Mixed Numbers**
With a Table

Name:_____

Date:_____

	Salt in a Bag of Potato Chips
Brand A	
Brand B	
Brand C	
Brand D	
	= 1 teaspoon

1. Which brand of potato chips is the saltiest? _____

2. Which brand has the least salt? _____

3. How much salt is in a bag of Brand B chips? _____

4. How much salt is in a bag of Brand C chips? _____

ACTIVITY 33 Improper Fractions to Mixed Numbers and Whole Numbers

Name:_____

Date:_____

When the numerator is equal to or larger than the denominator, the fraction is an improper fraction. This means that the value of the fraction is equal to or greater than 1.

Examples: $\frac{9}{3}$ $\frac{14}{5}$ $\frac{7}{2}$

You can change an improper fraction to a whole number or mixed number (a whole number plus a fraction). To change an improper fraction to a mixed number, divide the numerator by the denominator. Write the whole number. Write the remainder over the denominator. Combine the two numbers.

Example: $\frac{13}{3}$ $3\overline{)13}$ with quotient 4, -12, remainder 1 $\frac{13}{3} = 4 \text{ R1} = 4\frac{1}{3}$

Change these improper fractions to mixed numbers or whole numbers.

1. $\frac{5}{3}$ = _____

2. $\frac{7}{4}$ = _____

3. $\frac{9}{8}$ = _____

4. $\frac{17}{6}$ = _____

5. $\frac{31}{21}$ = _____

ACTIVITY 34 Improper Fractions to Mixed Numbers and Whole Numbers

Name:_____

Date:_____

Change these improper fractions to mixed numbers or whole numbers.

1. $\frac{101}{100}$ = _____

2. $\frac{47}{42}$ = _____

3. $\frac{12}{4}$ = _____

4. $\frac{8}{6}$ = _____

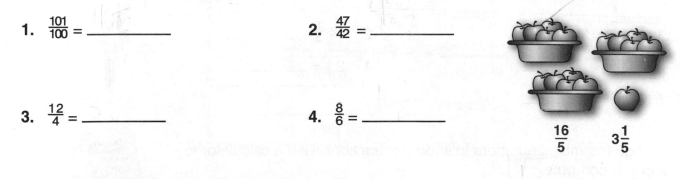

$\frac{16}{5}$ $3\frac{1}{5}$

5. Write an example of an improper fraction that is greater than 1. _____

6. Draw an image to represent your fraction.

ACTIVITY 35 Mixed Numbers and Whole Numbers to Improper Fractions

Name:_____

Date:_____

You can change a mixed number to an improper fraction. Multiply the whole number by the denominator. Add the product to the numerator. Write that sum over the denominator.

Example: $3\frac{1}{8}$ $3\frac{1}{8}$ $8 \times 3 = 24$ $24 + 1 = 25$ $\frac{25}{8}$ is the same as $3\frac{1}{8}$

Change the mixed numbers to improper fractions.

1. $4\frac{2}{3}$ = _____

2. $6\frac{5}{8}$ = _____

3. $100\frac{4}{5}$ = _____

4. 7 = _____

5. $9\frac{7}{12}$ = _____

6. $12\frac{2}{5}$ = _____

- -

ACTIVITY 36 Mixed Numbers and Whole Numbers to Improper Fractions

Name:_____

Date:_____

Change the mixed numbers to improper fractions. Use paper and pencil to compute.

1. $9\frac{2}{16}$ = _____

2. $11\frac{1}{3}$ = _____

3. $1\frac{17}{18}$ = _____

4. $2\frac{2}{5}$ = _____

5. $4\frac{3}{7}$ = _____

Change the mixed numbers to improper fractions. Use a calculator to help you compute.

6. $6\frac{3}{5}$ = _____

7. $35\frac{1}{2}$ = _____

8. $7\frac{1}{3}$ = _____

9. $3\frac{7}{13}$ = _____

10. $5\frac{3}{4}$ = _____

ACTIVITY 37) Review

Name:_____

Date:_____

Circle *T* for true or *F* for false.

1. T   F   Seven inches is another way of saying $\frac{7}{12}$ of a foot.

2. T   F   Five months is the same as $\frac{5}{12}$ of the year.

3. T   F   A mixed number is two fractions added together.

4. T   F   A mixed number is always larger than 1.

5. T   F $\frac{7}{3}$ is an example of a mixed number.

6. T   F   An improper fraction can be changed to a whole number or mixed number.

7. T   F   All improper fractions can be changed to whole numbers.

8. T   F   An improper fraction is equal to or greater than 1.

9. T   F   When changing a mixed number to a fraction, the answer will always be an improper fraction.

10. T   F $\frac{9}{4}$ is equal to $2\frac{1}{4}$.

- -

ACTIVITY 38) Review

Name:_____

Date:_____

Write a mixed number for the model.

1. _____

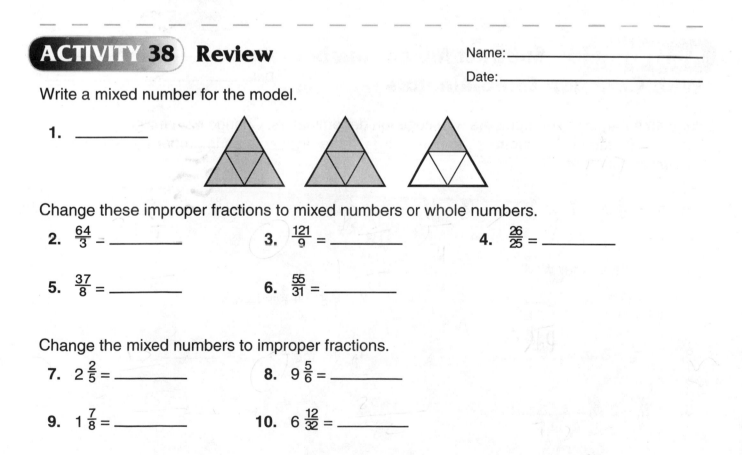

Change these improper fractions to mixed numbers or whole numbers.

2. $\frac{64}{3}$ _____

3. $\frac{121}{9}$ = _____

4. $\frac{26}{25}$ = _____

5. $\frac{37}{8}$ = _____

6. $\frac{55}{31}$ = _____

Change the mixed numbers to improper fractions.

7. $2\frac{2}{5}$ = _____

8. $9\frac{5}{6}$ = _____

9. $1\frac{7}{8}$ = _____

10. $6\frac{12}{32}$ = _____

**ACTIVITY 39 Add Mixed Numbers
With Common Denominators**

Name:_____

Date:_____

You can add mixed numbers with common denominators. Add the whole numbers. Then add the fractions. If the answer is an improper fraction, change it to a mixed number. Add it to the whole number.

Example: $1\frac{2}{3} + 2\frac{2}{3} = 3\frac{4}{3} = 3 + 1\frac{1}{3} = 4\frac{1}{3}$

Add. Show your work.

1. $4\frac{2}{8} + 2\frac{7}{8} =$ _____

2. $3\frac{5}{7} + 6\frac{6}{7} =$ _____

3. $4\frac{2}{3} + 9\frac{1}{3} =$ _____

4. $11\frac{3}{9} + 2\frac{5}{9} =$ _____

5. $18\frac{1}{2} + 9\frac{1}{2} =$ _____

6. $7\frac{9}{32} + 11\frac{19}{32} =$ _____

**ACTIVITY 40 Subtract Mixed Numbers
With Common Denominators**

Name:_____

Date:_____

You can subtract mixed numbers with common denominators. Change both mixed numbers to improper fractions and subtract the numerators. If the answer is an improper fraction, write it as a mixed number.

Example: $4\frac{2}{3} - 3\frac{1}{3} =$ $4\frac{2}{3} = \frac{14}{3}$ $3\frac{1}{3} = \frac{10}{3}$ $= \frac{14}{3} - \frac{10}{3} = \frac{4}{3} = 1\frac{1}{3}$

Subtract. Show your work.

1. $6\frac{3}{8} - 3\frac{7}{8} =$ _____

2. $9\frac{1}{5} - 4\frac{4}{5} =$ _____

3. $11\frac{9}{16} - 8\frac{11}{16} =$ _____

4. $12\frac{44}{100} - 4\frac{54}{100} =$ _____

5. $7\frac{3}{10} - 2\frac{5}{10} =$ _____

6. $81\frac{2}{6} - 72\frac{3}{6} =$ _____

ACTIVITY 41   Compare Fractions Using Fraction Strips

Name: _____

Date: _____

Use the Fraction Strip Chart on page 79.

Circle the fraction in each group that is greatest.

1. $\frac{1}{2}$ $\frac{1}{3}$ $\frac{1}{4}$

2. $\frac{2}{3}$ $\frac{2}{4}$ $\frac{2}{5}$

3. $\frac{4}{10}$ $\frac{2}{5}$ $\frac{3}{6}$

4. $\frac{3}{4}$ $\frac{7}{8}$ $\frac{1}{2}$

Circle the fraction in each group that is least.

5. $\frac{2}{3}$ $\frac{1}{2}$ $\frac{3}{4}$

6. $\frac{2}{5}$ $\frac{2}{10}$ $\frac{2}{8}$

7. $\frac{3}{10}$ $\frac{2}{3}$ $\frac{6}{8}$

8. $\frac{7}{8}$ $\frac{3}{5}$ $\frac{2}{6}$

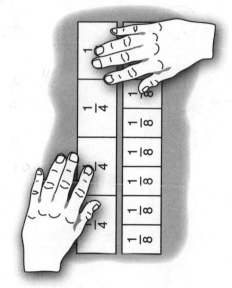

ACTIVITY 42   Compare Fractions Using Fraction Strips

Name: _____

Date: _____

Use the Fraction Strip Chart on page 79.

Circle the fractions in each group that are equal.

1. $\frac{3}{4}$ $\frac{2}{3}$ $\frac{6}{8}$

2. $\frac{4}{10}$ $\frac{2}{5}$ $\frac{5}{8}$

3. $\frac{5}{10}$ $\frac{3}{6}$ $\frac{4}{8}$

4. $\frac{1}{3}$ $\frac{2}{6}$ $\frac{1}{2}$

Use the rectangles below for the following.

5. Divide one rectangle into eighths.

6. Divide the second rectangle into tenths.

7. Color parts of each rectangle to show two equal fractions.

23

ACTIVITY 43 **Compare and Order Fractions Using Fraction Strips**

Name:_____

Date:_____

Use the Fraction Strips on page 79. Write >, <, or = between each pair of fractions.

1. $\frac{1}{2}$ ◯ $\frac{1}{3}$ 2. $\frac{5}{10}$ ◯ $\frac{6}{8}$

3. $\frac{2}{3}$ ◯ $\frac{3}{4}$ 4. $\frac{5}{6}$ ◯ $\frac{7}{8}$

5. $\frac{7}{8}$ ◯ $\frac{9}{10}$ 6. $\frac{3}{8}$ ◯ $\frac{2}{3}$

7. $\frac{3}{6}$ ◯ $\frac{4}{8}$ 8. $\frac{9}{10}$ ◯ $1\frac{1}{2}$

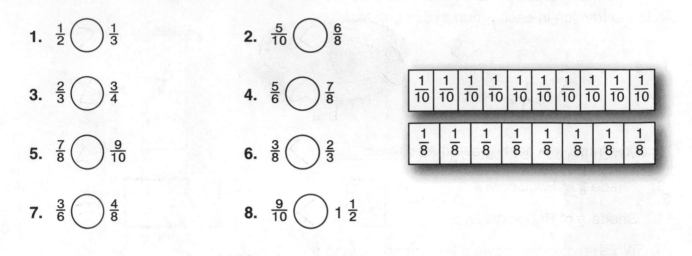

ACTIVITY 44 **Compare and Order Fractions Using Fraction Strips**

Name:_____

Date:_____

Use the Fraction Strips on page 79.
Rewrite each group of fractions in order from least to greatest.

1. $\frac{1}{3}$ $\frac{1}{5}$ $\frac{2}{4}$ $\frac{3}{8}$ $\frac{2}{3}$ $\frac{5}{6}$

____ ____ ____ ____ ____ ____

2. $\frac{1}{2}$ $\frac{2}{3}$ $\frac{7}{8}$ $\frac{2}{6}$ $\frac{9}{10}$ $\frac{4}{5}$

____ ____ ____ ____ ____ ____

3. Bret worked on his science project for $\frac{3}{8}$ of an hour. Jess spent $\frac{1}{3}$ of an hour on his project. Who worked longer on his science fair project? _____

4. Bret tossed a football to Jess for $\frac{2}{5}$ of an hour. Was that more or less time than he spent on his science fair project? _____

ACTIVITY 45 **Compare and Order**
Fractions

Name:_____

Date:_____

1. Which amount of pie is smaller? _____

A   B

2. Which fraction is greater: $\frac{1}{3}$ or $\frac{2}{3}$? _____

3. Shade $\frac{3}{8}$ of Rectangle A.   A. ☐   B. ☐

4. Shade $\frac{1}{2}$ of Rectangle B.

5. Which rectangle shows a larger part shaded? _____

6. Which is less: $\frac{1}{2}$ or $\frac{3}{8}$? _____

ACTIVITY 46 **Compare and Order**
Mixed Numbers Using Fraction Strips

Name:_____

Date:_____

When comparing two mixed numbers, compare the whole numbers first. If they are equal, compare the fractions to determine which is greater. But watch out for improper fractions!

Use the Fraction Strips on page 79. Write >, <, or = between each pair of mixed numbers.

1. $2\frac{1}{3}$ ◯ $3\frac{1}{10}$ 2. $7\frac{9}{10}$ ◯ $7\frac{3}{4}$ 3. $1\frac{4}{6}$ ◯ $1\frac{5}{8}$

4. $4\frac{3}{6}$ ◯ $4\frac{1}{2}$ 5. $8\frac{1}{8}$ ◯ $7\frac{3}{8}$ 6. $3\frac{6}{8}$ ◯ $4\frac{2}{3}$

Rewrite each group of mixed numbers in order from least to greatest.

7. $2\frac{3}{4}$ $2\frac{5}{6}$ $2\frac{5}{8}$ $1\frac{1}{2}$ $3\frac{1}{8}$ $1\frac{3}{4}$

____ ____ ____ ____ ____ ____

8. $6\frac{7}{8}$ $6\frac{2}{3}$ $5\frac{1}{3}$ $5\frac{2}{8}$ $6\frac{3}{4}$ $5\frac{3}{4}$

____ ____ ____ ____ ____ ____

ACTIVITY 47 Equivalent Fractions

Name: _____

Date: _____

Equivalent fractions are fractions that are equal.
$\frac{1}{2}$ and $\frac{2}{4}$ are equivalent fractions.
You can use a fraction strip chart or draw pictures to find equivalent fractions. Follow these steps to find equivalent fractions by drawing pictures.

Example: Find an equivalent fraction of $\frac{2}{3}$ with a denominator of 6. Draw a shape. Divide the shape into the number of parts equal to the denominator. Color the number of parts equal to the numerator.

Draw lines to divide the shape into the number of parts for the new denominator. Count the number of colored parts.

1. What fraction with a denominator of 6 is equal to $\frac{2}{3}$? _____

- -

ACTIVITY 48 Equivalent Fractions

Name: _____

Date: _____

Divide the rectangles to help you find the equivalent fractions.

1. What fraction with a denominator of 12 is equal to $\frac{3}{4}$? _____

2. What fraction with a denominator of 9 is equal to $\frac{1}{3}$? _____

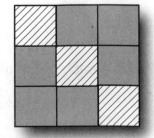

3. What fraction with a denominator of 16 is equal to $\frac{1}{4}$? _____

ACTIVITY 49 Equivalent Fractions

Name:_____

Date:_____

Find equivalent fractions with a denominator of 8.

1. $\frac{1}{2}$ = _____

2. $\frac{3}{4}$ = _____

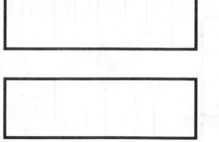

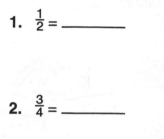

Find equivalent fractions with a denominator of 12.

3. $\frac{2}{3}$ = _____   4. $\frac{5}{6}$ = _____

5. $\frac{3}{4}$ = _____   6. $\frac{1}{4}$ = _____

ACTIVITY 50 Equivalent Fractions

Name:_____

Date:_____

Find equivalent fractions with a denominator of 20.

1. $\frac{3}{10}$ = _____   2. $\frac{3}{5}$ = _____   3. $\frac{1}{2}$ = _____   4. $\frac{3}{4}$ = _____

Write the missing numerator or denominator.

5. $\frac{1}{11} = \frac{3}{\Box}$ 6. $\frac{18}{\Box} = \frac{9}{16}$ 7. $\frac{2}{5} = \frac{\Box}{50}$

8. $\frac{7}{98} = \frac{1}{\Box}$ 9. $\frac{2}{3} = \frac{\Box}{21}$ 10. $\frac{1}{4} = \frac{25}{\Box}$

ACTIVITY 51 Create a Table/ Use Data From a Table

Name: _____

Date: _____

Take a poll of your classmates and fill in the chart. Then answer the questions.

Eye Color	Girls	Boys
Blue		
Green		
Brown		

1. How many students are in your class? _____

2. What fraction of the girls have blue eyes? _____

3. What fraction of the class has brown eyes? _____

4. What fraction of the boys have green eyes? _____

5. Which fraction is greater, boys with blue eyes or girls with brown eyes? _____

ACTIVITY 52 Create a Table/ Use Data From a Table

Name: _____

Date: _____

Take another poll using three other options. Fill in the chart.

	Girls	Boys

Write three statistics using data from your table.

Example: $\frac{2}{12}$ of the girls like blue more than green.

1. _____

2. _____

3. _____

ACTIVITY 53 Review

Name: _____

Date: _____

1. Write three examples of mixed numbers.

_____   _____   _____

2. Write three examples of improper fractions.

_____   _____   _____

IMPROPER

$\frac{24}{5}$

PROPER

$6\frac{1}{4}$

Change the mixed numbers to improper fractions.

3. $3\frac{5}{9}$ = _____

4. $2\frac{4}{7}$ = _____

5. $13\frac{3}{10}$ = _____

Change the improper fractions to mixed or whole numbers.

6. $\frac{41}{3}$ = _____

7. $\frac{17}{5}$ = _____

8. $\frac{24}{6}$ = _____

ACTIVITY 54 Review

Name: _____

Date: _____

Write >, <, or = between the two numbers.

1. $\frac{7}{3}$ ◯ $3\frac{1}{3}$

2. $2\frac{3}{15}$ ◯ $\frac{51}{15}$

3. $6\frac{4}{7}$ ◯ $\frac{28}{7}$

4. Draw and shade a diagram to show the fraction of a square with a denominator of 16 equal to $\frac{3}{4}$.

Find equivalent fractions with a denominator of 16.

5. $\frac{3}{4}$ = _____

6. $\frac{1}{8}$ = _____

7. $\frac{1}{2}$ = _____

8. $\frac{5}{8}$ = _____

29

ACTIVITY 55 **Greatest Common Factors** Name:_____

Date:_____

Every number has factors. These are the numbers that can be multiplied by other numbers to equal the number in question.

Examples: The factors of 8 are 1, 8, 2, and 4. $1 \times 8 = 8$ $2 \times 4 = 8$
The factors of 10 are 1, 10, 2, and 5. $1 \times 10 = 10$ $2 \times 5 = 10$

The **greatest common factor** is the largest number that is a factor of two or more numbers. In the example above, the greatest common factor of 8 and 10 is 2 because 2 is the greatest number that they have in common as a factor.

1. What is the greatest common factor of 8 and 10? _____

2. Fill in the charts to show the factors of 12 and 16.

Factors of 12	
1	
2	
	4

Factors of 16	
2	

3. Circle all factors that appear in both charts.

4. What is the greatest common factor of 12 and 16? _____

- -

ACTIVITY 56 **Greatest Common Factors** Name:_____

Date:_____

Fill in the charts to show the factors of each pair of numbers.

Factors of 25	

Factors of 30	
1	

1. The greatest common factor of 25 and 30 is _____.

Factors of 16	

Factors of 20	

2. The greatest common factor of 16 and 20 is _____.

ACTIVITY 57 Simplify Fractions

Name:_____

Date:_____

If the numerator and denominator have no common factors other than one, a fraction is in its simplest form.

Are these fractions in their simplest form? Circle *yes* or *no.*

1. $\frac{2}{3}$ yes   no

2. $\frac{7}{14}$ yes   no

3. $\frac{3}{9}$ yes   no

4. $\frac{7}{15}$ yes   no

5. $\frac{4}{6}$ yes   no

6. $\frac{2}{21}$ yes   no

7. $\frac{25}{100}$ yes   no

8. $\frac{4}{11}$ yes   no

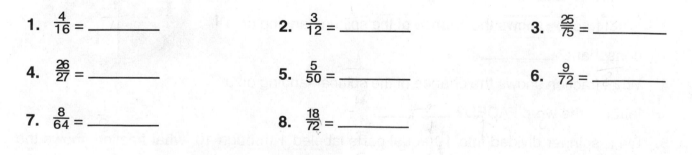

Simplify:

$$\frac{10}{100} = \frac{1}{10}$$

$$\frac{4}{12} = \frac{1}{3}$$

ACTIVITY 58 Simplify Fractions

Name:_____

Date:_____

If a fraction is not in simplest form, you can reduce it.
Determine the greatest common factor of the numerator and denominator. Divide the numerator by the greatest common factor. Divide the denominator by the same number. Rewrite the fraction.

Example: Reduce $\frac{4}{12}$ to simplest form. The greatest common factor of 4 and 12 is 4.

$$\frac{4}{12} \div \frac{4}{4} = \frac{1}{3}$$ The simplest form of $\frac{4}{12}$ is $\frac{1}{3}$.

If the fraction is not in its simplest form, simplify it.

1. $\frac{4}{16}$ = _____

2. $\frac{3}{12}$ = _____

3. $\frac{25}{75}$ = _____

4. $\frac{26}{27}$ = _____

5. $\frac{5}{50}$ = _____

6. $\frac{9}{72}$ = _____

7. $\frac{8}{64}$ = _____

8. $\frac{18}{72}$ = _____

ACTIVITY 59 Fraction Patterns

Name:_____

Date:_____

Follow the rule. Fill in the blanks to complete the pattern.

1. **Rule:** Add $1\frac{1}{2}$

   $\frac{1}{2}$ 2   ____   ____   ____   8   ____   11

2. **Rule:** Subtract $\frac{1}{12}$

   $\frac{11}{12}$ ____   ____   ____ $\frac{7}{12}$ ____   ____ $\frac{4}{12}$

3. **Rule:** Add $\frac{2}{6}$

   $3\frac{1}{6}$ ____ $3\frac{5}{6}$ ____   ____   ____

Fill in the pattern. Then write the rule.

4. $\frac{1}{8}$ $\frac{3}{8}$ ____ $\frac{7}{8}$ ____ $1\frac{3}{8}$

   Rule: _____

5. $\frac{89}{100}$ $\frac{86}{100}$ ____   ____ $\frac{77}{100}$ ____

   Rule: _____

ACTIVITY 60 Probability With Fractions

Name:_____

Date:_____

Fractions express probability. The chances of a coin landing

on heads are 1 in 2. The ratio is 1:2. The ratio can be written as the fraction $\frac{1}{2}$.

Use the spinner to answer the questions. Simplify the fractions.

1. What fraction represents the chance of the spinner landing

   on a D? _____

2. What fraction shows the chance of the spinner landing on a

   vowel? _____

3. What fraction shows the chance of the spinner landing on a

   consonant? _____

4. What fraction shows the chance of the spinner landing on a

   letter in the word FACED? _____

5. On a spinner divided into 10 equal parts labeled 1 through 10, what fraction shows the

   chance of the spinner landing on an even number? _____

ACTIVITY 61 Compare Fractions Without Common Denominators

Name: _____

Date: _____

If fractions do not have a common denominator, you can change them so they are easier to compare, add, and subtract. Find a new denominator that both old denominators will divide into evenly. Multiply the denominators to produce that number as the product. Multiply the numerators by the same number as the denominator for each fraction. Rewrite the fractions with a common denominator. Compare the numerators.

Example: Compare $\frac{3}{4}$ and $\frac{4}{5}$. $\frac{3}{4} \times \frac{5}{5} = \frac{15}{20}$ $\frac{4}{5} \times \frac{4}{4} = \frac{16}{20}$

16 is greater than 15, so $\frac{4}{5}$ is greater than $\frac{3}{4}$.

Use this method to compare the fractions. Show your work.

1. Which is greater: $\frac{2}{3}$ or $\frac{3}{5}$? _____

2. Which is less: $\frac{7}{8}$ or $\frac{5}{6}$? _____

ACTIVITY 62 Compare Fractions Without Common Denominators

Name: _____

Date: _____

The least common denominator is the smallest number that both of the original denominators are a factor of. Find the least common denominator for each set of fractions, and then compare the fractions. Show your work.

1. What is the least common denominator of $\frac{2}{3}$ and $\frac{3}{8}$? _____

   Which is greater: $\frac{2}{3}$ or $\frac{3}{8}$? _____

2. What is the least common denominator of $\frac{3}{5}$ and $\frac{4}{7}$? _____

   Which is greater: $\frac{3}{5}$ or $\frac{4}{7}$? _____

3. What is the least common denominator of $\frac{1}{10}$ and $\frac{2}{100}$? _____

   Which is less: $\frac{1}{10}$ or $\frac{2}{100}$? _____

4. What is the least common denominator of $\frac{6}{12}$ and $\frac{4}{10}$? _____

   Which is less: $\frac{6}{12}$ or $\frac{4}{10}$? _____

5. What is the least common denominator of $\frac{2}{3}$, $\frac{5}{6}$, and $\frac{1}{12}$? _____

   Which is greatest: $\frac{2}{3}$, $\frac{5}{6}$, or $\frac{1}{12}$? _____

LEAST COMMON DENOMINATOR

ACTIVITY 63   Least Common Multiple

Name:_____

Date:_____

Another way to compare fractions is to find the least common multiple. The least common multiple is the smallest number that two or more numbers will divide into evenly. Find multiples of both denominators. Determine the lowest number that is a multiple of both numbers. Multiply the denominator by whatever factor will produce the least common multiple as a product. Multiply the numerator by the same number as the denominator. Rewrite the fractions with the common denominator. Compare the numerators.

Example: Compare $\frac{2}{3}$ and $\frac{3}{7}$.

Multiples of 3 are 3, 6, 9, 12, 15, 18, 21, 24, 27, etc.

Multiples of 7 are 7, 14, 21, 28, 35, 42, etc.

21 is the least common multiple.

$\frac{2}{3} \times \frac{\times 7}{\times 7} = \frac{14}{21}$ $\frac{3}{7} \times \frac{\times 3}{\times 3} = \frac{9}{21}$ 14 is greater than 9, so $\frac{2}{3}$ is greater than $\frac{3}{7}$.

Use this method to compare the fractions. Show your work on your own paper.

1. What is the least common multiple for $\frac{3}{4}$ and $\frac{2}{5}$? _____ Which is greater: $\frac{3}{4}$ or $\frac{2}{5}$? _____

2. What is the least common multiple for $\frac{2}{3}$ and $\frac{4}{9}$? _____ Which is less: $\frac{2}{3}$ or $\frac{4}{9}$? _____

ACTIVITY 64   Least Common Multiple

Name:_____

Date:_____

Compare the fractions. Show your work.

1. What is the least common multiple of $\frac{5}{12}$ and $\frac{3}{10}$? _____

   Which is greater: $\frac{5}{12}$ or $\frac{3}{10}$? _____

2. What is the least common multiple of $\frac{1}{3}$ and $\frac{3}{4}$? _____

   Which is greater: $\frac{1}{3}$ or $\frac{3}{4}$? _____

3. What is the least common multiple of $\frac{3}{9}$ and $\frac{2}{18}$? _____

   Which is less: $\frac{3}{9}$ or $\frac{2}{18}$? _____

4. What is the least common multiple of $\frac{3}{12}$ and $\frac{3}{8}$? _____

   Which is less: $\frac{3}{12}$ or $\frac{3}{8}$? _____

ACTIVITY 65　Equivalent Fractions

Name:_____

Date:_____

If you multiply the numerator and the denominator of a fraction by the same number, the answer will be an equivalent fraction.

Example: $\frac{3}{4} \times \frac{4}{4} = \frac{12}{16}$　　$\frac{3}{4}$ and $\frac{12}{16}$ are equal.

If you divide the numerator and the denominator of a fraction by the same number, the answer will be an equivalent fraction.

Example: $\frac{6}{10} \div \frac{2}{2} = \frac{3}{5}$　　$\frac{6}{10}$ and $\frac{3}{5}$ are equal.

You also can find an equivalent fraction with a specific denominator.

Example: Find an equivalent fraction of $\frac{25}{40}$ with a denominator of 8.　$\frac{25}{40} \div \frac{5}{5} = \frac{5}{8}$

Find equivalent fractions with a denominator of 10. Show your work.

1. $\frac{3}{30}$ = _____

2. $\frac{20}{50}$ = _____

3. $\frac{70}{100}$ = _____

ACTIVITY 66　Equivalent Fractions

Name:_____

Date:_____

Find equivalent fractions with a denominator of 8.

1. $\frac{9}{24}$ = _____

2. $\frac{8}{64}$ = _____

3. $\frac{6}{16}$ = _____

Find equivalent fractions with a denominator of 12.

4. $\frac{16}{24}$ = _____

5. $\frac{9}{36}$ = _____

6. $\frac{4}{6}$ = _____

Determine if each pair is equivalent. Explain why or why not.

7. $\frac{2}{4}$　$\frac{3}{12}$　　yes　　no

_____

8. $\frac{3}{9}$　$\frac{9}{27}$　　yes　　no

_____

ACTIVITY 67 Fraction Analogies

Name:_____

Date:_____

Study the first set of fractions to find how they are related.
Write a fraction in the second set that is related in the same way. Briefly explain your answer.

Example: $\frac{1}{2}$ is to $\frac{2}{4}$ as $\frac{3}{6}$ is to $\frac{6}{12}$.

$\frac{1}{2}$ and $\frac{2}{4}$ are equivalent fractions. The numerators and denominators of the first fraction are doubled to equal the second fraction.

1. $\frac{1}{3}$ is to $\frac{3}{9}$ as $\frac{2}{3}$ is to _____.

_____

2. $\frac{3}{8}$ is to $\frac{8}{3}$ as $\frac{5}{8}$ is to _____.

_____

3. $\frac{5}{10}$ is to $\frac{50}{100}$ as $\frac{30}{300}$ is to _____.

_____

4. $\frac{8}{10}$ is to $\frac{2}{10}$ as $\frac{4}{5}$ is to _____.

_____

ACTIVITY 68 Classify Fractions

Name:_____

Date:_____

Look at each group of fractions. Write at least one property
that all the fractions in the group have in common.

Example: What properties do these fractions have in common: $\frac{1}{3}$, $\frac{1}{5}$, $\frac{1}{11}$, $\frac{1}{13}$?

The numerators are 1.
The denominators are odd numbers.
The denominators are prime numbers.

1. What property do these fractions have in common: $\frac{2}{4}$, $\frac{25}{50}$, $\frac{100}{200}$, $\frac{9}{18}$?

_____

2. What property do these fractions have in common: $\frac{8}{3}$, $\frac{5}{2}$, $\frac{7}{4}$, $\frac{83}{17}$?

_____

3. What property do these fractions have in common: $\frac{3}{8}$, $\frac{7}{24}$, $\frac{9}{16}$, $\frac{5}{32}$?

_____

4. What property do these fractions have in common: $\frac{25}{100}$, $\frac{3}{12}$, $\frac{4}{16}$, $\frac{6}{24}$?

_____

ACTIVITY 69 **Add Fractions Without Common Denominators**

Name:_____

Date:_____

You can add fractions that do not have a common denominator. Find the least common multiple for the denominators, and then rewrite the equivalent fractions with that number as the denominator. Add the numerators. Write the sum over the denominator. If the answer is an improper fraction, change it to a mixed number.

Example: $\frac{2}{3} + \frac{1}{4} =$ The least common multiple is 12.

$$\frac{2}{3} \times \frac{4}{4} = \frac{8}{12} \qquad \frac{1}{4} \times \frac{3}{3} = \frac{3}{12} \qquad \frac{8}{12} + \frac{3}{12} = \frac{11}{12}$$

Add. Reduce the answer to lowest terms.

1. $\frac{5}{6} + \frac{2}{3} =$ _____

2. $\frac{3}{10} + \frac{3}{15} =$ _____

3. $\frac{2}{9} + \frac{5}{6} =$ _____

4. $\frac{7}{8} + \frac{3}{16} =$ _____

5. $\frac{7}{10} + \frac{3}{4} =$ _____

6. $\frac{2}{3} + \frac{5}{12} =$ _____

ACTIVITY 70 **Add Fractions Without Common Denominators**

Name:_____

Date:_____

Add. Reduce the answer to lowest terms.

1. Rachel ate $\frac{2}{9}$ of the peppermints in a bag. Her brother ate $\frac{5}{12}$ of the peppermints. What fraction of the peppermints did they eat in all? _____

2. Sonja walked $\frac{3}{12}$ of a mile on Saturday and $\frac{4}{16}$ of a mile on Sunday. What fraction of a mile did she walk in all? _____

3. Mom left a pan of brownies on the counter. The boys came along and ate $\frac{6}{9}$ of the pan. Their sister wanted a smaller piece and cut out a piece that was $\frac{1}{4}$ of the pan. What fraction of the pan of brownies was eaten in all? _____

4. The jump-rope team had jumpers stay in the air for $\frac{1}{2}$ of a minute, $\frac{55}{60}$ of a minute, and $\frac{25}{30}$ of a minute. What was their total air time? _____

5. A baby learning to crawl first went $\frac{1}{3}$ of a yard, then $\frac{4}{12}$ of a yard, and then $\frac{2}{12}$ of a yard. What fraction of a yard did he go in all, and how many inches was it? _____

ACTIVITY 71 Subtract Fractions Without Common Denominators

Name: _____

Date: _____

You can subtract fractions that do not have a common denominator. Find the least common multiple. Rewrite the fractions with the same denominator. Subtract the numerators. Write the answer over the denominator.

Example: $\frac{7}{8} - \frac{1}{4} =$ The least common multiple is 8.

$\frac{7}{8}$ stays the same. $\frac{1}{4} \times \frac{2}{2} = \frac{2}{8}$ $\frac{7}{8} - \frac{2}{8} = \frac{5}{8}$

Subtract. Reduce the answer to lowest terms.

1. $\frac{3}{4} - \frac{5}{16} =$ _____

2. $\frac{19}{24} - \frac{3}{4} =$ _____

3. $\frac{7}{6} - \frac{5}{12} =$ _____

Estimate. Compare each number to $\frac{1}{2}$. Is the answer more or less than $\frac{1}{2}$? Then solve. Reduce the answer to lowest terms.

4. $\frac{7}{8} - \frac{2}{3} =$ _____

5. $\frac{7}{10} - \frac{3}{15} =$ _____

6. $\frac{5}{6} - \frac{2}{3} =$ _____

Estimate: _____   Estimate: _____   Estimate: _____

- -

ACTIVITY 72 Subtract Fractions Without Common Denominators

Name: _____

Date: _____

1. Rachel ate $\frac{2}{9}$ of the peppermints in a bag. Her brother ate $\frac{5}{12}$ of the peppermints. What fraction equals the peppermints left in the bag? _____

2. Laura made a salad for her school picnic. The salad bowl was $\frac{3}{4}$ full when the picnic started; by the end, it was $\frac{1}{5}$ full. What fraction was eaten?

     _____

3. Brent wanted to throw his Frisbee $\frac{1}{4}$ of a mile. On his first try, he threw it $\frac{2}{16}$ of a mile. How much farther did he have to go to reach his goal? _____

4. The veterinarian told John that she thought his dog would grow to be about $\frac{2}{3}$ of a yard tall. If the dog is $\frac{3}{6}$ of a yard tall now, what fraction of a yard does he have left to grow?

     _____

5. Renae bought a piece of fabric that was $\frac{3}{4}$ of a yard long. She cut off $\frac{2}{12}$ of a yard to make a headband and $\frac{1}{4}$ of a yard to make a belt. How much fabric does she have left?

     _____

ACTIVITY 73 Multiply Fractions

Name:_____

Date:_____

When multiplying fractions, it doesn't matter if they have a common denominator. Multiply the numerators. Then multiply the denominators. Write the answers as a fraction. Simplify the fraction if needed. Use the same method for improper fractions.

Example: $\frac{3}{4} \times \frac{2}{3} =$ $\frac{3}{4} \times \frac{2}{3} = \frac{6}{12} = \frac{1}{2}$

$\frac{2}{9} \times \frac{5}{8}$ ✗ $\frac{1}{4} \times \frac{3}{7}$

Multiply. Write the answers in simplest form.

1. $\frac{3}{8} \times \frac{5}{8} =$ _____

2. $\frac{4}{7} \times \frac{4}{8} =$ _____

3. $\frac{11}{9} \times \frac{6}{7} =$ _____

4. $\frac{10}{12} \times \frac{8}{10} =$ _____

5. $\frac{7}{2} \times \frac{2}{3} =$ _____

6. $\frac{11}{3} \times \frac{8}{16} =$ _____

ACTIVITY 74 Multiply Fractions

Name:_____

Date:_____

Multiply in your head. Write the answers in simplest form.

1. $\frac{1}{3} \times \frac{1}{2} =$ _____

2. $\frac{2}{3} \times \frac{1}{5} =$ _____

3. $\frac{2}{4} \times \frac{2}{3} =$ _____

4. $\frac{1}{2} \times \frac{2}{4} =$ _____

5. $\frac{8}{12} \times \frac{3}{6} =$ _____

6. $\frac{10}{12} \times \frac{1}{6} =$ _____

7. $\frac{3}{6} \times \frac{7}{5} =$ _____

8. $\frac{10}{5} \times \frac{3}{5} =$ _____

9. $\frac{7}{5} \times \frac{5}{9} =$ _____

10. $\frac{11}{20} \times \frac{3}{8} =$ _____

ACTIVITY 75 Multiply Mixed Numbers and Whole Numbers by Fractions

Name:_____

Date:_____

To multiply a mixed number by a fraction, convert the mixed number to an improper fraction, then follow the steps for multiplying fractions.

Example: $2\frac{3}{4} \times \frac{1}{4} =$ $2\frac{3}{4} = \frac{11}{4}$ $\frac{11}{4} \times \frac{1}{4} = \frac{11}{16}$

To multiply a whole number by a fraction, write the whole number as the numerator and 1 as the denominator. Then follow the steps for multiplying fractions.

Example: $7 \times \frac{5}{8} =$ $\frac{7}{1} \times \frac{5}{8} = \frac{35}{8} = 4\frac{3}{8}$

Multiply. Write the answers in simplest form.

1. $3\frac{1}{2} \times \frac{2}{3} =$ _____

2. $7 \times \frac{5}{6} =$ _____

3. $\frac{7}{9} \times 6 =$ _____

4. $1\frac{1}{2} \times 1\frac{1}{2} =$ _____

5. $\frac{13}{2} \times 4\frac{1}{3} =$ _____

6. $4\frac{3}{8} \times 6\frac{1}{2} =$ _____

- -

ACTIVITY 76 Multiply Mixed Numbers and Whole Numbers by Fractions

Name:_____

Date:_____

Sometimes estimation helps you solve. For each problem, use mental math to round each mixed number to the nearest whole number, then multiply. Next, multiply and solve the problem on your own paper. Simplify if needed. If your answer is close to your estimate, it is probably correct.

1. $3 \times \frac{3}{4} =$ _____

   Estimate: _____

2. $12 \times \frac{8}{5} =$ _____

   Estimate: _____

3. $\frac{5}{8} \times 11 =$ _____

   Estimate: _____

4. $1\frac{5}{7} \times 4\frac{1}{2} =$ _____

   Estimate: _____

5. $3\frac{1}{4} \times 6\frac{7}{8} =$ _____

   Estimate: _____

6. $8\frac{1}{2} \times 2\frac{5}{6} =$ _____

   Estimate: _____

7. $2 \times 1\frac{1}{2} =$ _____

   Estimate: _____

8. $5\frac{3}{9} \times 8 =$ _____

   Estimate: _____

9. $3\frac{9}{10} \times 1\frac{1}{2} =$ _____

   Estimate: _____

10. $2\frac{2}{7} \times 5 =$ _____

   Estimate: _____

ACTIVITY 77 **Fraction Word Problems** Name:_____

Date:_____

Use any method to solve.

1. $\frac{2}{9}$ of the 18 students in a class have red hair. How many have red hair? _____

2. Dominic is 24. His brother is $\frac{2}{3}$ as old. How old is Dominic's brother? _____

3. Rachel read $\frac{5}{9}$ of a 63-page book. How many pages did she read? _____

4. $\frac{3}{4}$ of 28 balloons are red. How many balloons are red? _____

5. Jeanine made a beaded necklace. $\frac{6}{7}$ of the 49 beads she used were purple. How many were not purple? _____

6. $\frac{5}{6}$ of 42 seventh-grade students ate pizza in the school cafeteria on Monday. How many ate pizza? _____

7. Jake and Zach ate $\frac{5}{6}$ of a dozen donuts. How many are left? _____

ACTIVITY 78 **Fraction Word Problems** Name:_____

Date:_____

Use any method to solve. Write the answers in lowest terms.

1. Jon has a collection of 60 caps. $\frac{3}{10}$ of his caps are from Major League baseball teams. How many are not from Major League baseball teams? _____

2. Carla jogged for $\frac{2}{6}$ of an hour. How many minutes did Carla jog? _____

3. Grandma used $\frac{3}{5}$ of a 25-pound bag of flour to bake holiday cookies. How many pounds of flour did she use? _____

4. $\frac{2}{3}$ of 33 penguins at the zoo are female. How many are female? _____

5. Grant received $100 as a special birthday gift from his grandparents. He spent $\frac{3}{5}$ of the money. How much money does Grant have left? _____

6. Tasha planted 35 seeds. Only $\frac{4}{7}$ of them sprouted. How many sprouted? _____

7. Of the 21 pieces of mail Cal received this week, $\frac{6}{7}$ was junk mail. How many pieces of junk mail did Cal receive? _____

ACTIVITY 79   Review

Name:_____

Date:_____

Fill in the blanks.

1. _____ are whole numbers that can be multiplied to equal a given number.

2. The factors of 24 are: _____.

3. The factors of 36 are: _____.

4. If the numerator and denominator of a fraction have no common factors other than _____, a fraction is in its simplest form.

5. Is $\frac{7}{8}$ in its simplest form? _____ Why or why not? _____
   _____

6. Is $\frac{15}{20}$ in its simplest form? _____ Why or why not? _____
   _____

7. The _____ common multiple of two fractions is the smallest number that is a multiple of both denominators.

8. What is the least common multiple of 12 and 9? _____

9. Two fractions are equivalent if they are _____.

10. Are $\frac{3}{4}$ and $\frac{2}{3}$ equivalent fractions? _____ Why or why not? _____
    _____

ACTIVITY 80   Review

Name:_____

Date:_____

Write the answers in lowest terms.

Ray has 2 half-dollars, 4 quarters, 10 dimes, 20 nickels, and 8 pennies.

1. What fraction of his coins are nickels? _____

2. What fraction of his coins are pennies? _____

3. What fraction of his coins are half-dollars? _____

4. What fraction of his coins are not pennies? _____

5. Write a math story question that uses fractions.

_____

_____

_____

_____

_____

6. Trade with a partner, solve your partner's problem, and then check the answers.

ACTIVITY 81 Divide Fractions

Name:_____

Date:_____

1. Half of a pizza was left after supper. Draw half of a pizza. Don ate $\frac{1}{4}$ of the leftover pizza before bed. Shade in the part of the pizza Don ate before bed. How much of the whole pizza did Don eat before bed? _____

2. Jon made a dozen chocolate chip cookies. Draw a dozen cookies. Jon ate $\frac{2}{6}$ of the cookies for lunch. Cross off $\frac{2}{6}$ of the cookies. He ate $\frac{1}{8}$ of the rest of the cookies after supper. Circle the number of cookies Jon ate after supper. What fraction of the dozen cookies did Jon eat after supper? _____

3. The guests at great-great-grandpa's birthday party ate $\frac{2}{3}$ of the cake. Draw the amount of his great-great big cake that was left. Three great-great grandsons arrived late. They each ate an equal part of the leftover cake. Divide the leftover cake into 3 equal parts to show how much each one ate. What fraction of the whole cake did each great-great grandson eat? _____

- -

ACTIVITY 82 Divide Fractions
by Fractions

Name:_____

Date:_____

When dividing, it does not matter if fractions have a common denominator. To divide two fractions, invert the divisor (invert means to turn it upside down). Change the division sign to a multiplication sign, and rewrite the equation. Multiply the numerators. Multiply the denominators. Write the product of the numerators over the product of the denominators. Simplify the fraction if needed.

Example: $\frac{3}{4} \div \frac{2}{3} = \quad \frac{3}{4} \times \frac{3}{2} = \frac{9}{8} = 1\frac{1}{8}$

Divide and simplify. Use mental math to complete the multiplication.

1. $\frac{3}{8} \div \frac{4}{5} = $ _____

2. $\frac{1}{3} \div \frac{5}{9} = $ _____

3. $\frac{1}{2} \div \frac{1}{3} = $ _____

4. $\frac{1}{3} \div \frac{2}{7} = $ _____

5. $\frac{2}{8} \div \frac{4}{5} = $ _____

6. $\frac{2}{5} \div \frac{1}{7} = $ _____

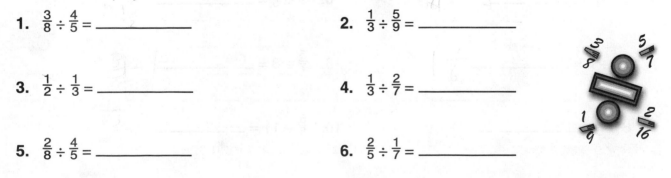

ACTIVITY 83 Divide Fractions and Whole Numbers

Name:_____

Date:_____

To divide fractions and whole numbers, change the whole number to a fraction. Invert the divisor. Change the sign to multiplication and rewrite. Multiply the numerators. Multiply the denominators. Write the product of the numerators over the product of the denominators. Simplify the fraction if necessary.

Example: $\frac{3}{4} \div 7 =$ $\frac{3}{4} \div \frac{7}{1} =$ $\frac{3}{4} \times \frac{1}{7} = \frac{3}{28}$

Divide. Reduce to lowest terms.

1. $7 \div \frac{3}{4} =$ _____

2. $\frac{2}{8} \div 5 =$ _____

3. $\frac{3}{5} \div 5 =$ _____

4. $\frac{5}{7} \div 4 =$ _____

5. $12 \div \frac{2}{3} =$ _____

6. $4 \div \frac{4}{9} =$ _____

ACTIVITY 84 Divide Fractions and Whole Numbers

Name:_____

Date:_____

Divide. Reduce to lowest terms.

1. $12 \div \frac{8}{5} =$ _____

2. $\frac{1}{3} \div 2 =$ _____

3. $\frac{1}{6} \div 4 =$ _____

4. $\frac{2}{5} \div 2 =$ _____

5. $1 \div \frac{1}{2} =$ _____

6. $9 \div \frac{4}{5} =$ _____

7. $12 \div \frac{5}{8} =$ _____

8. $\frac{5}{7} \div 3 =$ _____

9. $6 \div \frac{5}{6} =$ _____

10. $\frac{5}{8} \div 11 =$ _____

ACTIVITY 85 Divide Mixed Numbers

Name:_____

Date:_____

To divide a whole number and a mixed number, change the mixed number to an improper fraction. Follow the steps for dividing a whole number and a fraction.

Divide.

1. $8 \div 3\frac{2}{3} =$ _____

2. $4\frac{1}{9} \div 4 =$ _____

To divide a mixed number by a mixed number, change both mixed numbers to improper fractions. Follow the steps for dividing fractions by fractions.

Divide.

3. $2\frac{3}{7} \div 1\frac{1}{4} =$ _____

4. $8\frac{1}{3} \div 3\frac{5}{8} =$ _____

To divide a mixed number and a fraction, change the mixed number to an improper fraction. Follow the steps for dividing fractions by fractions.

Divide.

5. $5\frac{1}{5} \div \frac{3}{5} =$ _____

6. $\frac{2}{9} \div 3\frac{1}{8} =$ _____

- -

ACTIVITY 86 Divide Mixed Numbers

Name:_____

Date:_____

Estimate. First, round all numbers to the nearest whole number. Then use mental math to divide the two whole numbers. Then solve the orginal problem on your own paper, using your estimate to help you decide if your answer is reliable. Reduce your answers to lowest terms.

1. $3\frac{1}{3} \div 2 =$ _____

Estimate: _____

2. $3\frac{1}{6} \div 4\frac{2}{3} =$ _____

Estimate: _____

3. $3\frac{9}{10} \div 1\frac{1}{2} =$ _____

Estimate: _____

4. $6\frac{1}{8} \div 4 =$ _____

Estimate: _____

5. $7 \div 4\frac{1}{3} =$ _____

Estimate: _____

6. $2 \div 8\frac{1}{2} =$ _____

Estimate: _____

7. $2\frac{7}{10} \div 9 =$ _____

Estimate: _____

8. $4\frac{2}{5} \div \frac{1}{4} =$ _____

Estimate: _____

9. $4\frac{5}{9} \div \frac{1}{6} =$ _____

Estimate: _____

10. $12 \div 4\frac{1}{4} =$ _____

Estimate: _____

ACTIVITY 87 Review

Name: _____

Date: _____

Divide.

1. $\frac{3}{7} \div \frac{2}{7} =$ _____

2. $\frac{7}{8} \div \frac{1}{8} =$ _____

3. $8 \div \frac{2}{3} =$ _____

4. $3 \div \frac{3}{5} =$ _____

5. $\frac{7}{1} \div 9 =$ _____

6. $\frac{7}{8} \div 3 =$ _____

7. $\frac{2}{9} \div 8\frac{1}{3} =$ _____

8. $\frac{2}{5} \div 5\frac{1}{5} =$ _____

9. $4\frac{1}{2} \div \frac{3}{4} =$ _____

10. $3\frac{1}{8} \div \frac{2}{7} =$ _____

ACTIVITY 88 Review

Name: _____

Date: _____

Divide.

1. $21 \div 1\frac{1}{7} =$ _____

2. $6 \div 2\frac{4}{9} =$ _____

3. $\frac{2}{3} \div \frac{4}{7} =$ _____

4. $8 \div \frac{1}{5} =$ _____

5. $5\frac{1}{4} \div 1\frac{3}{4} =$ _____

6. $9 \div \frac{1}{2} =$ _____

7. $20 \div \frac{2}{5} =$ _____

8. $\frac{1}{8} \div 3 =$ _____

9. $\frac{1}{5} \div \frac{1}{4} =$ _____

10. $3\frac{3}{5} \div 1\frac{1}{5} =$ _____

ACTIVITY 89 **Create a Pie Chart**   Name:_____

Date:_____

Each section of the circle represents one hour.
Color the sections of the circle to show how you spend a typical school day.
Save your pie chart to use with the next activity.

Green = Time spent in school
(include the time it takes to
get there and back)
Red = Time spent sleeping
Blue = Time spent preparing, eating,
and cleaning up after meals
Yellow = Time spent doing homework
and chores
Purple = Time spent relaxing, reading,
or enjoying sports and games
White = Other

ACTIVITY 90 **Fractions on a Pie Chart** Name:_____

Date:_____

Use the information on the pie chart you made in the
previous activity to answer the questions. Write fractions in lowest terms.

1. What fraction of the day do you spend sleeping? _____

2. What fraction of the day do you spend in school? _____

3. What fraction of the day do you spend preparing, eating, and
cleaning up after meals? _____

4. What fraction of the day do you spend doing homework and chores? _____

5. What fraction of the day do you spend relaxing, reading, or enjoying sports and games?

_____

6. What do you do during the rest of the day? _____

7. What fraction of the day do you spend doing other things besides sleeping and going to
school? _____

8. If it weren't a school day, how would the chart change? _____

_____

ACTIVITY 91 Measurement With Fractions

Name:_____

Date:_____

Read carefully. Then solve the problems. Reduce all fractions to lowest terms.

1. Ellen likes raisins. She is making a recipe that calls for $\frac{2}{3}$ cup of raisins. If she doubles the amount of raisins, how many cups of raisins will she use? _____

2. If one serving of cereal is $1\frac{1}{4}$ ounces, how many servings would be in a 10-ounce box of cereal? _____

3. If eight apples weigh 3 pounds, what is the average weight of each apple? _____

4. A large can of dogfood contains $22\frac{3}{4}$ ounces. If each can contains $3\frac{1}{2}$ servings, how many ounces equals one serving? _____

5. Jeremy bought $1\frac{3}{4}$ pounds of cherries. He ate the same amount of cherries each day for four days. How many ounces of cherries did he eat each day if he ate all of the cherries? _____

6. Trisha bought $259\frac{1}{2}$ inches of ribbon. She cut it into equal lengths to tie onto 17 helium balloons. How many inches of ribbon did she use for each balloon? _____

ACTIVITY 92 Measurement With Fractions

Name:_____

Date:_____

Read carefully. Then solve the problems. Reduce all fractions to lowest terms.

1. Janice bought $2\frac{3}{4}$ pounds of ground beef and made it into 9 hamburgers. How many ounces did each hamburger weigh? _____

2. Bob bought a 35-ounce bag of plaster of Paris to make dinosaur models. He used $\frac{1}{3}$ of the bag to make five small dinosaurs. How many ounces did he use for each dinosaur? _____

3. Randy wants to make a 20-foot path of stepping stones. Each stepping stone is $\frac{10}{12}$ of a foot long. How many stepping stones will he need? _____

4. Pete plans to fence in a rectangular area for his dog. It will be $4\frac{6}{13}$ feet by $5\frac{7}{13}$ feet. How many feet of fencing does Pete need? _____

5. Marnie needs to line up square crates in a warehouse. Each crate is $34\frac{1}{2}$ inches. How many crates can she fit along a wall that is 15 feet long? _____

ACTIVITY 93   Fractions With a Bar Graph

Name:_____

Date:_____

One hundred students voted for their favorite pizza topping. Use the information from the graph to answer the questions. Write fractions in lowest terms.

1. Which topping received the most votes? _____
   What fraction of the students preferred that topping?
   _____

2. Which topping received the fewest votes? _____
   What fraction of the students preferred this topping?
   _____

3. What fraction of the students preferred onions or olives?
   _____

4. What fraction of the students did not choose pepperoni?
   _____

5. What fraction of the students preferred sausage or mushrooms? _____

6. What fraction of the students preferred pizzas without meat? _____

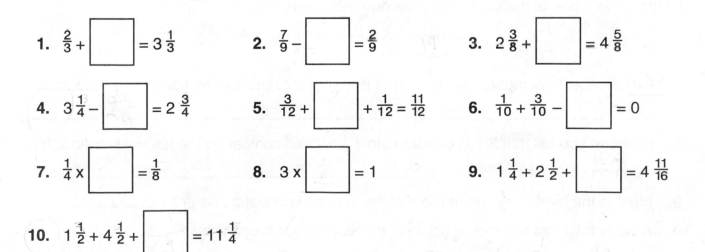

ACTIVITY 94   Fraction Algebra

Name:_____

Date:_____

Fill in the missing fractions. Remember, addition and subtraction are inverse operations. Draw diagrams or use another reliable method to solve the equations.

Example: $\frac{3}{4} - \frac{2}{4} = \frac{1}{4}$ and $\frac{1}{4} + \frac{2}{4} = \frac{3}{4}$

1. $\frac{2}{3} + \boxed{} = 3\frac{1}{3}$

2. $\frac{7}{9} - \boxed{} = \frac{2}{9}$

3. $2\frac{3}{8} + \boxed{} = 4\frac{5}{8}$

4. $3\frac{1}{4} - \boxed{} = 2\frac{3}{4}$

5. $\frac{3}{12} + \boxed{} + \frac{1}{12} = \frac{11}{12}$

6. $\frac{1}{10} + \frac{3}{10} - \boxed{} = 0$

7. $\frac{1}{4} \times \boxed{} = \frac{1}{8}$

8. $3 \times \boxed{} = 1$

9. $1\frac{1}{4} + 2\frac{1}{2} + \boxed{} = 4\frac{11}{16}$

10. $1\frac{1}{2} + 4\frac{1}{2} + \boxed{} = 11\frac{1}{4}$

ACTIVITY 95 Fraction Test

Name:_____

Date:_____

Write the mixed numbers as improper fractions.

1. $7\frac{4}{5} =$ _____

2. $4\frac{3}{6} =$ _____

3. $9\frac{3}{15} =$ _____

4. $81\frac{1}{2} =$ _____

5. $8\frac{2}{3} =$ _____

6. $4\frac{1}{3} =$ _____

Write the improper fractions as mixed numbers or whole numbers. Simplify all the fractions.

7. $\frac{7}{3} =$ _____

8. $\frac{96}{82} =$ _____

9. $\frac{14}{8} =$ _____

10. $\frac{114}{2} =$ _____

11. $\frac{16}{9} =$ _____

12. $\frac{14}{7} =$ _____

- -

ACTIVITY 96 Fraction Test

Name:_____

Date:_____

Write the factors of each pair of numbers.
Circle the greatest common factor.

1. 9 and 18   _____   _____

2. 21 and 28   _____   _____

Compare each pair of fractions. Circle the one that is greater.

3. $\frac{3}{7}$ $\frac{4}{6}$

4. $\frac{8}{15}$ $\frac{7}{30}$

5. $\frac{7}{21}$ $\frac{2}{3}$

6. $\frac{94}{100}$ $\frac{9}{10}$

7. Explain how to compare two fractions if the denominators are the same. _____

_____

8. How can you tell that $2\frac{3}{4}$ is greater than $1\frac{7}{8}$ without comparing the fractions or finding a

common denominator? _____

9. What is the least common multiple of the denominators of $\frac{5}{6}$ and $\frac{3}{11}$? _____

10. What is the least common multiple of the denominators of $\frac{3}{9}$ and $\frac{4}{27}$? _____

ACTIVITY 97 Fraction Test

Name:_____

Date:_____

Write equivalent fractions with a denominator of 9.

1. $\frac{2}{3}$ = _____

2. $\frac{18}{27}$ = _____

3. $\frac{9}{81}$ = _____

Simplify the fractions.

4. $\frac{14}{16}$ = _____

5. $\frac{7}{21}$ = _____

6. $\frac{22}{32}$ = _____

7. $\frac{75}{100}$ = _____

8. $\frac{4}{16}$ = _____

9. $\frac{8}{10}$ = _____

10. $\frac{36}{48}$ = _____

ACTIVITY 98 Fraction Test

Name:_____

Date:_____

Add. Write the answers in simplest form.

1. $\frac{3}{8} + \frac{4}{7}$ = _____

2. $\frac{4}{9} + \frac{7}{18}$ = _____

3. $\frac{7}{14} + \frac{2}{7}$ = _____

Subtract. Write the answers in simplest form.

4. $\frac{3}{5} - \frac{1}{6}$ = _____

5. $\frac{1}{3} - \frac{1}{6}$ = _____

6. $\frac{2}{3} - \frac{3}{5}$ = _____

Multiply. Write the answers in simplest form.

7. $\frac{6}{9} \times \frac{3}{5}$ = _____

8. $7 \times \frac{2}{7}$ = _____

9. $3\frac{1}{2} \times \frac{1}{4}$ = _____

Divide. Write the answers in simplest form.

10. $2\frac{5}{7} \div 1\frac{1}{3}$ = _____

11. $\frac{1}{16} \div \frac{1}{2}$ = _____

12. $10 \div 4\frac{3}{8}$ = _____

13. At a track meet, Rachel and Rhonda each took first place in $\frac{1}{4}$ of the events they entered. Rachel won 2 blue ribbons. Rhonda won 5 blue ribbons. Explain how this could be true.

_____

_____

ACTIVITY 99 Decimals and Monetary Notation

Name:_____

Date:_____

Decimals are fractional numbers written after a period called a decimal point. A familiar use of decimals is with money.

One penny is worth $\frac{1}{100}$ of a dollar. We write $\frac{1}{100}$ of a dollar as 1¢ or $0.01.

One dime is worth $\frac{1}{10}$ of a dollar. We write $\frac{1}{10}$ of a dollar as 10¢ or $0.10.

Write the amount of cents using a dollar sign and decimal point.

Example: 47¢ = $0.47

1. 53¢ = _____

2. 75¢ = _____

3. 49¢ = _____

4. 7¢ = _____

5. 82¢ = _____

6. 4¢ = _____

ACTIVITY 100 Decimals and Monetary Notation

Name:_____

Date:_____

For amounts over one dollar, write the whole number to the left of the decimal. 716¢ is the same as seven dollars and sixteen cents. It is written as $7.16.

Write the amount of cents using a dollar sign and decimal point.

1. 487¢ = _____

2. 1827¢ = _____

3. 2045¢ = _____

4. 2936¢ = _____

5. 798¢ = _____

6. 135¢ = _____

7. 1199¢ = _____

8. 1583¢ = _____

ACTIVITY 101 **Place Value of Decimals** Name:_____

Date:_____

The place value of a decimal is determined by the number of digits to the right of the decimal point.

Decimal	Place Value	Words	Fraction Value
0.2	tenths	two-tenths	2/10
0.02	hundredths	two-hundredths	2/100
0.002	thousandths	two-thousandths	2/1,000
0.0002	ten thousandths	two-ten-thousandths	2/10,000

Rewrite the decimals on the place value chart.

	Ones	Tenths	Hundredths	Thousandths
1. 0.7	0.			
2. 0.92	0.			
3. 0.107	0.			
4. 0.635	0.			
5. 0.809	0.			

ACTIVITY 102 **Place Value of Decimals** Name:_____

Date:_____

Write the decimal numbers to match the words.

1. six-tenths = _____

2. thirty-four-hundredths = _____

3. six-hundredths = _____

4. seventy-three-hundredths = _____

5. eight-thousandths = _____

6. one-thousandth = _____

7. eight hundred fourteen-thousandths = _____

8. four hundred twenty-six-thousandths = _____

Write the words for the decimal numbers.

9. 0.68 = _____

10. 0.306 = _____

ACTIVITY 103 Decimals on a Grid

Name:_____

Date:_____

Decimals can be shown on a grid. Each grid equals one whole. Each small square equals $\frac{1}{100}$ or 0.01.

Shade in the right number of squares to show the decimals.

1. 0.75

2. 0.33

- -

ACTIVITY 104 Decimals and Fractions

Name:_____

Date:_____

All decimals can be written as fractions. The number of places to the right of the decimal point indicates the number of zeros in the numerator of the fraction. If the decimal does not contain a whole number, always write a zero to the left of the decimal point.

Examples: $0.4 = \frac{4}{10}$ $0.55 = \frac{55}{100}$ $0.222 = \frac{222}{1000}$ $0.8888 = \frac{8888}{10000}$

Rewrite the decimals as fractions.

1. 0.05 _____

2. 0.252 _____

3. 0.16 _____

Like fractions, decimals can be combined with whole numbers. A decimal with a whole number is like a mixed number.

Examples: $4.2 = 4\frac{2}{10}$ $17.65 = 17\frac{65}{100}$

Rewrite the decimals with whole numbers as mixed numbers.

4. 8.24 _____

5. 13.44 _____

6. 121.011 _____

ACTIVITY 105   Compare Decimals

Name:_____

Date:_____

To compare decimals, look first at the whole numbers.
The one with the greater whole number is larger.

Example: 5.22 is greater than 4.22.

1. Which is greater: 3.14 or 2.999? _____
2. Which is less: 7.001 or 9.999? _____
3. Which is greatest: 7.22, 6.91, or 5.02? _____

If the whole numbers are equal, compare the digits in the tenths place.

Example: 7.11 is greater than 7.01.

4. Which is greater: 3.12 or 3.21? _____
5. Which is less: 4.12 or 4.01? _____
6. Which is greatest: 9.811, 9.901, or 9.999? _____

- -

ACTIVITY 106   Compare Decimals

Name:_____

Date:_____

If the whole numbers and digits in the tenths place are
equal, compare the digits in the hundredths place.

Example: 3.89 is greater than 3.87.

1. Which is greater: 5.555 or 5.565? _____
2. Which is less: 0.242 or 0.233? _____
3. Which is greatest: 1.111, 1.131, or 1.113? _____

Circle the greatest number in each set.

4. $5.24 $5.17 $5.71   5. $4.02 $5.00 $4.91

6. Write the decimal that is one-tenth more than 5.2. _____
7. Write the decimal that is $\frac{1}{100}$ less than 7.98. _____
8. Write a decimal that is between 0.024 and 0.026. _____

55

ACTIVITY 107 Compare Decimals and Fractions

Name: _____

Date: _____

You can compare decimals, fractions, mixed numbers, and whole numbers. To compare a decimal and a fraction, change the decimal to a fraction. Rewrite the fraction so it has a common denominator. Compare the two fractions.

Example: Which is greater: $\frac{2}{10}$ or 0.21? $\frac{2}{10} = \frac{20}{100}$ $0.21 = \frac{21}{100}$

0.21 is greater than $\frac{2}{10}$.

Circle the number in each set that is greater. Remember, when looking at a decimal, simply change it to a fraction, and then change the other fraction to a fraction with a common denominator to see which one is greater.

1. 0.34 $\frac{2}{10}$

2. $\frac{7}{10}$ 0.825

3. $\frac{4}{5}$ 0.75

4. $3\frac{1}{4}$ 3.26

5. 0.64 $\frac{63}{100}$

6. 1.89 $\frac{189}{100}$

7. Carol bought a 3.45-ounce bag of snacks for $3.00. Darryl bought a 1.75-ounce bag of the same items for $1.50. Which was the better buy? _____

- -

ACTIVITY 108 Compare Decimals and Fractions

Name: _____

Date: _____

Circle the number in each set that is greater.

1. 0.6 $\frac{3}{4}$

2. $\frac{4}{25}$ 0.85

3. 0.04 $\frac{3}{5}$

4. 0.23 $\frac{17}{20}$

5. $\frac{14}{100}$ 0.014

6. $\frac{1}{25}$ 2.5

7. Jeff had a $2\frac{1}{2}$-pound bag of marbles. When Sean weighed his bag of marbles, the scale said 2.25 pounds. Who had the most marbles? _____

8. Marjorie wanted to run about $5\frac{3}{4}$ miles. At the end of her run, her pedometer read 5.875 miles. Did she run more or less than $5\frac{3}{4}$ miles? _____

56

ACTIVITY 109   Round Decimals

Name:_____

Date:_____

To round a decimal to the nearest whole number, look at
the number in the tenths place. If it is 5 or more, round up to the nearest whole number. If it is
4 or less, round down.

Examples: Round 4.6 to 5.   Round 91.3 to 91.

Round these decimals to the nearest whole number.

1. 7.8   _____   **2.** 13.39   _____

3. 14.09   _____   **4.** 0.75   _____

To round a decimal to the nearest tenth, look at the number in the hundredths place. If it is 5 or
more, round up to the nearest tenth. If it is 4 or less, round down.

Examples: Round 4.67 to 4.7.   Round 91.73 to 91.7.

Round these decimals to the nearest tenth.

5. 0.24   _____   **6.** 4.352   _____

7. 3.991   _____   **8.** 11.011   _____

ACTIVITY 110   Round Decimals

Name:_____

Date:_____

Newspapers often round numbers used in headlines to
make them easier to read. Round the number and rewrite each headline.

1.   3.782 Million Vote in State Primary Election

_____

2.   Accidents Increased 0.8934% Per Week on New Bypass

_____

3.   Spinach Consumption Declined 49.6137%

_____

4.   Write a headline using a rounded decimal.

_____

_____

ACTIVITY 111) Classify Decimals

Name:_____

Date:_____

Write these decimals in the correct parts of the
Venn diagram.

0.317   0.249   0.733   0.273   0.1743   0.923   0.7   0.1644

**Decimals between
0.25 and 0.75**

**Decimals less
than 0.25**

**Decimals greater
than 0.75**

ACTIVITY 112) Decimals and Zeros

Name:_____

Date:_____

Zeros are important because they are placeholders.
There is a big difference between $5.25 and $500.25.

1. What's the difference between 3.001 and 3.1? _____

2. Why are the zeros important in this case? _____

_____

In decimals, a zero at the far right is not important and can be deleted.

3. What's the difference between 4.3100 and 4.31? _____

4. Why aren't these zeros important? _____

_____

When using monetary notation, zeros are left in the hundredths place, even though they aren't
needed as placeholders. We write $10.40, not $10.4.

5. Why do you think zeros are used in monetary notation? _____

_____

ACTIVITY 113 Add Decimals

Name:_____

Date:_____

Keep two things in mind when you add decimals. Always line up the decimal points before you start. Remember to bring the decimal point down in the answer.

Example: 0.25 + 7.85

$$\begin{array}{r} 0.25 \\ +\ 7.85 \\ \hline 8.10 \end{array}$$

Rewrite these addition problems to line up the decimal points. Then find the sums.

1. 3.64 + 2.071 =

2. 6 + 2.911 =

3. $71.17 + $17.71 =

4. 4.002 + 0.2 =

5. 0.013 + 0.1031 =

6. Colin spent $5.73 on socks and $12.51 for a cap.

    How much did he spend in all? _____

- -

ACTIVITY 114 Decimal Patterns

Name:_____

Date:_____

Follow the rule. Fill in the blanks to complete the pattern. Use a calculator to do the computation, if necessary.

1. Rule: Add 0.3

    1   1.3 _____ 1.9 _____ _____ _____ _____ 3.4

2. Rule: Subtract 0.05

    100   99.95 _____ 99.85 _____ _____ _____ _____ 99.6

3. Rule: Add 1.101

    7.103 _____ 9.305 _____ 11.507 _____ _____ 15.911

Fill in the pattern. Write the rule. Use a calculator to do the computation, if necessary.

4. 0.02   0.04 _____ 0.08 _____ 0.12 _____ _____ _____

    The rule is: _____

5. 3.667   6.667   9.667 _____ _____ _____ _____ _____ 27.667

    The rule is: _____

6. 0.89   0.86 _____ _____ 0.77 _____ _____ _____

    The rule is: _____

ACTIVITY 115 Subtract Decimals

Name:_____

Date:_____

Always line up the decimal points before you subtract.
Remember to bring the decimal point down in the answer.

Rewrite these subtraction equations. Line up the decimals and find the answer.

1. 41.35 – 22.06 =   **2.** 17.01 – 9.02 =   **3.** 0.083 – 0.078 =

4. Edgar spent $7.17 at the hardware store.

How much change did he get from a ten-dollar bill? _____

5. Angie spent $4.71 at the paint store.

How much change did she get from a five-dollar bill? _____

6. Esmeralda spent $6.42 for lunch and a tip.

How much change did she get from a twenty-dollar bill? _____

ACTIVITY 116 Subtract Decimals

Name:_____

Date:_____

Always line up the decimal points before you subtract.
Remember to bring the decimal point down in the answer.

Rewrite these subtraction equations. Line up the decimals and find the answer.

1. 31.0 – 2.75 =   **2.** 14.25 – 6.0 =

3. 3.02 – 2.81 =   **4.** 3.89 – 0.05 =

Write the math sentence you need to use, then solve.

5. Sonja bought a picture frame for $14.99 and wants to exchange it for one that costs $7.35.

How much money should she get back? _____

6. Erin's total grocery bill was $103.45. She had $8.50 in coupons. How much did she end

up paying? _____

60

ACTIVITY 117 Decimal Story Problems Name:_____

Date:_____

1. A customer at the party supply store buys 2 packages
of paper plates for $3.99 each and a package of plastic cups for $4.55. How much does
the customer spend in all? _____
If the customer pays with a $20 bill, how much change should she get back? _____

2. Ramona wanted to buy a stereo that was on sale for $59.99. She had $35.26 in her savings
account and she got $10 in the birthday card from her grandma. She also found $1.57 in
change in the couch cushions. How much money does she have in all? _____
Is it enough to buy the stereo, and if not, how much more does she need? _____

3. Chloe got $50 from her grandparents for a junior high school graduation gift. She needs
to pay her little brother $5.75 each week for the next month for cleaning out her hamster's
cage. How much money will she have left at the end of the month? _____

4. In the month of May, Joel recorded the following distances in miles on his bike: 42.6, 22.1,
24, and 56.7. How far did he bike in May? _____
If Joel's goal was to bike 150 miles in May, how far short did he fall? _____

**ACTIVITY 118 Write-Your-Own
Decimal Story Problems**   Name:_____

Date:_____

Write three story problems using addition or subtraction of decimals. Trade papers with a partner. Solve the story problems and check each other's answers.

1. _____
_____
_____
Answer: _____

2. _____
_____
_____
Answer: _____

3. _____
_____
_____
Answer: _____

ACTIVITY 119 Review

Name: _____

Date: _____

Rewrite the amounts using dollar signs and decimal points.

1. 456¢ _____   **2.** 72¢ _____

3. 1548¢ _____   **4.** 902¢ _____

Write the decimals as fractions. Reduce to lowest terms.

5. 0.78 _____   **6.** 0.625 _____

7. 0.99 _____   **8.** 0.26 _____

Reviewing Decimals

ACTIVITY 120 Review

Name: _____

Date: _____

Add.

1. 3.7 + 4.9 = _____   **2.** 2.9 + 11.4 = _____

3. 27.3 + 4.7 = _____   **4.** 11.4 + 9.5 = _____

Write the equivalent decimals.

5. eight-hundredths _____   **6.** eleven and twelve-hundredths _____

7. eighty-one-hundredths _____   **8.** fourteen and six-tenths _____

9. twenty-one-hundredths _____   **10.** seven and seven-hundredths _____

ACTIVITY 121   Review

Name: _____

Date: _____

1. Complete the temperature chart.

	Noon	Midnight	Difference
a.	98.5	78.7	
b.	84.6	59.8	
c.	71.3	67.5	
d.	78	67.2	

Write the equivalent mixed numbers. Reduce fractions to lowest terms.

2. 3.7 = _____

3. 4.62 = _____

4. 11.1 = _____

5. 9.65 = _____

ACTIVITY 122   Review

Name: _____

Date: _____

Round decimals to the nearest whole number.

1. 17.357 _____

2. 0.5021 _____

3. 1,237.7321 _____

Round the decimals to the nearest tenth.

4. 17.357 _____

5. 0.5021 _____

6. 1,237.7321 _____

Write the place value for the underlined digit.

7. 8.21359 _____

8. 0.001 _____

9. 1,237.7321 _____

10. 25.03696 _____

ACTIVITY 123 Add Whole Numbers and Decimals

Name:_____

Date:_____

To add a whole number and a decimal, add a decimal point and zeros after the whole number. Line up the numbers and add.

Example: 6 + 4.35 =

$$\begin{array}{r} 6.00 \\ + \ 4.35 \\ \hline 10.35 \end{array}$$

Rewrite each whole number so that it is shown with a decimal point and zeros to show the place value indicated.

1. 6   tenths place _____

2. 3   thousandths place _____

3. 11   hundredths place _____

4. 8   ten-thousandths place _____

5. 24   hundredths place _____

6. Does adding a decimal point and zeros after the decimal to a whole number change the value of the number? Why or why not? _____

_____

Rewrite and solve the equations. Round the answer to the nearest tenth.

7. $7 + $9.20 = _____

8. 2.145 + 6 = _____

ACTIVITY 124 Add Whole Numbers and Decimals

Name:_____

Date:_____

Rewrite and solve the equations. Round the answer to the nearest tenth.

1. 21.327 + 42 = _____

2. $8.02 + $11 = _____

3. 5.43 + 354 = _____

4. 8 + 9.25134 = _____

5. 32.61 + 21 = _____

Use a calculator to solve. Round the answers to the nearest tenth.

6. $2.81 + $83 = _____

7. 6.09 + 29 = _____

8. 41.40 + 4 = _____

9. $37 + $3.19 = _____

10. $50 + $6.01 = _____

ACTIVITY 125 Subtract Decimals and Whole Numbers

Name:_____

Date:_____

To subtract a decimal from a whole number, or a whole number from a decimal, add a decimal point and zeros to the whole number. Line up the numbers and subtract.

Example: 17 − 4.5 =

$$
\begin{array}{r}
\overset{6\;10}{1\cancel{7}.0} \\
-\quad 4.5 \\
\hline
12.5
\end{array}
$$

Use the place value chart to help you line up the numbers for subtraction. Then solve beside the chart.

1. $53.36 − $19 = _____

Tens	Ones	Decimal	Tenths	Hundredths
		.		
		.		

2. 41 − 2.9 = _____   3. 745 − 238.6327 = _____

- -

ACTIVITY 126 Subtract Decimals and Whole Numbers

Name:_____

Date:_____

Use the place value chart to help you line up the numbers for subtraction. Then solve beside the chart.

1. 24.461 − 18 = _____

Tens	Ones	Decimal	Tenths	Hundredths	Thousandths
		.			
		.			

Rewrite and solve the equations. Round the answers to the nearest hundredth.

2. 7.3 − 2 = _____   3. 25 − 0.46875 = _____

4. $14.55 − $3 = _____   5. $145 − $33.75 = _____

Use a calculator to solve. Round the answers to the nearest whole number.

6. $41.07 − $21 = _____   7. 231.756489 − 142 = _____

8. 10.625 − 2 = _____

ACTIVITY 127 Multiply Decimals by Whole Numbers

Name:_____

Date:_____

To multiply a decimal and a whole number, line up the numbers and multiply. When you finish, count the number of decimal places in the factors. Starting from the right of the product, count back the same number of places and add a decimal point.

Example: 4.23 x 7 =

$$\begin{array}{r} {\scriptstyle 1\ 2} \\ 4.23 \\ \underline{x\quad 7} \\ 2961 \end{array}$$

There are 2 decimal places in the factors, so the answer is 29.61.

Look at each problem. Write how many decimal places the product will have. You do not need to solve.

1. 4.1 x 3 = _____ decimal places

2. 65.003 x 5 = _____ decimal places

3. 6.80 x 35 = _____ decimal places

Rewrite each problem vertically, then solve.

4. 0.34 x 6 = _____

5. 2.17 x 4 = _____

6. 1.307 x 8 = _____

ACTIVITY 128 Multiply Decimals by Whole Numbers

Name:_____

Date:_____

Rewrite each problem vertically, then solve.

1. 0.036 x 10 = _____

2. 1.5 x 15 = _____

3. 76.828 x 4 = _____

4. 42.24 x 12 = _____

5. At a party, Keith poured 42 cups of punch. Each cup contained 4.25 ounces. How many ounces of punch did Keith pour? _____

6. Marsha fed the ducks at the park. She threw them pieces of 12 loaves of stale bread. Each loaf weighed 1.15 pounds. How many pounds of bread did Marsha feed the ducks? _____

ACTIVITY 129 Multiply Decimals by Decimals

Name:_____

Date:_____

To multiply two decimals, line up the numbers and multiply. When you finish, count the number of decimal places in both numbers. Starting from the right of the product, count back the same number of places and add a decimal point.

Example: 4.23 x 7.1 =

$$
\begin{array}{r}
1\,2 \\
4.23 \\
\times\quad 7.1 \\
\hline
1\,1\;423 \\
2961 \\
\hline
30033
\end{array}
$$

There are 3 decimal places in the factors, so the answer is 30.033.

Multiply.

1. 0.7 x 0.2 = _____

2. 1.5 x 2.3 = _____

3. 5.12 x 2.4 = _____

4. Steve paid 16¢ per ounce for fresh spinach.

   How much did a half pound of spinach cost? _____

ACTIVITY 130 Multiply Decimals by Decimals

Name:_____

Date:_____

Neal is hanging framed art on the wall and needs to know the area of each picture. Use the formula *l* x *w* (length x width) to find the area of each frame. Write your answer inside the shape. Area is written in square units, such as in².

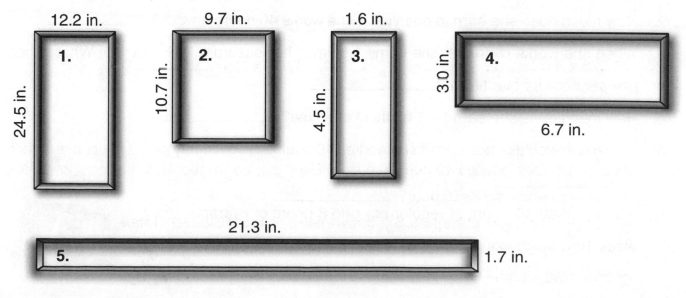

ACTIVITY 131 Decimal Word Problems

Name:_____

Date:_____

Solve. Use a calculator to help you.

1. Eduardo ordered three items from the menu at the Hungry Dragon Café. Each item cost $1.59. How much did the three items cost all together?

    _____

2. The Hungry Dragon Café served an average of 9.5 lemon cream pies a day. How many pies did the café serve in two weeks? _____

3. The manager of the Hungry Dragon Café knows that the average customer spends $3.25 for breakfast. If 42 people eat breakfast there, how much will they spend? _____

4. Doughnuts at the Hungry Dragon Café cost 79¢ each. What is the cost per dozen?

    _____

5. Marge worked 5.7 hours at the Hungry Dragon Café on Monday. She worked 4.2 hours on Tuesday and 6.4 hours on Wednesday, Friday, and Saturday. How many hours in all did she work? _____

- -

ACTIVITY 132 Everyday Decimals

Name:_____

Date:_____

Solve. Use a calculator to help you.

1. Grace earns $9.56 per hour as a cook at the Hungry Dragon Café. How much does she earn for 40 hours? _____

2. How much does she earn in one year if she works 40 hours a week? _____

3. When she works overtime, she earns 1.5 times her base pay. ($9.56 x 1.5) What is her pay per hour for overtime? _____

4. How much does she earn for 8 hours of overtime? _____

5. How much would Grace earn if she worked 40 hours at regular pay plus 8 hours overtime?

    _____

6. If she worked 40 hours at regular pay and 8 hours of overtime every week, how much would Grace earn in a year? _____

ACTIVITY 133 Fractions to Decimals

Name:_____

Date:_____

To change a fraction to a decimal, divide the numerator by
the denominator. Remember to add a zero to the left of the decimal place in the quotient when
the decimal does not include a whole number.

Example: $\frac{1}{5}$ is equal to what decimal?

$$5 \overline{)\begin{array}{c} 0.2 \\ 1.0 \\ -1.0 \\ \hline 0 \end{array}}$$

Write the fractions as decimals. Show your work on paper.

1. $\frac{3}{4}$ = _____

2. $\frac{5}{8}$ = _____

3. $\frac{7}{8}$ = _____

Write the fractions as decimals. Use a calculator to help you.

4. $\frac{4}{32}$ = _____

5. $\frac{7}{10}$ = _____

6. $\frac{3}{12}$ = _____

ACTIVITY 134 Fractions to Decimals

Name:_____

Date:_____

The fraction $\frac{1}{3}$ is an example of a fraction with a
repeating decimal. If you divide 1 by 3, the answer will be 0.33333333…. It will never be a quotient with no remainder.

1. What answer do you get if you change $\frac{5}{6}$ to a decimal? _____

When a fraction results in a repeating decimal, round the number to the desired place value
(tenths, hundredths, thousandths, etc.).

Write the decimal for each fraction. Round answers to the nearest hundredth.

2. $\frac{1}{3}$ = _____

3. $\frac{5}{6}$ = _____

4. $\frac{5}{9}$ = _____

5. Cal jogged $\frac{7}{8}$ of a mile. Write $\frac{7}{8}$ as a decimal rounded to the nearest tenth.

_____

6. Sal did homework for $\frac{11}{60}$ of an hour. Write $\frac{11}{60}$ as a decimal rounded to the

nearest tenth. _____

ACTIVITY 135 Mixed Numbers to Decimals

Name:_____

Date:_____

To change a mixed number to a decimal, change the fraction to a decimal and write it to the right of the decimal point. If the fraction results in a repeating decimal, round to the desired place value.

Example: $9\frac{3}{4} = 9.75$

Change these mixed numbers to decimals. Round answers to the nearest hundredth.

1. $6\frac{3}{8} = $ _____

2. $9\frac{1}{9} = $ _____

3. $8\frac{3}{7} = $ _____

4. $4\frac{3}{11} = $ _____

5. $7\frac{4}{5} = $ _____

6. $3\frac{6}{16} = $ _____

7. Mike drove $238\frac{3}{4}$ miles to the state park. Write the decimal. _____

8. He hiked a trail that was $7\frac{6}{10}$ miles long. Write the decimal. _____

ACTIVITY 136 Mixed Numbers to Decimals

Name:_____

Date:_____

Change these mixed numbers to decimals. Round answers to the nearest hundredth.

1. $11\frac{3}{4} = $ _____

2. $7\frac{1}{3} = $ _____

3. $2\frac{2}{5} = $ _____

4. $35\frac{1}{2} = $ _____

5. $6\frac{8}{9} = $ _____

6. $4\frac{3}{7} = $ _____

7. Dan used up $5\frac{1}{5}$ gallons of gas on his trip. Write the decimal. _____

8. Barb baked $8\frac{2}{24}$ batches of cookies. Write the decimal. _____

    If a batch is 12 cookies, how many cookies did she bake? _____

9. In January, Sara turned $13\frac{2}{6}$ years old. Write the decimal. _____

    How many years and months old is she? _____

10. Yaron took the train to Chicago to visit his grandfather and traveled $180\frac{8}{10}$ miles. Write the decimal. _____

ACTIVITY 137 Fraction/Decimal Equivalents

Name:_____

Date:_____

Fill in the fraction/decimal equivalency charts. Round to the nearest thousandth.
You may use a calculator.

Fraction	Decimal
$\frac{1}{4}$	
$\frac{2}{4}$	
$\frac{3}{4}$	
$\frac{1}{3}$	
$\frac{2}{3}$	
$\frac{1}{2}$	
$\frac{1}{5}$	
$\frac{2}{5}$	

Fraction	Decimal
$\frac{3}{5}$	
$\frac{4}{5}$	
$\frac{1}{6}$	
$\frac{2}{6}$	
$\frac{3}{6}$	
$\frac{4}{6}$	
$\frac{5}{6}$	

ACTIVITY 138 Fraction/Decimal Equivalents

Name:_____

Date:_____

Fill in the fraction/decimal equivalency charts. Round to the nearest thousandth.
You may use a calculator.

Fraction	Decimal
$\frac{1}{8}$	
$\frac{2}{8}$	
$\frac{3}{8}$	
$\frac{4}{8}$	
$\frac{5}{8}$	
$\frac{6}{8}$	
$\frac{7}{8}$	
$\frac{1}{10}$	

Fraction	Decimal
$\frac{2}{10}$	
$\frac{3}{10}$	
$\frac{4}{10}$	
$\frac{5}{10}$	
$\frac{6}{10}$	
$\frac{7}{10}$	
$\frac{8}{10}$	
$\frac{9}{10}$	

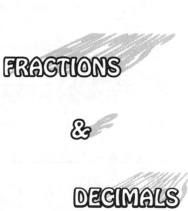

FRACTIONS

&

DECIMALS

71

ACTIVITY 139 Review

Name:_____

Date:_____

1. How much does it cost for 2 peanut butter and banana sandwiches and a Brussels sprouts soda? _____ How much change would be given from a $10 bill? _____

2. How much does it cost for radishes and mustard with cheese on a bun and 3 slices of lima bean pie? _____ How much change would be given from a $5 bill? _____

Hungry Dragon Café Kids' Menu

Peanut butter and banana sandwich	$2.75
Radishes and mustard on a bun	$1.90
Jelly and ham sandwich	$3.25
Slice of cheese	35¢
Lima bean pie	75¢
Brussels sprouts soda	$1.15
Spinach ice cream bar	90¢
Chocolate chips	22¢ a handful

3. How much does it cost for 3 jelly and ham sandwiches and 3 spinach ice cream bars? _____ How much change would be given from a $20 bill? _____

4. Jake had exactly the right amount of money to buy $6\frac{1}{2}$ handfuls of chocolate chips. How much money did he have? _____

ACTIVITY 140 Review

Name:_____

Date:_____

Rewrite and solve the equations.
Round the answer to the nearest tenth.

1. $1.75 + $20 = _____

2. 0.34 + 471 = _____

3. 120 − 2.5 = _____

4. $29.36 − $11 = _____

5. $4.25 x $59 = _____

6. 119 x 0.95 = _____

7. 4.4 x 1.4 = _____

8. 27.44 x 3 = _____

Change these fractions or mixed numbers to decimals. Round answers to the nearest tenth.

9. $\frac{8}{24}$ = _____

10. $2\frac{1}{3}$ = _____

11. $\frac{4}{5}$ = _____

12. $3\frac{9}{10}$ = _____

ACTIVITY 141 **Divide a Decimal by a**   Name:_____
Whole Number   Date:_____

Dividing a decimal by a whole number is similar to dividing two whole numbers.
Divide the same way you would with whole numbers. When you finish, put a decimal point in the quotient above where it is in the dividend.

$$\begin{array}{r} 0.05 \\ 7\overline{)0.35} \\ -35 \\ \hline 0 \end{array}$$

Example: 0.35 ÷ 7 =

Rewrite the equations and divide. Round to the nearest hundredth.

1. 2.25 ÷ 7   **2.** 22.6 ÷ 13   **3.** 21.12 ÷ 6

Write the equations and the answers.

4. Meg biked 19.6 miles last week. She rode the same number of miles each day. How far did Meg ride each day? _____

5. Greg drove 292.5 miles on 15 gallons of gas. What were his average miles per gallon?

_____

- -

ACTIVITY 142 **Divide a Decimal by a**   Name:_____
Whole Number   Date:_____

Rewrite the equations and divide. Round to the nearest hundredth.

1. 193.5 ÷ 9   **2.** 5.232 ÷ 8   **3.** 36.6 ÷ 6

4. 14.18 ÷ 4   **5.** 199.8 ÷ 6   **6.** 266.65 ÷ 5

Write the equations and the answers. You may use a calculator to solve.

7. Mrs. Reyes wants to compare the prices of different brands of baby food, but each jar contains a different amount. Help her find the best buy by finding the price per ounce for each brand and choosing the least expensive.

Brand A $1.99 per jar   3 oz. jar   _____

Brand B $2.09 per jar   4 oz. jar   _____

Brand C $1.79 per jar   2 oz. jar   _____

Least expensive brand: _____

ACTIVITY 143   Divide a Decimal by a Decimal

Name:_____

Date:_____

Dividing a decimal by a decimal is similar to dividing two whole numbers. Change the divisor to a whole number by multiplying it by 10, 100, or 1,000, etc. Multiply the dividend by the same number. (An easy way to do this is to move the decimal point to the right of the divisor and move the decimal point of the dividend the same number of places.) Divide the way you would with whole numbers. When you finish, put the decimal point in the quotient directly above the decimal point in the dividend.

Example: 7.9625 ÷ 2.45

$$
\begin{array}{r}
3.25 \\
245\overline{)796.25} \\
-735 \\
\hline
612 \\
-490 \\
\hline
1225 \\
-1225 \\
\hline
0
\end{array}
$$

Rewrite the equations on your own paper and divide. Write the answers below.

1. 23.4375 ÷ 6.25   2. 24.612 ÷ 8.4   3. 12.5847 ÷ 7.11

_____   _____   _____

4. Josh spent $5.95 for 3.5 pounds of pineapple. What was the cost per pound? _____

- -

ACTIVITY 144   Divide a Decimal by a Decimal

Name:_____

Date:_____

Rewrite the equations on your own paper and divide. Write the answers below. Round to the nearest hundredth if needed.

1. 6.0 ÷ 1.5   2. 7.2 ÷ 0.036   3. 40.05 ÷ 10.5

_____   _____   _____

4. 113.88 ÷ 2.1   5. 0.4998 ÷ 14.3   6. 3.6 ÷ 15.3

_____   _____   _____

Write the equations and the answers. You may use a calculator to solve.

7. The following shows the foods Tonya bought. Find out how many pounds or ounces she purchased. The price per pound and the total cost are shown (total costs are rounded to the nearest hundredth). Round to the nearest hundredth.

Broccoli $3.99/pound   total: $5.99   _____

Bananas $0.49/pound   total: $1.59   _____

Grapes $1.39/pound   total: $2.43   _____

ACTIVITY 145 **Decimals and Measurement**

Name:_____

Date:_____

1. Joa's red oval beads are 0.75 inches long. The blue square ones are 0.875 inches long. How much longer are the blue beads than the red ones? _____

2. Joa strung six blue beads and four red beads together for a necklace. What was the total length of the beads? _____

3. It is 2.3 miles from Joa's house to the bead shop where she works. How far does she travel there and back in five days? _____

4. It snowed 13.2 inches in January, 4.75 inches in February, and 1.9 inches in March. How much did it snow during those three months? _____

5. When Joa's 12-inch ruler broke, one section was 4.25 inches long. How long was the other piece? _____

6. Joa jogged 3.7 miles every day for a week. How far did she jog in one week?

_____

ACTIVITY 146 **Decimal Division Word Problems**

Name:_____

Date:_____

1. Toby used 8.7 gallons of gas to drive 478 miles. How many miles to a gallon did he get? Round your answer to the nearest hundredths. _____

2. Tony spent $23.70 on ice cream bars in June. Ice cream bars cost 79¢ each. How many did he buy? _____

3. Sandy, Randy, and Mandy split the cost of a computer game that cost $31.38. How much did it cost each of them? _____

4. It took Andy 50.37 hours to install a fence that was 34.5 feet 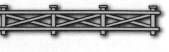 long. How many feet of fence did he install per hour? _____

5. Wendy used 73.2 feet of lumber to build a raised square flower box. How long was each side of the box? _____

6. Ben bought 110.36 square feet of carpeting for his office. The room is 8.9 feet long. How wide is it? _____

75

ACTIVITY 147 Review

Name:_____

Date:_____

Write the decimals as fractions or mixed numbers.
Do not reduce to lowest terms.

1. 0.86 = _____

2. 0.091 = _____

3. 0.200 = _____

4. 3.725 = _____

5. 51.004 = _____

6. 7.130 = _____

Circle the number in each group that is greatest.

7. $\frac{7}{10}$ $\frac{3}{5}$ 0.675

8. $5.82 $5.28 $8.52

9. 0.35 $\frac{3}{10}$ 0.533

10. $7\frac{2}{5}$ 7.08   7.45

ACTIVITY 148 Review

Name:_____

Date:_____

Round the decimals to the nearest tenth.

1. 4.499   _____

2. 0.5002   _____

3. 7.037   _____

Add.

4. $41.25 + $3.59 = _____

5. 82.28 + 11.82 = _____

6. $7.98 + $14.99 = _____

7. 148.03 + 5.99 = _____

ACTIVITY 149 **Decimal Test**

Name:_____

Date:_____

Write the amount of cents using monetary notation.

1. 350800¢ = _____
2. 1250¢ = _____
3. 295¢ = _____
4. 1048¢ = _____

Write the decimal numbers to match the words.

5. forty-hundredths = _____
6. six-tenths = _____

Write the words for the decimal numbers.

7. 0.25 = _____

8. 0.375 = _____

Round these decimals to the nearest tenth.

9. 98.34 _____
10. 2.7707 _____

11. Which is greater: 5.67 or 5.067? _____

12. Which is less: 84.9 or 0.849? _____

ACTIVITY 150 **Decimal Test**

Name:_____

Date:_____

Circle the number in each set that is greater.

1. $\frac{20}{40}$ 0.6
2. 0.81 $\frac{1}{6}$

3. 0.15 $\frac{2}{3}$
4. $\frac{3}{7}$ 0.622

Write the decimal for each fraction. Round answers to the nearest hundredth.

5. $\frac{8}{20}$ = _____
6. $\frac{14}{50}$ = _____
7. $\frac{5}{10}$ = _____

Change these mixed numbers to decimals. Round answers to the nearest hundredth.

8. $5\frac{3}{4}$ = _____
9. $4\frac{3}{7}$ = _____
10. $7\frac{1}{3}$ = _____

ACTIVITY 151 Decimal Test

Name: _____

Date: _____

Rewrite these equations on your own paper to line up
the decimal points. Then find the sum or difference. Write the answers below.

1. 3.545 + 83.4 = _____

2. 7.1 + 66.76 = _____

3. 53.33 − 17.25 = _____

4. 401.5 − 199.8 = _____

5. 583.8 − 7 = _____

6. 86.25 + 5 = _____

7. 193.5 + 6 = _____

8. 5.232 − 2 = _____

9. Stephanie bought new school supplies for $15.67, new jeans for $35.46, and
a new backpack for $24.50. How much did she spend in all? _____
If she paid with a $100 bill, what was her change? _____

10. Sean made a goal to collect $500.00 for charity. He earned $105.50 in a fund-raising
car wash and collected $162.77 from family and friends. He also contributed one of his
paychecks from work, which was $145.57. How much money has he collected in all?
_____ How much more money does he need to reach his goal? _____

ACTIVITY 152 Decimal Test

Name: _____

Date: _____

Rewrite each problem vertically on your own paper.
Then solve and write the answers below.

1. 27.43 x 4 = _____

2. 3 x 15.3 = _____

3. 2.5 x 6.5 = _____

4. 6.1 x 17.3 = _____

5. Marilyn is training for a 5 kilometer race. Each day for a week she runs 5 kilometers (3.1
miles). How many miles does she run that week? _____

6. 3.6 ÷ 15 = _____

7. 199.8 ÷ 6 = _____

8. 4.56 ÷ 0.1 = _____

9. 78.9 ÷ 1.2 = _____

10. Steven wanted to buy some first-class stamps at the post office. The charge for a book of
stamps was $8.20. Steven couldn't tell how many stamps were in a book. If the value of 1
stamp is $0.41, how many stamps are in one book? _____

Fraction Strips

1

$\frac{1}{2}$	$\frac{1}{2}$

$\frac{1}{3}$	$\frac{1}{3}$	$\frac{1}{3}$

$\frac{1}{4}$	$\frac{1}{4}$	$\frac{1}{4}$	$\frac{1}{4}$

$\frac{1}{5}$	$\frac{1}{5}$	$\frac{1}{5}$	$\frac{1}{5}$	$\frac{1}{5}$

$\frac{1}{6}$	$\frac{1}{6}$	$\frac{1}{6}$	$\frac{1}{6}$	$\frac{1}{6}$	$\frac{1}{6}$

$\frac{1}{7}$	$\frac{1}{7}$	$\frac{1}{7}$	$\frac{1}{7}$	$\frac{1}{7}$	$\frac{1}{7}$	$\frac{1}{7}$

$\frac{1}{8}$	$\frac{1}{8}$	$\frac{1}{8}$	$\frac{1}{8}$	$\frac{1}{8}$	$\frac{1}{8}$	$\frac{1}{8}$	$\frac{1}{8}$

$\frac{1}{9}$	$\frac{1}{9}$	$\frac{1}{9}$	$\frac{1}{9}$	$\frac{1}{9}$	$\frac{1}{9}$	$\frac{1}{9}$	$\frac{1}{9}$	$\frac{1}{9}$

$\frac{1}{10}$	$\frac{1}{10}$	$\frac{1}{10}$	$\frac{1}{10}$	$\frac{1}{10}$	$\frac{1}{10}$	$\frac{1}{10}$	$\frac{1}{10}$	$\frac{1}{10}$	$\frac{1}{10}$

$\frac{1}{11}$	$\frac{1}{11}$	$\frac{1}{11}$	$\frac{1}{11}$	$\frac{1}{11}$	$\frac{1}{11}$	$\frac{1}{11}$	$\frac{1}{11}$	$\frac{1}{11}$	$\frac{1}{11}$	$\frac{1}{11}$

$\frac{1}{12}$	$\frac{1}{12}$	$\frac{1}{12}$	$\frac{1}{12}$	$\frac{1}{12}$	$\frac{1}{12}$	$\frac{1}{12}$	$\frac{1}{12}$	$\frac{1}{12}$	$\frac{1}{12}$	$\frac{1}{12}$	$\frac{1}{12}$

Answer Keys

Activity 1: Parts of a Whole (p. 3)

1. $\frac{3}{8}$

2. The shaded part is not $\frac{2}{3}$ of the triangle because the triangle is not divided into equal parts.

3. $\frac{5}{6}$

Activity 2: Parts of a Whole (p. 3)

1. 3   2. 4   3. $\frac{2}{4}$
4. $\frac{4}{10}$ 5. $\frac{2}{3}$ 6. $\frac{7}{12}$

Activity 3: Parts of a Whole (p. 4)

1.  or

2.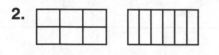

3. $\frac{1}{6}$ should be red, and $\frac{3}{6}$ should be gray.

4. $\frac{2}{6}$ should be red, and $\frac{2}{6}$ should be gray.

Activity 4: Parts of a Whole (p. 4)

1. Image should show $\frac{1}{2}$ of a pie.

2. Image should show $\frac{1}{3}$ of a glass of juice.

3. Image should show $\frac{1}{4}$ of a cookie.

4. Image should show $\frac{1}{2}$ of an apple.

5. Image should show $\frac{3}{4}$ of a sandwich.

6. Image should show $\frac{2}{3}$ of a bottle of water.

7. 6

Acitivity 5: Parts of a Group (p. 5)

1. numerator   2. denominator

3. 3   4. $\frac{3}{7}$

5. $\frac{6}{11}$ 6. $\frac{5}{11}$

Activity 6: Parts of a Group (p. 5)

1.–3. Answers will vary.

4. 6   5. $\frac{12}{18}$

Activity 7: Parts of a Group/Use a Table (p. 6)

1. 6   2. $\frac{2}{6}$ 3. $\frac{4}{6}$
4. $\frac{3}{6}$ 5. 55   6. $\frac{8}{55}$
7. $\frac{16}{55}$

Activity 8: Fractional Parts of a Whole and a Group (p. 6)

1. $\frac{5}{8}$ 2. $\frac{3}{8}$ 3. $\frac{3}{4}$
4. $\frac{1}{4}$ 5.–6. Answers will vary.

Activity 9: Fraction Words (p. 7)

1. three-fourths   2. two-sevenths
3. seven-ninths   4. three-tenths
5. two-sixths   6. eight-elevenths
7. $\frac{11}{20}$ 8. $\frac{4}{100}$
9. $\frac{6}{18}$ 10. $\frac{9}{32}$

Activity 10: Fraction Words (p. 7)

1. 11   2. 6   3. 13
4. 20   5. $\frac{9}{11}$ 6. $\frac{1}{9}$

Activity 11: Review (p. 8)

1. Answer should show a shape divided into 8 equal parts with 7 parts colored.
2. $\frac{5}{5}$ 3. $\frac{7}{8}$ 4. $\frac{2}{6}$
5. $\frac{7}{7}$ 6. $\frac{14}{14}$ 7. $\frac{9}{9}$
8. $\frac{100}{100}$

Activity 12: Review (p. 8)

1. Answer should show a group of 15 objects with 6 of the objects colored.
2. $\frac{8}{17}, \frac{9}{17}$ 3. $\frac{15}{52}$
4. $\frac{35}{48}$ 5. $\frac{1}{2}$

Activity 13: Review (p. 9)
1. 2   2. 12   3. 30
4. 32   5. 5   6. 100
7. Six watermelon seeds should be circled.

Activity 14: Review (p. 9)
1. 92   2. 76   3. $\frac{3}{15}$
4. $\frac{11}{14}$ 5. $\frac{2}{100}$ 6. $\frac{2}{3}$
7. one-fourth   8. eighteen-thirtieths
9. five-eighths   10. twelve-hundredths

Activity 15: Everyday Math With Fractions (p. 10)
1. $\frac{5}{7}$ 2. $\frac{3}{12}$ 3. $\frac{8}{24}$
4. $\frac{6}{16}$ 5. $\frac{3}{12}$ 6. $\frac{1}{2}$

Activity 16: Everyday Math With Fractions (p. 10)
1. $\frac{13}{16}$ 2. $\frac{5}{31}$ 3. $\frac{2}{5}$
4. $\frac{3}{7}$ 5. $\frac{5}{14}$ 6. 4 ounces

Activity 17: Estimate With Fractions (p. 11)
1. $\frac{1}{2}$ 2. $\frac{1}{3}$ 3. $\frac{3}{4}$
4. $\frac{2}{3}$ 5. $\frac{1}{4}$ 6. $\frac{2}{3}$

Activity 18: Estimate With Fractions (p. 11)
1. $\frac{2}{8}$ or $\frac{1}{4}$ 2. $\frac{2}{6}$ or $\frac{1}{3}$

3. $\frac{3}{9}$ or $\frac{1}{3}$ 4. $\frac{1}{2}$
5. Answer should show a glass that is about $\frac{1}{3}$ full.
6. Answer should show a cake cut into 5 pieces with 1 piece gone.

Activity 19: Compare and Order Fractions With Common Denominators (p. 12)
1. 4   2. $\frac{6}{7}$ 3. <   4. >
5. >   6. $\frac{1}{8}, \frac{2}{8}, \frac{3}{8}, \frac{5}{8}, \frac{6}{8}, \frac{7}{8}$

Activity 20: Compare and Order Fractions With Common Denominators (p. 12)
1. Answer should show number line with $\frac{2}{10}, \frac{3}{10}, \frac{4}{10}, \frac{5}{10}, \frac{6}{10}, \frac{7}{10}, \frac{8}{10},$ and $\frac{9}{10}$ written in order.
2. Answer should show number line with $\frac{1}{8}, \frac{2}{8}, \frac{4}{8}, \frac{5}{8}, \frac{6}{8},$ and $\frac{7}{8}$ written in order.
3. Answer should show number line with $\frac{1}{12}, \frac{3}{12}, \frac{4}{12}, \frac{5}{12}, \frac{6}{12}, \frac{7}{12}, \frac{8}{12}, \frac{9}{12}, \frac{10}{12},$ and $\frac{11}{12}$ written in order.

Activity 21: Add Fractions With Common Denominators (p. 13)
1. $\frac{3}{5}$ 2. $\frac{14}{100}$ 3. $\frac{17}{24}$
4. $\frac{5}{7}$ 5. 6 innings

Activity 22: Add Fractions With Common Denominators (p. 13)
1. $\frac{6}{6}$ 2. $\frac{7}{8}$ 3. $\frac{4}{5}$
4. $\frac{3}{4}$ 5. $\frac{66}{99}$ 6. $\frac{36}{40}$
7. $\frac{6}{20}$ 8. $\frac{11}{12}$ 9. $\frac{2}{3}$
10. $\frac{9}{9}$

Activity 23: Subtract Fractions With Common Denominators (p. 14)
1. $\frac{5}{10}$ 2. $\frac{4}{14}$ 3. $\frac{40}{100}$
4. $\frac{4}{16}$ 5. $\frac{15}{64}$ 6. $\frac{4}{19}$

Activity 24: Subtract Fractions With Common Denominators (p. 14)
1. $\frac{8}{16}$ 2. $\frac{18}{24}$ 3. 3 days
4. $\frac{5}{8}$ 5. $\frac{5}{12}$ 6. $\frac{26}{98}$

Activity 25: Add and Subtract Fractions With Common Denominators (p. 15)
1. $\frac{6}{13}$ 2. $\frac{10}{11}$
3. $\frac{14}{32}$ 4. $\frac{9}{15}$

5. $\frac{83}{100}$ 6. $\frac{17}{64}$

7. $\frac{55}{60}$ 8. $\frac{15}{60}$

9. 20 minutes   10. $\frac{3}{10}$

Activity 26: Review (p. 15)
1. F   2. T   3. F   4. T
5. T   6. F   7. F   8. T
9. T   10. F   11. $\frac{15}{32}$ 12. 5 days

Activity 27: Measurement With Fractions (p. 16)
1. $\frac{4}{12}$ 2. $\frac{5}{8}$ 3. $\frac{11}{16}$
4. $\frac{16}{36}$ 5. $\frac{7}{12}$ 6. 7 inches
7. 3 ounces 8. 21 inches 9. 3 days
10. 3 eggs

Activity 28: Measurement With Fractions (p. 16)
1. $\frac{1}{16}$ 2. $\frac{1}{3}$ 3. $\frac{1}{3}$
4. $\frac{1}{12}$ 5. $\frac{1}{365}$ 6. $\frac{1}{3600}$
7. $\frac{1}{10}$ 8. $\frac{1}{16}$ 9. $\frac{1}{2}$
10. $\frac{1}{52}$

Activity 29: Round Fractions (p. 17)
Answers will vary.

Activity 30: Estimate (p. 17)
Answers will vary.

Activity 31: Mixed Numbers (p. 18)
1. $2\frac{2}{3}$ 2. $3\frac{1}{2}$ 3. $5\frac{1}{4}$ 4. $8\frac{1}{3}$

Activity 32: Mixed Numbers With a Table (p. 18)
1. Brand B   2. Brand A
3. $3\frac{1}{2}$ teaspoons   4. $2\frac{1}{2}$ teaspoons

Activity 33: Improper Fractions to Mixed Numbers and Whole Numbers (p. 19)
1. $1\frac{2}{3}$ 2. $1\frac{3}{4}$ 3. $1\frac{1}{8}$
4. $2\frac{5}{6}$ 5. $1\frac{10}{21}$

Activity 34: Improper Fractions to Mixed Numbers and Whole Numbers (p. 19)
1. $1\frac{1}{100}$ 2. $1\frac{5}{42}$ 3. 3
4. $1\frac{2}{6}$
5.–6.   Answers will vary.

Activity 35: Mixed Numbers and Whole Numbers to Improper Fractions (p. 20)
1. $\frac{14}{3}$ 2. $\frac{53}{8}$ 3. $\frac{504}{5}$
4. Answers may vary; $\frac{49}{7}$
5. $\frac{115}{12}$ 6. $\frac{62}{5}$

Activity 36: Mixed Numbers and Whole Numbers to Improper Fractions (p. 20)
1. $\frac{146}{16}$ 2. $\frac{34}{3}$ 3. $\frac{35}{18}$
4. $\frac{12}{5}$ 5. $\frac{31}{7}$ 6. $\frac{33}{5}$
7. $\frac{71}{2}$ 8. $\frac{22}{3}$ 9. $\frac{46}{13}$
10. $\frac{23}{4}$

Activity 37: Review (p. 21)
1. T   2. T   3. F   4. T
5. F   6. T   7. F   8. T
9. T   10. T

Activity 38: Review (p. 21)
1. $2\frac{1}{4}$ 2. $21\frac{1}{3}$ 3. $13\frac{4}{9}$
4. $1\frac{1}{25}$ 5. $4\frac{5}{8}$ 6. $1\frac{24}{31}$
7. $\frac{12}{5}$ 8. $\frac{59}{6}$ 9. $\frac{15}{8}$
10. $\frac{204}{32}$

Activity 39: Add Mixed Numbers With Common Denominators (p. 22)

1. $7\frac{1}{8}$ 2. $10\frac{4}{7}$ 3. 14
4. $13\frac{8}{9}$ 5. 28 6. $18\frac{28}{32}$

Activity 40: Subtract Mixed Numbers With Common Denominators (p. 22)

1. $2\frac{4}{8}$ 2. $4\frac{2}{5}$ 3. $2\frac{14}{16}$
4. $7\frac{90}{100}$ 5. $4\frac{8}{10}$ 6. $8\frac{5}{6}$

Activity 41: Compare Fractions Using Fraction Strips (p. 23)

1. $\frac{1}{2}$ 2. $\frac{2}{3}$ 3. $\frac{3}{6}$
4. $\frac{7}{8}$ 5. $\frac{1}{2}$ 6. $\frac{2}{10}$
7. $\frac{3}{10}$ 8. $\frac{2}{6}$

Activity 42: Compare Fractions Using Fraction Strips (p. 23)

1. $\frac{3}{4}$ and $\frac{6}{8}$ 2. $\frac{4}{10}$ and $\frac{2}{5}$
3. $\frac{5}{10}, \frac{3}{6}$, and $\frac{4}{8}$ 4. $\frac{1}{3}$ and $\frac{2}{6}$
5. Rectangle should be divided into 8 equal parts.
6. Rectangle should be divided into 10 equal parts.
7. Answers will vary.

Activity 43: Compare and Order Fractions Using Fraction Strips (p. 24)

1. $>$ 2. $<$ 3. $<$ 4. $<$
5. $<$ 6. $<$ 7. $=$ 8. $<$

Activity 44: Compare and Order Fractions Using Fraction Strips (p. 24)

1. $\frac{1}{5}, \frac{1}{3}, \frac{3}{8}, \frac{2}{4}, \frac{2}{3}, \frac{5}{6}$
2. $\frac{2}{6}, \frac{1}{2}, \frac{2}{3}, \frac{4}{5}, \frac{7}{8}, \frac{9}{10}$
3. Bret
4. more

Activity 45: Compare and Order Fractions (p. 25)

1. B   2. $\frac{2}{3}$
3. $\frac{3}{8}$ of rectangle A should be shaded.
4. $\frac{1}{2}$ of rectangle B should be shaded.
5. rectangle B   6. $\frac{3}{8}$

Activity 46: Compare and Order Mixed Numbers Using Fraction Strips (p. 25)

1. $<$ 2. $>$ 3. $>$ 4. $=$
5. $>$ 6. $<$
7. $1\frac{1}{2}, 1\frac{3}{4}, 2\frac{5}{8}, 2\frac{3}{4}, 2\frac{5}{6}, 3\frac{1}{8}$
8. $5\frac{2}{8}, 5\frac{1}{3}, 5\frac{3}{4}, 6\frac{2}{3}, 6\frac{3}{4}, 6\frac{7}{8}$

Activity 47: Equivalent Fractions (p. 26)

1. $\frac{4}{6}$

Activity 48: Equivalent Fractions (p. 26)

1. $\frac{9}{12}$ 2. $\frac{3}{9}$ 3. $\frac{4}{16}$

Activity 49: Equivalent Fractions (p. 27)

1. $\frac{4}{8}$ 2. $\frac{6}{8}$ 3. $\frac{8}{12}$
4. $\frac{10}{12}$ 5. $\frac{9}{12}$ 6. $\frac{3}{12}$

Activity 50: Equivalent Fractions (p. 27)

1. $\frac{6}{20}$ 2. $\frac{12}{20}$ 3. $\frac{10}{20}$
4. $\frac{15}{20}$ 5. 33 6. 32
7. 20 8. 14 9. 14
10. 100

Activity 51: Create a Table/Use Data From a Table (p. 28)
Answers will vary.

Activity 52: Create a Table/Use Data From a Table (p. 28)
Answers will vary.

Activity 53: Review (p. 29)
1. Answers will vary.
2. Answers will vary.
3. $\frac{32}{9}$ 4. $\frac{18}{7}$ 5. $\frac{133}{10}$
6. $13\frac{2}{3}$ 7. $3\frac{2}{5}$ 8. 4

Activity 54: Review (p. 29)
1. <   2. <   3. >
4. Diagram should show $\frac{12}{16}$ $(\frac{3}{4})$.
5. $\frac{12}{16}$ 6. $\frac{2}{16}$ 7. $\frac{8}{16}$
8. $\frac{10}{16}$

Activity 55: Greatest Common Factors (p. 30)
1. 2
2. Missing numbers from top to bottom, left to right are: 12, 6, 3 and 1, 16, 8, 4, and 4.
3. 1, 2, 4
4. 4

Activity 56: Greatest Common Factors (p. 30)
1. Missing numbers from top to bottom, left to right are: 1, 25, 5, and 5 and 1, 30, 2, 15, 3, 10, 5, and 6; GCF = 5
2. Missing numbers from top to bottom, left to right are: 1, 16, 2, 8, 4, and 4 and 1, 20, 2, 10, 4, and 5; GCF = 4

Activity 57: Simplify Fractions (p. 31)
1. yes   2. no   3. no
4. yes   5. no   6. yes
7. no   8. yes

Activity 58: Simplify Fractions (p. 31)
1. $\frac{1}{4}$ 2. $\frac{1}{4}$ 3. $\frac{1}{3}$
4. simplest form   5. $\frac{1}{10}$
6. $\frac{1}{8}$ 7. $\frac{1}{8}$ 8. $\frac{1}{4}$

Activity 59: Fraction Patterns (p. 32)
1. Missing numbers are: $3\frac{1}{2}$, 5, $6\frac{1}{2}$, $9\frac{1}{2}$
2. Missing numbers are: $\frac{10}{12}$, $\frac{9}{12}$, $\frac{8}{12}$, $\frac{6}{12}$, $\frac{5}{12}$
3. Missing numbers are: $3\frac{3}{6}$, $3\frac{7}{6}$ or $4\frac{1}{6}$, $3\frac{9}{6}$ or $4\frac{3}{6}$, $3\frac{11}{6}$ or $4\frac{5}{6}$
4. Add $\frac{2}{8}$; Missing numbers are: $\frac{5}{8}$, $\frac{9}{8}$, or $1\frac{1}{8}$
5. Subtract $\frac{3}{100}$; Missing numbers are: $\frac{83}{100}$, $\frac{80}{100}$ or $\frac{8}{10}$, $\frac{74}{100}$

Activity 60: Probability With Fractions (p. 32)
1. $\frac{1}{8}$ 2. $\frac{1}{4}$ 3. $\frac{3}{4}$
4. $\frac{5}{8}$ 5. $\frac{1}{2}$

Activity 61: Compare Fractions Without Common Denominators (p. 33)
1. $\frac{2}{3} = \frac{10}{15}$ and $\frac{3}{5} = \frac{9}{15}$; $\frac{2}{3}$ is greater.
2. $\frac{7}{8} = \frac{21}{24}$ and $\frac{5}{6} = \frac{20}{24}$; $\frac{5}{6}$ is less.

Activity 62: Compare Fractions Without Common Denominators (p. 33)
1. 24; $\frac{2}{3}$ is greater.   2. 35; $\frac{3}{5}$ is greater.
3. 100; $\frac{2}{100}$ is less.   4. 60; $\frac{4}{10}$ is less.
5. 12; $\frac{5}{6}$ is greatest.

Activity 63: Least Common Multiple (p. 34)
1. 20; $\frac{3}{4}$ is greater.   2. 9; $\frac{4}{9}$ is less.

Activity 64: Least Common Multiple (p. 34)
1. 60; $\frac{5}{12}$ 2. 12; $\frac{3}{4}$ 3. 18; $\frac{2}{18}$
4. 24; $\frac{3}{12}$

Activity 65: Equivalent Fractions (p. 35)
1. $\frac{1}{10}$ 2. $\frac{4}{10}$ 3. $\frac{7}{10}$

Activity 66: Equivalent Fractions (p. 35)
1. $\frac{3}{8}$ 2. $\frac{1}{8}$ 3. $\frac{3}{8}$
4. $\frac{8}{12}$ 5. $\frac{3}{12}$ 6. $\frac{8}{12}$
7. no; $\frac{2}{4}$ with a denominator of 12 is $\frac{6}{12}$.
8. yes; To compare $\frac{3}{9}$ and $\frac{9}{27}$, multiply the 9 in the denominator by 3 to get 27 and multiply the numerator by 3 to get 9.

Activity 67: Fraction Analogies (p. 36)
1. $\frac{6}{9}$ 2. $\frac{8}{5}$ 3. $\frac{300}{3000}$
4. $\frac{1}{5}$

Activity 68: Classify Fractions (p. 36)
1. Each fraction equals $\frac{1}{2}$.
2. Each is an improper fraction.
3. Each has a denominator that is a multiple of 8, and they cannot be reduced.
4. Each equals $\frac{1}{4}$.

Activity 69: Add Fractions Without Common Denominators (p. 37)
1. $1\frac{1}{2}$ 2. $\frac{1}{2}$ 3. $1\frac{1}{18}$
4. $1\frac{1}{16}$ 5. $1\frac{9}{20}$ 6. $1\frac{1}{12}$

Activity 70: Add Fractions Without Common Denominators (p. 37)
1. $\frac{23}{36}$
2. $\frac{1}{2}$ mile
3. $\frac{11}{12}$ of the pan
4. $2\frac{1}{4}$ minutes or 135 seconds
5. $\frac{5}{6}$ of a yard; 30 inches

Activity 71: Subtract Fractions Without Common Denominators (p. 38)
1. $\frac{7}{16}$ 2. $\frac{1}{24}$ 3. $\frac{3}{4}$
4. $\frac{5}{24}$; less   5. $\frac{1}{2}$; half   6. $\frac{1}{6}$; less

Activity 72: Subtract Fractions Without Common Denominators (p. 38)
1. $\frac{13}{36}$ 2. $\frac{11}{20}$ 3. $\frac{1}{8}$ mile
4. $\frac{1}{6}$ yard   5. $\frac{4}{12}$ yard or $\frac{1}{3}$ yard

Activity 73: Multiply Fractions (p. 39)
1. $\frac{15}{64}$ 2. $\frac{2}{7}$ 3. $1\frac{1}{21}$
4. $\frac{2}{3}$ 5. $2\frac{1}{3}$ 6. $1\frac{5}{6}$

Activity 74: Multiply Fractions (p. 39)
1. $\frac{1}{6}$ 2. $\frac{2}{15}$ 3. $\frac{1}{3}$
4. $\frac{1}{4}$ 5. $\frac{1}{3}$ 6. $\frac{5}{36}$
7. $\frac{7}{10}$ 8. $1\frac{1}{5}$ 9. $\frac{7}{9}$
10. $\frac{33}{160}$

Activity 75: Multiply Mixed Numbers and Whole Numbers by Fractions (p. 40)
1. $2\frac{1}{3}$ 2. $5\frac{5}{6}$ 3. $4\frac{2}{3}$
4. $4\frac{1}{2}$ 5. $28\frac{1}{6}$ 6. $28\frac{7}{16}$

Activity 76: Multiply Mixed Numbers and Whole Numbers by Fractions (p. 40)
1. $2\frac{1}{4}$ 2. $19\frac{1}{5}$ 3. $6\frac{7}{8}$
4. $7\frac{5}{7}$ 5. $22\frac{11}{32}$ 6. $24\frac{1}{12}$
7. 3   8. $42\frac{2}{3}$ 9. $5\frac{17}{20}$
10. $11\frac{3}{7}$

Activity 77: Fraction Word Problems (p. 41)
1. 4 students
2. 16 years old
3. 35 pages
4. 21 red balloons
5. 7 beads
6. 35 students
7. 2 donuts

Activity 78: Fraction Word Problems (p. 41)

1. 42
2. 20 minutes
3. 15 pounds
4. 22 female penguins
5. $40
6. 20 seeds sprouted
7. 18 pieces of junk mail

Activity 79: Review (p. 42)

1. factors
2. 1, 2, 3, 4, 6, 8, 12, 24
3. 1, 2, 3, 4, 6, 9, 12, 18, 36
4. 1
5. yes; 7 cannot be divided by any other number than 1.
6. no; Both 15 and 20 can be divided by 5 to reduce the fraction to $\frac{3}{4}$.
7. least
8. 36
9. equal
10. no; If $\frac{3}{4}$ and $\frac{2}{3}$ are given the common denominator of 12, they equal $\frac{9}{12}$ and $\frac{8}{12}$ respectively.

Activity 80: Review (p. 42)

1. $\frac{5}{11}$ 2. $\frac{2}{11}$ 3. $\frac{1}{22}$ 4. $\frac{9}{11}$
5–6. Answers will vary.

Activity 81: Divide Fractions (p. 43)

1. $\frac{1}{8}$ 2. $\frac{1}{12}$ 3. $\frac{1}{9}$

Activity 82: Divide Fractions by Fractions (p. 43)

1. $\frac{15}{32}$ 2. $\frac{3}{5}$ 3. $1\frac{1}{2}$ 4. $1\frac{1}{6}$
5. $\frac{5}{16}$ 6. $2\frac{4}{5}$

Activity 83: Divide Fractions by Whole Numbers (p. 44)

1. $9\frac{1}{3}$ 2. $\frac{1}{20}$ 3. $\frac{3}{25}$
4. $\frac{5}{28}$ 5. 18 6. 9

Activity 84: Divide Fractions by Whole Numbers (p. 44)

1. $7\frac{1}{2}$ 2. $\frac{1}{6}$ 3. $\frac{1}{24}$
4. $\frac{1}{5}$ 5. 2 6. $11\frac{1}{4}$
7. $19\frac{1}{5}$ 8. $\frac{5}{21}$ 9. $7\frac{1}{5}$
10. $\frac{5}{88}$

Activity 85: Divide Mixed Numbers (p. 45)

1. $2\frac{2}{11}$ 2. $1\frac{1}{36}$ 3. $1\frac{33}{35}$
4. $2\frac{26}{87}$ 5. $8\frac{2}{3}$ 6. $\frac{16}{225}$

Activity 86: Divide Mixed Numbers (p. 45)

1. $1\frac{2}{3}$ 2. $\frac{19}{28}$ 3. $2\frac{3}{5}$
4. $1\frac{17}{32}$ 5. $1\frac{8}{13}$ 6. $\frac{4}{17}$
7. $\frac{3}{10}$ 8. $17\frac{3}{5}$ 9. $27\frac{1}{3}$
10. $2\frac{14}{17}$

Activity 87: Review (p. 46)

1. $1\frac{1}{2}$ 2. 7 3. 12
4. 5 5. $\frac{7}{9}$ 6. $\frac{7}{24}$
7. $\frac{2}{75}$ 8. $\frac{1}{13}$ 9. 6
10. $10\frac{15}{16}$

Activity 88: Review (p. 46)

1. $18\frac{3}{8}$ 2. $2\frac{5}{11}$ 3. $1\frac{1}{6}$
4. 40 5. 3 6. 18
7. 50 8. $\frac{1}{24}$ 9. $\frac{4}{5}$
10. 3

Activity 89: Create a Pie Chart (p. 47)

Answers will vary.

Activity 90: Fractions on a Pie Chart (p. 47)

Answers will vary.

Activity 91: Measurement With Fractions (p. 48)

1. $1\frac{1}{3}$ c.
2. 8 servings
3. $\frac{3}{8}$ lb.
4. $6\frac{1}{2}$ oz.
5. 7 oz.
6. $15\frac{9}{34}$ in.

Activity 92: Measurement With Fractions (p. 48)

1. $4\frac{8}{9}$ oz.
2. $2\frac{1}{3}$ oz.
3. 24 stones
4. 20 feet
5. $5\frac{5}{23}$ crates

Activity 93: Fractions With a Bar Graph (p. 49)

1. pepperoni; $\frac{1}{2}$
2. olives; $\frac{3}{100}$
3. $\frac{7}{100}$
4. $\frac{1}{2}$
5. $\frac{43}{100}$
6. $\frac{1}{5}$

Activity 94: Fraction Algebra (p. 49)

1. $2\frac{2}{3}$
2. $\frac{5}{9}$
3. $2\frac{1}{4}$ or $2\frac{2}{8}$
4. $\frac{2}{4}$ or $\frac{1}{2}$
5. $\frac{7}{12}$
6. $\frac{4}{10}$
7. $\frac{1}{2}$
8. $\frac{1}{3}$
9. $\frac{15}{16}$
10. $5\frac{1}{4}$

Activity 95: Fraction Test (p. 50)

1. $\frac{39}{5}$
2. $\frac{27}{6}$
3. $\frac{138}{15}$
4. $\frac{163}{2}$
5. $\frac{26}{3}$
6. $\frac{13}{3}$
7. $2\frac{1}{3}$
8. $1\frac{7}{41}$
9. $1\frac{3}{4}$
10. 57
11. $1\frac{7}{9}$
12. 2

Activity 96: Fraction Test (p. 50)

1. 1, 3, 9 and 1, 2, 3, 6, 9, 18; the GCF is 9.
2. 1, 3, 7, 21 and 1, 2, 4, 7, 14, 28; the GCF is 7.
3. $\frac{4}{6}$
4. $\frac{8}{15}$
5. $\frac{2}{3}$
6. $\frac{94}{100}$

7. If the denominators are the same, look at the numerators of the fractions.
8. Compare the whole numbers.
9. 66   10. 27

Activity 97: Fraction Test (p. 51)

1. $\frac{6}{9}$
2. $\frac{6}{9}$
3. $\frac{1}{9}$
4. $\frac{7}{8}$
5. $\frac{1}{3}$
6. $\frac{11}{16}$
7. $\frac{3}{4}$
8. $\frac{1}{4}$
9. $\frac{4}{5}$
10. $\frac{3}{4}$

Activity 98: Fraction Test (p. 51)

1. $\frac{53}{56}$
2. $\frac{5}{6}$
3. $\frac{11}{14}$
4. $\frac{13}{30}$
5. $\frac{1}{6}$
6. $\frac{1}{15}$
7. $\frac{2}{5}$
8. 2
9. $\frac{7}{8}$
10. $2\frac{1}{28}$
11. $\frac{1}{8}$
12. $2\frac{2}{7}$
13. $\frac{1}{4}$ is relative only to the number of events for each individual girl. So, Rachel entered 8 events and won 2 ($\frac{1}{4}$ of 8) and Rhonda entered 20 events and won 5 ($\frac{1}{4}$ of 20).

Activity 99: Decimals and Monetary Notation (p. 52)

1. $0.53
2. $0.75
3. $0.49
4. $0.07
5. $0.82
6. $0.04

Activity 100: Decimals and Monetary Notation (p. 52)

1. $4.87
2. $18.27
3. $20.45
4. $29.36
5. $7.98
6. $1.35
7. $11.99
8. $15.83

Activity 101: Place Value of Decimals (p. 53)

	Ones	Tenths	Hundredths	Thousandths
1.	0.	7		
2.	0.	9	2	
3.	0.	1	0	7
4.	0.	6	3	5
5.	0.	8	0	9

Activity 102: Place Value of Decimals (p. 53)

1. 0.6   2. 0.34   3. 0.06
4. 0.73   5. 0.008   6. 0.001
7. 0.814   8. 0.426
9. sixty-eight hundredths
10. three hundred six-thousandths

Activity 103: Decimals on a Grid (p. 54)

1. Grid should have 75 squares shaded.
2. Grid should have 33 squares shaded.

Activity 104: Decimals and Fractions (p. 54)

1. $\frac{5}{100}$ 2. $\frac{252}{1000}$ 3. $\frac{16}{100}$
4. $8\frac{24}{100}$ 5. $13\frac{44}{100}$ 6. $121\frac{11}{1000}$

Activity 105: Compare Decimals (p. 55)

1. 3.14   2. 7.001   3. 7.22
4. 3.21   5. 4.01   6. 9.999

Activity 106: Compare Decimals (p. 55)

1. 5.565   2. 0.233   3. 1.131
4. $5.71   5. $5.00   6. 5.3
7. 7.97   8. 0.025

Activity 107: Compare Decimals and Fractions (p. 56)

1. 0.34   2. 0.825   3. $\frac{4}{5}$
4. 3.26   5. 0.64   6. equal
7. Darryl's

Activity 108: Compare Decimals and Fractions (p. 56)

1. $\frac{3}{4}$ 2. 0.85   3. $\frac{3}{5}$
4. $\frac{17}{20}$ 5. $\frac{14}{100}$ 6. 2.5
7. Jeff   8. more

Activity 109: Round Decimals (p. 57)

1. 8   2. 13   3. 14
4. 1   5. 0.2   6. 4.4
7. 4.0   8. 11.0

Activity 110: Round Decimals (p. 57)

1. 4 Million   2. 1%
3. 50%   4. Answers will vary.

Activity 111: Classify Decimals (p. 58)

Decimals less than 0.25: 0.249, 0.1743, 0.1644
Decimals greater than 0.75: 0.923
Decimals Between 0.25 and 0.75: 0.317, 0.733, 0.273, 0.7

Activity 112: Decimals and Zeros (p. 58)

1. 0.099; One number has a 1 in the thousandths place, the other has a 1 in the tenths place.
2. The zeros determine the place value of the 1.
3. There is no difference; they are equal.
4. Since a zero indicates that there is no value in those place value positions, and no number follows them, they can be deleted.
5. Our monetary system is based on hundredths (1 penny is $\frac{1}{100}$ of a dollar).

Activity 113: Add Decimals (p. 59)

1. 5.711   2. 8.911   3. $88.88
4. 4.202   5. 0.1161   6. $18.24

Activity 114: Decimal Patterns (p. 59)

1. Missing numbers are: 1.6, 2.2, 2.5, 2.8, 3.1
2. Missing numbers are: 99.9, 99.8, 99.75, 99.7, 99.65
3. Missing numbers are: 8.204, 10.406, 12.608, 13.709, 14.81
4. Add 0.02; Missing numbers are: 0.06, 0.1, 0.14, 0.16, 0.18, 0.2
5. Add 3; Missing numbers are: 12.667, 15.667, 18.667, 21.667, 24.667
6. Subtract 0.03; Missing numbers are: 0.83, 0.8, 0.74, 0.71, 0.68

Activity 115: Subtract Decimals (p. 60)
1. 19.29   2. 7.99   3. 0.005
4. $2.83   5. $0.29   6. $13.58

Activity 116: Subtract Decimals (p. 60)
1. 28.25   2. 8.25   3. 0.21
4. 3.84
5. $14.99 − $7.35 = $7.64
6. $103.45 − $8.50 = $94.95

Activity 117: Decimal Story Problems (p. 61)
1. $12.53; $7.47
2. $46.83; No, $13.16
3. $27.00
4. 145.4 miles; 4.6 miles

Activity 118: Write-Your-Own Decimal Story Problems (p. 61)
Answers will vary.

Activity 119: Review (p. 62)
1. $4.56   2. $0.72   3. $15.48
4. $9.02   5. $\frac{39}{50}$ 6. $\frac{5}{8}$
7. $\frac{99}{100}$ 8. $\frac{13}{50}$

Activity 120: Review (p. 62)
1. 8.6   2. 14.3   3. 32
4. 20.9   5. 0.08   6. 11.12
7. 0.81   8. 14.6   9. 0.21
10. 7.07

Activity 121: Review (p. 63)
1. a. 19.8   b. 24.8   c. 3.8   d. 10.8
2. $3\frac{7}{10}$ 3. $4\frac{31}{50}$ 4. $11\frac{1}{10}$
5. $9\frac{13}{20}$

Activity 122: Review (p. 63)
1. 17   2. 1   3. 1,238
4. 17.4   5. 0.5   6. 1,237.7
7. thousandths
8. tenths
9. hundredths
10. ten-thousandths

Activity 123: Add Whole Numbers and Decimals (p. 64)
1. 6.0   2. 3.000   3. 11.00
4. 8.0000   5. 24.00
6. No; since the zeros indicate no added value, it does not matter how many there are, so the whole number remains the same.
7. $16.2   8. 8.1

Activity 124: Add Whole Numbers and Decimals (p. 64)
1. 63.3   2. $19.0   3. 359.4
4. 17.3   5. 53.6   6. $85.8
7. 35.1   8. 45.4   9. 40.2
10. 56.0

Activity 125: Subtract Decimals and Whole Numbers (p. 65)
1. $34.36   2. 38.1
3. 506.3673

Activity 126: Subtract Decimals and Whole Numbers (p. 65)
1. 6.461   2. 5.30
3. 24.53   4. $11.55
5. $111.25   6. $20
7. 90   8. 9

Activity 127: Multiply Decimals by Whole Numbers (p. 66)
1. 1 decimal place
2. 3 decimal places
3. 2 decimal places
4. 2.04
5. 8.68
6. 10.456

Activity 128: Multiply Decimals by Whole Numbers (p. 66)
1. 0.360   2. 22.5
3. 307.312   4. 506.88
5. 178.5 ounces   6. 13.8 pounds

89

Activity 129: Multiply Decimals by Decimals (p. 67)
1. 0.14
2. 3.45
3. 12.288
4. $1.28

Activity 130: Multiply Decimals by Decimals (p. 67)
1. 298.9 in.²
2. 103.79 in.²
3. 7.2 in.²
4. 20.1 in.²
5. 36.21 in.²

Activity 131: Decimal Word Problems (p. 68)
1. $4.77
2. 133 pies
3. $136.50
4. $9.48
5. 29.1 hours

Activity 132: Everyday Decimals (p. 68)
1. $382.40
2. $19,884.80
3. $14.34
4. $114.72
5. $497.12
6. $25,850.24

Activity 133: Fractions to Decimals (p. 69)
1. 0.75
2. 0.625
3. 0.875
4. 0.125
5. 0.7
6. 0.25

Activity 134: Fractions to Decimals (p. 69)
1. 0.83
2. 0.33
3. 0.83
4. 0.56
5. 0.9
6. 0.2

Activity 135: Mixed Numbers to Decimals (p. 70)
1. 6.38
2. 9.11
3. 8.43
4. 4.27
5. 7.80
6. 3.38
7. 238.75
8. 7.60

Activity 136: Mixed Numbers to Decimals (p. 70)
1. 11.75
2. 7.33
3. 2.40
4. 35.50
5. 6.89
6. 4.43
7. 5.20
8. 8.08; 97 cookies
9. 13.33; 13 years and 4 months
10. 180.80

Activity 137: Fraction/Decimal Equivalents (p. 71)

Fraction	Decimal
$\frac{1}{4}$	0.250
$\frac{2}{4}$	0.500
$\frac{3}{4}$	0.750
$\frac{1}{3}$	0.333
$\frac{2}{3}$	0.667
$\frac{1}{2}$	0.500
$\frac{1}{5}$	0.200
$\frac{2}{5}$	0.400
$\frac{3}{5}$	0.600
$\frac{4}{5}$	0.800
$\frac{1}{6}$	0.167
$\frac{2}{6}$	0.333
$\frac{3}{6}$	0.500
$\frac{4}{6}$	0.667
$\frac{5}{6}$	0.833

Activity 138: Fraction/Decimal Equivalents (p. 71)

Fraction	Decimal
$\frac{1}{8}$	0.125
$\frac{2}{8}$	0.250
$\frac{3}{8}$	0.375
$\frac{4}{8}$	0.500
$\frac{5}{8}$	0.625
$\frac{6}{8}$	0.750
$\frac{7}{8}$	0.875
$\frac{1}{10}$	0.100
$\frac{2}{10}$	0.200
$\frac{3}{10}$	0.300
$\frac{4}{10}$	0.400
$\frac{5}{10}$	0.500
$\frac{6}{10}$	0.600
$\frac{7}{10}$	0.700
$\frac{8}{10}$	0.800
$\frac{9}{10}$	0.900

Activity 139: Review (p. 72)

1. $6.65; $3.35
2. $4.50; $0.50
3. $12.45; $7.55
4. $1.43

Activity 140: Review (p. 72)

1. $21.8
2. 471.3
3. 117.5
4. $18.4
5. $250.8
6. 113.1
7. 6.2
8. 82.3
9. 0.3
10. 2.3
11. 0.8
12. 3.9

Activity 141: Divide a Decimal by a Whole Number (p. 73)

1. 0.32
2. 1.74
3. 3.52
4. $19.6 \div 7 = 2.8$ miles
5. $292.5 \div 15 = 19.5$ miles per gallon

Activity 142: Divide a Decimal by a Whole Number (p. 73)

1. 21.50
2. 0.65
3. 6.10
4. 3.55
5. 33.30
6. 53.33
7. Brand A: $1.99 \div 3 = $0.663 per oz.
   Brand B: $2.09 \div 4 = $0.5225 per oz.
   Brand C: $1.79 \div 2 = $0.895 per oz.
   Brand B is the least expensive.

Activity 143: Divide a Decimal by a Decimal (p. 74)

1. 3.75
2. 2.93
3. 1.77
4. $1.70

Activity 144: Divide a Decimal by a Decimal (p. 74)

1. 4
2. 200
3. 3.81
4. 54.23
5. 0.03
6. 0.24
7. broccoli—$5.99 \div $3.99 = 1.50 pounds
   bananas—$1.59 \div $0.49 = 3.24 pounds
   grapes—$2.43 \div $1.39 = 1.75 pounds

Activity 145: Decimals and Measurement (p. 75)

1. 0.125 inches
2. 8.25 inches
3. 23 miles
4. 19.85 inches
5. 7.75 inches
6. 25.9 miles

Activity 146: Decimal Division Word Problems (p. 75)

1. 54.94 miles per gallon
2. 30
3. $10.46
4. 1.46 feet
5. 18.3 feet
6. 12.4 feet

Activity 147: Review (p. 76)

1. $\frac{86}{100}$ 2. $\frac{91}{1000}$
3. $\frac{200}{1000}$ 4. $3\frac{725}{1000}$
5. $51\frac{4}{1000}$ 6. $7\frac{130}{1000}$
7. $\frac{7}{10}$ 8. $8.52
9. 0.533   10. 7.45

Activity 148: Review (p. 76)

1. 4.5   2. 0.5
3. 7.0   4. $44.84
5. 94.1   6. $22.97
7. 154.02

Activity 149: Decimal Test (p. 77)

1. $3,508.00
2. $12.50
3. $2.95
4. $10.48
5. 0.40
6. 0.6
7. twenty-five-hundredths
8. three hundred seventy-five-thousandths
9. 98.3
10. 2.8
11. 5.67
12. 0.849

Activity 150: Decimal Test (p. 77)

1. 0.6   2. 0.81   3. $\frac{2}{3}$
4. 0.622   5. 0.40   6. 0.28
7. 0.50   8. 5.75   9. 4.43
10. 7.33

Activity 151: Decimal Test (p. 78)

1. 86.945
2. 73.86
3. 36.08
4. 201.7
5. 576.8
6. 91.25
7. 199.5
8. 3.232
9. $75.63; $24.37
10. $413.84; $86.16

Activity 152: Decimal Test (p. 78)

1. 109.72
2. 45.9
3. 16.25
4. 105.53
5. 21.7 miles
6. 0.24
7. 33.3
8. 45.6
9. 65.75
10. 20 stamps